Dedicated to helping people
more easily appreciate mountain
grandeur, in hope that it will
enrich their lives and inspire
their commitment to preserve
what little wilderness remains.

Mt. Shuksan from Yellow Aster Butte trail

Don't Waste Your Time™
in the **NORTH CASCADES**

An Opinionated Hiking Guide to help you get the most from this magnificent Wilderness

Boot-tested and written by
Kathy & Craig Copeland

WILDERNESS PRESS
BERKELEY

Library of Congress Card Number 96-13488
ISBN 0-89997-182-2

Manufactured in the United States of America
Published by Wilderness Press
              2440 Bancroft Way
              Berkeley, CA 94704
              (800) 443-8080
              FAX (510) 548-1355

              Write, call or fax for a free catalog

♺ Printed on recycled paper, 20% post-consumer waste

Library of Congress Cataloging-in-Publication Data

Copeland, Kathy, 1959–
    Don't waste your time in the North Cascades : an opinionated
hiking guide to help you get the most from this magnificent
wilderness / Kathy and Craig Copeland. — 1st ed.
        p.   cm.
    Includes index.
    ISBN 0-89997-182-2
    1. Hiking—Washington (State)—Guidebooks. 2. Hiking—Cascade
Range—Guidebooks. 3. Washington (State)—Guidebooks. 4. Cascade
Range—Guidebooks. I. Copeland, Craig, 1955– . II. Title.
GV199.42.W2C66 1996
796.5'22'09797—dc20   96-13488

Front cover photo: View northeast from Liberty Cap.
Back cover photo: Mt. Shuksan from Mt. Larrabee.

Contents

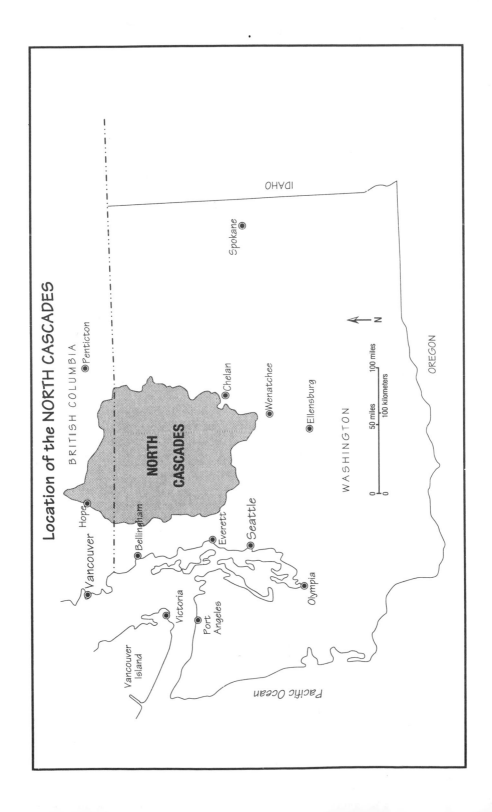

Location of the NORTH CASCADES

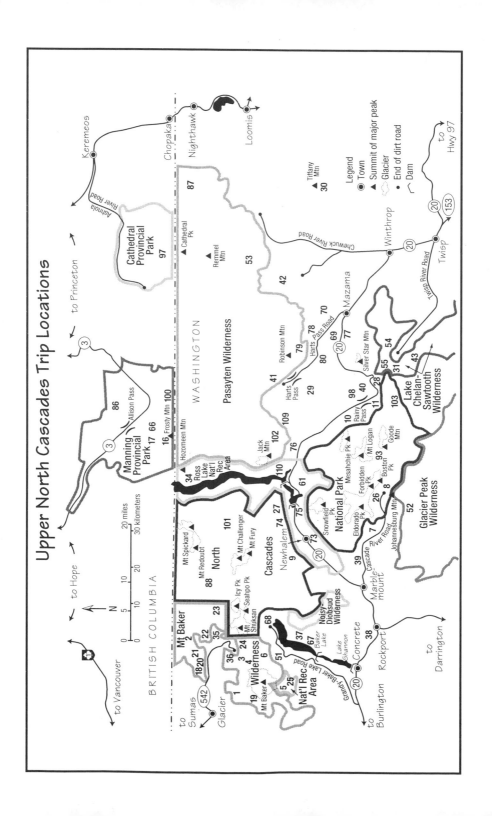

Upper North Cascades Trips

Lower North Cascades Trip Locations

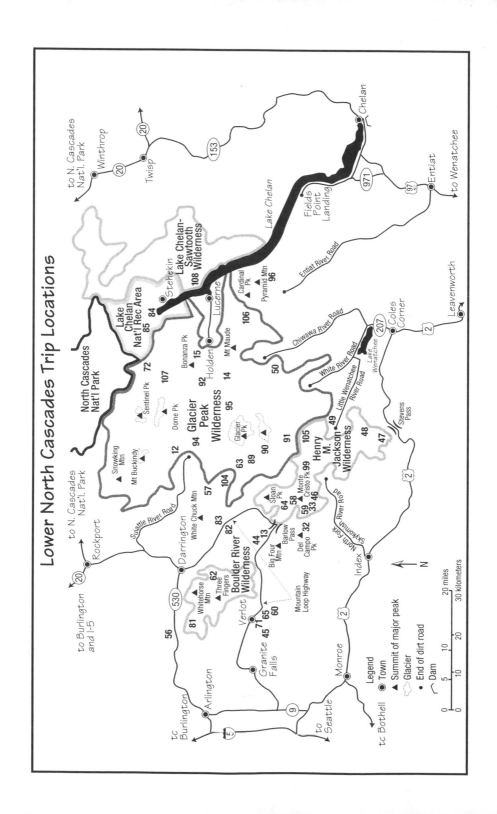

Lower North Cascades Trips

Time is Precious

A disappointing trip leaves a psychic dent. Sometimes it can't be helped. But often it can, by knowing where to go instead of guessing. Too many people toil up scenically deprived trails to lackluster destinations when they could be dancing with delight before one of North America's premier mountain panoramas. That's been our motivation: to save you from wasting your precious time. Even in this glorious mountain kingdom, not all scenery is created equal. Some places are simply more striking, more intriguing, more inspiring than others. Now you can be certain you're choosing a rewarding trail for your weekend or vacation.

These are our boot-tested opinions on which are the best hikes in the North Cascades, which ones you should avoid, and why. This isn't a catalog of every trail in the range. Some don't deserve consideration. We describe the exceptional dayhikes and backpack trips and rate them **Premier, Outstanding, or Worthwhile.** The **Don't Do** trips are trudgemills that, if you didn't know better, might tempt you.

This kind of advice is available only from the *Don't Waste Your Time* guidebook series. Think of it as an honest friend who has vast hiking experience and wants you to enjoy a memorable adventure. With other guidebooks, deciphering which hikes offer superior scenery, then choosing one, can be a slow, difficult process. We've made it fast and easy.

Our opinions are unusually strong, but they're based on widely shared, common-sense criteria. **To help you understand our commentary, here are our preferences:**

- A hike isn't emotionally rewarding solely because of the destination. Variety is what we're after. We want to be wowed along the way by mammoth trees, luxuriant understory, profuse wildflowers, plunging gorges, rocky escarpments. We're deeply moved by sacred, ancient forests. We find solitude to be a sustaining necessity of life. Watching a stream charge on its journey excites us. Observing wild creatures is a primal joy. We love walking trails carved into rugged mountainsides. Life-bright meadows have a magnetic effect on us. The closer we get to gleaming glaciers and piercing peaks, the more ecstatic we feel. High, awe-inspiring, soul-expanding perches thrill us most of all.

• Spending a sunny summer day entirely in forest, even ancient forest, doesn't appeal to us. We're discouraged by views of only rounded, forest-shrouded, nondescript mountains. Long stretches of trail through disenchanted forest (scraggly trees, particularly lodgepole pine or Englemann spruce) are downright depressing. When the scenery gets monotonous and the trail cantankerous, it's trudgery; all we want to do is finish. Although we'll push ourselves far higher for jolting scenery, we don't like climbing over 3500 feet a day for anything less.

Hiker-accessible camp between Deming and Easton glaciers

This is the guidebook we wish we'd had when we first drove Highway 20 through North Cascades National Park and peered up at 4000 vertical feet of forest. It was daunting. We couldn't imagine ourselves penetrating those thick bastions. Views from the highway near Colonial Creek and Washington Pass only hinted at possibilities. Where were all the other peaks and glaciers? The meadows? The alpine vistas?

We've long since learned that the North Cascades are a world of wonders for hikers of all levels. Mountain magic is here in staggering abundance, if you know where to look. Our complete, precise directions will tell you. Our discerning opinions will warn you away from inferior trips and empower you to choose worthier ones.

We also hope our suggestions compel you to get out even more often than you have. Do it to cultivate your wild self. It will give you perspective. Do it because the mountains teach simplicity and self-reliance, qualities that make life more fulfilling. Do it to remind yourself why wilderness needs and deserves your protection. A bolder conservation ethic develops naturally in the mountains. And do it to rediscover the fundamental but easily forgotten truth that there's little of importance outside simple, raw experience.

Trail-Rating System

PREMIER

Here's where you'll enjoy the most spectacular terrain: rugged peaks, sheer cliffs, extensive meadows, tumbling glaciers. The panoramic vistas have startling impact. You'll attain views soon (within 3 miles on dayhikes, 5 to 7 miles on backpack trips). Most of the dayhikes are quickly gratifying because they start at higher elevations. Many of the backpack trips entail little elevation gain or offer long ridge-walks. You'll want to come back again and again.

OUTSTANDING

These are stunning, exhilarating trails. But they're not superlative. Either they require you to work harder and longer to achieve astounding views, or the scenery never reaches an intense climax. They might have earned a Premier rating if the backpack trips offered a more sustained alpine experience, or the dayhikes led you closer to vertical topography.

WORTHWHILE

You'll see beautiful scenery here, just not the kind that leaves an image blazed in your memory. The dayhikes are enjoyable, revealing a special aspect of the area. On the backpack trips, you'll trek a long way before it's obvious why you came, but you'll be glad you did.

DON'T DO

We have nothing good to say about these cursed trails. They're tedious and have little interesting scenery, or too miserably demanding for the reward they offer. Repeat a Premier or an Outstanding hike rather than waste your time here.

Shoulder-Season Hiking

Extend your hiking season in the North Cascades by trying some trails as early as March or as late as November. On the drier east side of the range, open forest and strong sun exposure ensure many trails are snow-free in May. On the west side, lower elevations and mild, wet weather keep a few trails snow-free most of the year. With the exception of Chelan Lakeshore (Trip 108), scenery on shoulder-season trails isn't awesome, but it doesn't have to be. At these times of year, it's thrill enough just to be out hiking. Of course, shoulder-season dayhikes can also be short backpack trips.

Some of the long, river-valley trails in the North Cascades are hikeable in shoulder season. Options include Thunder Creek (Trip 93) as far as McAllister Camp, Suiattle River (Trip 94) as far as Canyon Creek Camp, and North Fork Sauk River (Trip 90) as far as McKinaw Shelter. They're not listed separately as shoulder-season trips. Read about these trail sections in the full trip descriptions. Completing these hikes isn't possible until summer, but in spring or late fall you can savor the lower reaches through glorious, ancient forest. Even in spring you won't have to fight brush on these broad, well-defined trails.

In case you're able to hike only a few times during shoulder season, we've forced ourselves to rank these trips. Remember: shoulder-season rankings are specific to that time of year; they're not equivalent to rankings for prime hiking season. A Premier shoulder-season trip might be merely Worthwhile in mid-summer. A Worthwhile shoulder-season trip could be a Don't Do in mid-summer.

Shoulder Season: Premier means the trail is remarkably scenic compared to others available in spring or late fall and offers a greater sense of adventure or completion.

Shoulder Season: Outstanding means the trail is punctuated by notable scenery. It might offer a high viewpoint or distinct destination but is otherwise typical of spring or late-fall options.

Shoulder Season: Worthwhile means the trail simply provides an opportunity to hike in spring or late fall. The scenery is enjoyable but not special.

Dayhiking versus Backpacking

To help speed your decision making, we've separated the trips roughly according to round-trip distance. Most backpack trips are longer than 16 miles. Most dayhikes are shorter than 12 miles. But there are exceptions. If a trip is longer than 12 miles but the overall elevation gain is reasonable, we might consider it a dayhike. Monte Cristo / Twin Lakes (Trip 33) is an example.

Don't necessarily limit yourself to our guidelines. Some dayhikes, like Rainbow Ridge (Trip 6) and Spider Meadow (Trip 14), make excellent backpack trips if you want or need a shorter option. Some backpack trips, like Snowy Lakes (Trip 98) and Pyramid Mountain (Trip 96), are hikeable in a day, if you're swift.

Dayhikes at a Glance

Trips in each category are listed according to geographic location: starting in the north and moving roughly from west to east. The distance in miles and the elevation gain in feet are in parentheses after each hike.

PREMIER
1 Skyline Divide (6.0 and 2150)
2 Winchester Mountain / Mt. Larrabee (3.4 and 1321 / 7.0 and 1460)
3 Table Mountain (3.0 and 600)
4 Ptarmigan Ridge (9.4 and 1000
5 Railroad Grade / Park Butte (6.0 and 2100 / 6.6 and 2100)
6 Rainbow Ridge (4.5 and 1200)
7 Hidden Lake Peaks (9.0 and 3200)
8 Cascade Pass / Sahale Arm (7.4 and 1800 / 12.4 and 4200)
9 Thornton Lakes / Trappers Peak (9.4 and 2360)
10 Easy Pass (7.2 and 2800)
11 Heather Pass / Maple Pass (6.5 and 2000)
12 Green Mountain (8.0 and 3000)
13 Mount Dickerman (8.6 and 3723)
14 Spider Meadow / Spider Gap (10.4 and 1100 / 16.4 and 3600)
15 Holden Lake (11.8 and 2100)

OUTSTANDING

16 Frosty Mountain (13.6 and 3800)
17 Skyline I and II (12.0 and 3000 / 10.3 and 2214)
18 Excelsior Mountain / High Divide / Welcome Pass
    (6.6 and 1550 / 10.0 and 2020)
19 Heliotrope Ridge (6.5 and 1900)
20 Church Mountain (8.4 and 3600)
21 Yellow Aster Butte / Tomyhoi Peak (6.0 and 2100)
22 Goat Mountain (8.0 and 3500)
23 Hannegan Pass (8.0 and 1966)
24 Lake Ann (8.2 and 900)
25 Scott Paul (7.9 and 1800)
26 Boston Basin (6.0 and 2600)
27 Sourdough Mountain (11.0 and 5100)
28 Blue Lake (4.4 and 1100)
29 Grasshopper Pass (11.0 and 660)
30 Tiffany Mountain (6.0 and 1742)
31 Twisp Pass (8.4 and 2400)
32 Gothic Basin (9.4 and 2640)
33 Monte Cristo / Twin Lakes (16.8 and 2640)

WORTHWHILE

34 Hozomeen Lake / Willow Lake (7.4 and 1150 / 10.2 and 1150)
35 Nooksack Cirque (12.0 and 600)
36 Galena Chain Lakes (6.5 and 900 / 8.0 and 1540)
37 Anderson Butte / Anderson and Watson lakes (7.0 and 2200)
38 Sauk Mountain (4.2 and 1200)
39 Lookout Mountain / Monogram Lake
    (9.4 and 4470 / 9.8 and 3950)
40 Cutthroat Pass (10.0 and 1920)
41 Windy Pass (7.4 and 1000)
42 Copper Glance Lake (7.6 and 2300)
43 Louis Lake (11.4 and 2200)
44 Perry Creek / Mount Forgotten (7.8 and 2900)
45 Mount Pilchuck (6.0 and 2224)
46 Blanca Lake (8.0 and 3300)
47 Lake Valhalla (10.8 and 1190)
48 Lake Janus / Grizzly Peak (15.6 and 2900)
49 Poe Mountain (5.0 and 3000)
50 Little Giant Pass / Napeequa Valley (10.0 and 3900)

DON'T DO

51 Boulder Ridge (8.0 and 1700)
52 South Fork Cascade River (5.0 and 400)
53 Black Lake (8.6 and 800)
54 North Lake (11.2 and 2200)
55 Copper Pass (11.4 and 3000)
56 Mt. Higgins (9.0 and 3450)
57 Crystal Lake (10.5 and 2185)
58 Monte Cristo / Glacier Basin (12.6 and 2140)
59 Monte Cristo / Silver Lake (12.4 and 2040)
60 Ashland Lakes / Bald Mountain (6.0 and 1500)

SHOULDER SEASON: PREMIER

61 Fourth of July Pass / Panther Creek
     (9.2 and 2300 / 11.4 and 2880)
62 Squire Creek Pass (6.8 and 2200)
63 Kennedy Hot Springs (10.4 and 1000)
64 Goat Lake (10.4 and 1300)
65 Lake Twentytwo (5.4 and 1300)

SHOULDER SEASON: OUTSTANDING

66 Lightning, Flash, Strike, and Thunder lakes (13.0 and 0)
67 Baker Lake East Bank (9.6 and 400)
68 Baker River (4.8 and 100)
69 Driveway Butte (9.0 and 3000)
70 Goat Peak Lookout (5.0 and 1400)
71 Heather Lake (4.0 and 1000)
72 Agnes Gorge (5.0 and 300)

SHOULDER SEASON: WORTHWHILE

73 Newhalem Creek (9.0 and 800)
74 Stetattle Creek (8.2 and 1100)
75 Pyramid Lake (4.2 and 1550)
76 Ruby Creek (3.5 and 300)
77 Cedar Creek (4.0 and 520)
78 Lost River (8.0 and 400)
79 Robinson Creek (8.0 and 400)
80 West Fork Methow River (4.6 and 0)
81 Boulder River (8.6 and 500)
82 Beaver Ponds (7.0 and 200)
83 White Chuck Bench (6.6 and 600)

84   Rainbow Loop (5.5 and 1000)
85   Company Creek (4.4 and 2000)

Backpack Trips at a Glance

The distance in miles and the elevation gain in feet are in parentheses after each hike.

PREMIER

86   Heather Trail (16.8 and 1855)
87   Horseshoe Basin / Boundary Trail
      (12.4 and 1200 / 26.4 and 1400)
88   Copper Ridge / Chilliwack River / Whatcom Pass
      (34.5 and 10160)
89   Lake Byrne (15.4 and 3300)
90   Red Pass / White Chuck River / Lost Creek Ridge Loop
      (33.1 and 8000)
91   Pilot Ridge / White Pass / North Fork Sauk River Loop
      (29.3 and 5800)
92   Railroad Creek / Lyman Lakes (18.6 and 2400)

OUTSTANDING

93   Thunder Creek / Park Creek Pass (36.5 and 8300)
94   Image Lake / Miners Ridge / Cloudy Pass
      (32.6 and 4400 / 44.0 and 5900)
95   Buck Creek Pass / High Pass (19.2 and 3100)
96   Pyramid Mountain (18.4 and 3900)

WORTHWHILE

97   Cathedral Provincial Park Core Area (17.4 and 3936)
98   Snowy Lakes (19.6 and 3180)
99   Skykomish Loops (18.3 and 2800 / 24.8 and 4200)

DON'T DO

100   Cascade Loop / Monuments 78 and 83 (33.8 and 4200)
101   Beaver Loop (27.0 and 3500)
102   McMillan Park / Devils Park / Jackita Ridge / Devils Dome
       (41.9 and 8350)
103   Bridge Creek (12.8 and 2320)
104   Meadow Mountain (18.9 and 3500

105   Meander Meadow / Cady Ridge (15.8 and 2900)
106   Ice Lakes / Entiat Meadows (26.8 and 3700)
107   South Fork Agnes Creek (19.8 and 4800)

SHOULDER SEASON: PREMIER
108   Chelan Lakeshore (17.0 and 2200)

SHOULDER SEASON: OUTSTANDING
109   Canyon Creek / Chancellor (18.0 and 1780)

SHOULDER SEASON: WORTHWHILE
110   Ross Lake East Bank (16.1 and 1300)

Trails not in this Book

We excluded many trails that we would have rated **Don't Do**. It seemed a waste of your time, as well as ours, to fill the book with undesirable options that you're unlikely to be drawn to anyway. Several are obscure, familiar only to locals. All are punishing, tedious, or both. Few people hike these trails. Specifically here's why:

(1) Mind-numbing monotony is the drawback to many trails on the eastern side of the range. You have to trudge too many dreary miles through long valley bottoms, only glimpsing rounded, cookie-cutter mountains through spindly, dry forest. Solitude is the only reward here, but not in fall when hunters swarm the area. The War Creek and Wolf Creek trails in the Lake Chelan-Sawtooth Wilderness are examples. So are the trails along the North Fork, Middle Fork, and East Fork Pasayten river, Andrews Creek, and other trails in Pasayten Wilderness.

(2) On some trails that receive little or no maintenance, hiking is certain to be miserable due to obstacles like deadfall and high brush. Examples include the Downey and Bachelor creek trails in Glacier Peak Wilderness, and the Dewdney-Whatcom Trail in British Columbia's Cascade Recreation Area.

(3) Where the scenery doesn't justify it, shredding your knees by climbing over 900 feet per mile for more than 4 miles is absurd. The Purple Pass trail in the Chelan Mountains is an example. Others are Dirty Face Peak above Lake Wenatchee, and Mt. Outram, near Manning Park, British Columbia.

(4) Trails frequented by horseback riders are obnoxiously dusty when dry, frustratingly muddy when wet, and always piled with manure. Add to that a lack of scenic variety, and many trails on the east side of the range are hard for hikers to enjoy. Examples are the Oval Creek trail in the Lake Chelan-Sawtooth Wilderness, and many trails in the Okanogan and Wenatchee national forests.

(5) The multiple-use policy in the Okanogan and Wenatchee national forests allows motorcycles to rampage trails, turning them into the very thing hikers seek to escape: noisy, busy roads. Hikers would far outnumber motorcyclists, but they've been literally driven off by noise, dust, and concern for their own safety. Horses are a problem, but loud, fume-spewing, highly destructive machines, often ridden by young, thoughtless, thrill seekers, are a travesty. Motorized travel is incompatible with wilderness. Hikers shouldn't have to constantly keep their ears cocked for motorcycles and leap out of the way when they approach. Some riders invade nearby hiker-only trails and even go cross-country. Motorcycles don't even have to be present to degrade your hiking experience. They grind trails into inches-deep dust. Your every footstep sends a choking cloud into the air. Dusty trails become slop troughs during rain. Motorcycle madness is worse on the eastern side of the range, between Twisp and Wenatchee. Examples include the Martin Creek, Eagle Lake, and North Fork Entiat River trails, as well as the south end of the Chelan Summit trail. Don't just avoid these places. Win them back. Write your elected representatives. Demand they stop using your tax dollars to "improve" trails for motorcycle use. Insist they ban motorcycles from hiking trails.

Crowded Trails

The west side of the North Cascades is within easy striking distance of several big cities, including the Everett-Seattle-Tacoma metropolis, and Vancouver, British Columbia. That makes solitude difficult to find, unless you hike on the east side of the range, in the Pasayten or Lake Chelan-Sawtooth wilderness areas. Trails off the Mountain Loop Highway and Mt. Baker Highway 542 are especially busy.

To avoid the throngs west of the Pacific Crest, you have several choices: go midweek, hike farther into the mountains than most people do, set off cross-country, or choose less scenic and there-fore less popular trails. We generally prefer to share Premier trails with other hikers than plod alone and disgruntled through unin-spiring terrain.

Don't let the crowds inhibit your enjoyment. Be glad they're out there. People who get close to nature develop reverence—an attitude that could help solve a lot of the world's problems. And the more hikers, the more of us who'll be working together to protect wild lands from resource extraction and development.

Elevation and Distance Figures

Various information sources such as maps, books, and hand-outs often state different elevation and distance figures for the same hike. But the discrepancies are usually small. And most hikers don't care whether an ascent is 2997 feet or 3010, or a trail is 5.4 miles or 5.5. Still, we made a supreme effort to give accurate figures.

Most of our figures are those printed on or calculated from the Green Trails maps—the best topographic maps available for the North Cascades. They're easy to read; trails are clearly marked in green ink; distances are indicated between points along the trails; and elevations are labeled at prominent locations. Sometimes, however, it was obvious the elevation figure on the map was significantly rounded off. For example, a figure might refer to a point halfway between contour lines. Then we added or sub-tracted half the contour interval, or used a figure from a govern-ment source, in order to be more exact. For a few peaks and passes, we use the more precise elevation figures provided by the National Park Service or the Forest Service.

Canada uses the metric system. So, for all trips in Canada, we've stated elevations in meters as well as feet, and distances in kilometers as well as miles.

Physical Capability

Until you gain experience judging your physical capability and that of your companions, these guidelines might be helpful. Any-thing longer than a 7-mile round-trip dayhike can be very taxing for someone who doesn't hike regularly. A 1400-foot elevation gain in that distance is challenging but possible for anyone in average physical condition. Very fit hikers are comfortable hiking 12 miles or more and gaining 3000-plus feet in a single day. Backpacking 12 miles in two days is a reasonable goal for most beginners. Hikers who backpack a couple times a season can enjoyably manage 18 miles in two days. Avid backpackers should find 24 miles in two days no problem. On three- to five-day trips, a typical backpacker prefers not to push beyond 10 miles a day. Remember it's always safer to underestimate your limits.

Wilderness Ethics

We hope you're already conscientious about respecting nature and other people. If not, don't be a bozo, keep reading.

Let wildflowers live. They blossom for only a few fleeting weeks. Uprooting them doesn't enhance your enjoyment, and it prevents others from seeing them at all. We've heard parents urge a string of children to pick as many different-colored flowers as they could find. It's a mistake to teach kids to entertain themselves by killing nature.

Stay on the trail. Shortcutting causes erosion. You probably won't save time anyway, unless you're incredibly strong.

Roam meadows with your eyes, not your boots. Again, stay on the trail. If it's braided, stick to the main path. When you're compelled to take a photo among the wildflowers, try to walk on rocks.

Leave the land unscarred. Avoid building fires. If you must, use an existing fire ring and keep the fire small. If there are no rings, build your fire on dirt or gravel. Never scorch meadows. Over time, tents can also leave scars. Pitch yours on an existing tent site whenever possible. If none is available, choose a patch of dirt, gravel, pine needles, or maybe a dried-up tarn. Never pitch your tent on grass, no matter how appealing it looks. If you do, and others follow, the grass will soon be gone.

Be quiet at backcountry campsites. Most of us are out there to enjoy silence and tranquility. If you want to party, go to a bar.

Pack out everything you bring. Never leave a scrap of trash anywhere. This includes toilet paper, nut shells, even cigarette butts. People who drop butts in the wilderness are buttheads.

They're buttheads in the city too, but it's worse in the wilds. Banana and orange peels are also trash. They take years to decompose, and wild animals won't eat them. If you bring fruit on your hike, you're responsible for the peels. And don't just pack out *your* trash. Leave nothing behind, whether you brought it or not. Clean up after others. Don't be hesitant or oblivious. Be proud. We always keep a small plastic bag handy, which makes picking up trash a habit instead of a pain. It's infuriating and disgusting to see what people toss on the trail. Often the tossing is mindless, but sometimes it's intentional. Anyone who leaves a pile of toilet paper and unburied feces should be banned from the wilderness.

Keep streams and lakes pristine. When brushing your teeth or washing yourself or your dishes with soap, do it well away from water sources, even if you use biodegradable soap. Carry water far enough so the waste water will percolate through soil and break down without directly polluting the wilderness water.

Respect the reverie of other hikers. In the busy North Cascades, don't feel it's necessary to communicate with everyone you pass on the trail. Most of us are seeking solitude, not a social scene. A simple greeting is sufficient to convey good will. Obviously, only you can judge what's appropriate at the time. But it's usually presumptuous and annoying to blurt out advice without being asked. "Boy, have you got a long way to go." "The views are much better up there." "Be careful, it gets rougher." If anyone wants to know, they'll ask. Some people are sly. They start by asking where you're going, so they can tell you all about it. Offer unsolicited information only to warn other hikers about conditions ahead that could seriously affect their trip.

Who's in Charge around Here?

The North Cascades comprise four distinct land jurisdictions: national park, national recreation areas, wilderness areas, and unprotected areas in national forest.

The mandate of **North Cascades National Park** is to protect the wilderness quality. Removing rocks and picking wildflowers are prohibited. Dogs and other pets are not allowed on trails—only on roads, and then only on a leash. Fishing is allowed, but you must have a license. Hunting is illegal.

National Recreation Areas allow more tourist development and permit leashed dogs and other pets on trails. Hunting and mining are prohibited. Horses are allowed on some trails, such as Ross Lake East Bank (Trip 110).

Wilderness Areas are supposed to be preserved in their wild state. Horseback riding, hunting, and fishing are allowed. New roads, mechanized equipment, commercial development, even mountain bikes are prohibited. Mining is allowed on some patented claims, but only after the Forest Service has conducted an impact study and elicited public response. Miners Ridge in Glacier Peak Wilderness has been threatened by plans for an open-pit copper mine.

Multiple-use is the key principle governing **National Forests.** Along with mining, logging, and commercial development, many forms of recreation are allowed, including mountain biking and motorcycle riding on some trails. But wilderness areas within national forests have the same limitations as outlined above.

Read the *Backcountry Permits* section below for details about camping in the national park and national recreation areas. Permits are not necessary elsewhere. In wilderness areas, rangers strongly urge you to camp only in designated campsites, although it's not a legal requirement. You can camp anywhere you want in national forests, but a lack of restrictions doesn't relieve you of responsibility. Always follow no-trace camping practices.

Backcountry Permits

North Cascades National Park, as well as Ross Lake National Recreation Area and Lake Chelan National Recreation Area, require you to have a permit for backcountry camping. You don't need one for dayhiking or car camping; only for overnight backpacking. The party size limit is 12. Elsewhere in the national forests and wilderness areas of the North Cascades, your group can be any size and you can camp wherever and whenever you want, but you should still do it lightly, leaving no trace of your stay.

It used to be you could reserve campsites prior to obtaining your permit, but not anymore. Now you have to show up in person no earlier than the day before your trip. First come, first served. The North Cascades National Park wilderness office in Marblemount is the best place to get a permit. It offers the most current and comprehensive information on backcountry conditions. But another office might be more convenient for you. Permits are available at the National Park / Forest Service office in Sedro Woolley, the Golden West visitor center in Stehekin, the Glacier public service center in Glacier, the North Cascades visitor center in Newhalem, the Marblemount wilderness office, the Hozomeen Ranger Station at the north end of Ross Lake, and the Forest Service ranger stations in Winthrop, Early Winters, Chelan, and Twisp. If you need to get a permit outside office hours, there's usually a self-register station.

Only with a permit in hand is your site at an official campground reserved. Camping elsewhere is prohibited, unless you get a permit for cross-country camping (1.0 mile from any official campground, 0.5 mile off trail, and 200 feet from water). Even cross-country camping is restricted to certain areas—usually brush-choked drainages—so following the rules can be difficult. If you try it, allow an extra couple hours of daylight at the end of your hike to find a site and set up camp.

Lupines are profuse in Cascade meadows

Permits can be a pain. If you request one for a popular area (e.g., Boston Basin, Cascade Pass, Monogram Lake, Thornton Lake, Copper Ridge, Ross Lake) in mid-season, you might find the campgrounds you want to stay at are full. If so, you must adjust your itinerary—hiking shorter or longer days than you'd prefer—to ensure you end up at a campground with an available site. Sticking to an itinerary, even a reasonable one, can be difficult in the backcountry. After all, once you leave the trailhead, you're on an adventure. Adventures, by definition, never fit neatly into rigid schedules. Besides, one of the joys of wilderness travel should be walking away from the constraints of modern civilization.

For the permit system to work well, every hiker must adhere to it, but some don't. Many simply fall behind schedule. Some change plans en route. Others just ignore the permit requirement from the outset. We've pitched our tent at backcountry campgrounds where none of the campers, us included, were sleeping where our permits said we should be.

So, just because you have a permit, don't assume an empty campsite is awaiting your arrival. You might have to make friends with other backpackers and share a site. Be reasonable and flexible. If at all possible, camp only according to your permit. Keep in mind: if a ranger catches you camping illegally, you'll be severely lectured and possibly fined. And never let your frustration with the permit system be an excuse for damaging the fragile mountain environment. Always follow minimal-impact practices.

The permit system is intended to ensure you enjoy a tranquil camping experience, and to protect the wilderness from the effects of an ever-increasing number of visitors. It's hypocritical to be part of the problem, yet not participate in the solution. For that reason alone, the system deserves our respect and cooperation.

Volunteer Trail Maintenance

Instead of just fighting your way through the dense vegetation that chokes many trails in the North Cascades, you could spend a weekend with a volunteer crew, helping maintain a trail so everyone can enjoy it.

The North Cascades trail network desperately needs maintenance. Yet the Forest Service budget for trail work in the Mt. Baker-Snoqualmie National Forest was slashed from $141,000 in 1995 to $81,000 in 1996. Legislators think cutbacks merely prevent expenditures for trail construction, which they consider unnecessary. They don't realize the previous budget was needed just to keep existing trails walkable.

Heavy rainfall and a temperate climate enable brush to grow profusely, swallowing some trails in a single summer. Dense forests mean lots of deadfall. Extremely steep grades allow serious erosion. Many trails were blazed by miners—obsessed with getting rich, not with providing recreation opportunities—which means the trails were poorly routed. Other trails were boot-built

Deadfall is a frequent obstacle in the North Cascades

by climbers who, likewise, were unconcerned about others following in their footsteps.

The Washington Trails Association schedules about 50 work parties a year, and you're invited. It's hard labor, but you'll be making a very valuable, much appreciated contribution. You'll also meet good people who share your interest in the outdoors. Call (206) 517-7032 to get involved. A $15 donation puts you on the WTA membership list. You'll be supporting their maintenance and advocacy work, and you'll receive their quarterly newsletter. Mail your check to Washington Trails Association, 1305 4th Avenue, Suite 512, Seattle, WA 98101.

Cascadian Climate

The volatile North Cascades climate will have you building shrines to placate the weather gods. Storms roll in off the Pacific Ocean, unleashing most of the precipitation on the west side and leaving the east side thirsty. Conditions can vary radically from day to day. On the west side, even during summer, it seems to rain half the time. Even many of the rain-free days are cloudy. So don't waste clear days on less scenic hikes. When you wake up to a blue sky, head for a premier trail and zoom up to an awesome vista. And remember that when it's socked-in and pouring on the west side, there's a chance it's merely overcast and pleasantly cool farther east. So instead of surrendering to the weather, try changing it by driving a few extra hours.

Summers are hot on both sides of the Pacific Crest. Daytime maximum temperatures average 75°F on the west, 85°F on the east. The mercury can soar as high 90°F on the west, higher on the east. To avoid the worst heat, hike early or late in the day, or plan to be at higher elevations or under dense forest cover in midday. Hot weather can be especially debilitating on the west side because of high humidity. But the sun's power is often tempered by cloudy skies and abundant shade. Stay away from the east side during summer—it's a furnace. The humidity is lower, but frequently clear skies and sparser forests make it difficult to find relief from the sun. Those same qualities, however, make the east side attractive for spring hiking. Fall would be equally enjoyable in the east if not for all the hunters roaming the hills.

Enough snow usually melts by early July to give you lots of dayhiking options throughout the range. The snow level then should be about 5500 feet on northern slopes, 6500 feet on southern. Just one week of clear, sunny weather can greatly increase trail accessibility. You can generally count on about three months of high-country hiking. The crux of any long, spectacular backpack trip probably isn't safely passable until late July, unless you're competent with an ice axe.

Snowstorms can hit the first week of September. An early wave of cold and snow, however, is often followed by warm days into mid-October. But then the days are shorter and the nights colder, so backpacking isn't as pleasant then. Fall colors usually reach full intensity by late September.

Scourge of the Cascades

You'll be tired, sweaty, thirsty. You'll stop for a rest. Within seconds, they'll be all over you: fingernail-sized, crunchy-to-the-touch black flies. A dozen or more will assault your legs, attack your arms, land on your neck, strafe your ears, crawl up your nose. And if you don't swat them, you'll feel the sharp, sudden prick of their vicious bite. Because they're sluggish, you'll easily kill many. Whap. Whap. Whap. But they're impossible to vanquish. They just keep coming, wave after endless wave. So you gulp a few sips of water and move on. Perpetual motion is your best defense. But there are a few other tactics you'll find helpful.

Black flies, as well as the larger deerflies and horseflies, usually appear in the North Cascades around late July. If the weather's been hot, they'll be a nuisance by mid-July. The blitz will continue until the weather cools, probably in September. Mosquitoes are bothersome too, of course, but no more so here than in most mountain ranges. Except in notoriously mosquito-infested areas, like Lyman Lakes, it's the black flies that will torment you.

In midsummer, when the flies are worst, begin long hikes at sunrise. Flies are aroused as the temperature rises. When the sun's heat penetrates the forest—about 9 A.M.—it's as if the flies hear their starting gun. Cooler temperatures subdue them, so consider starting backpack trips or very short dayhikes after 4 P.M.

Citronella bug repellent or eucalyptus oil might deter flies from biting you, but won't actually disperse them. They'll still swarm. Repellents containing DEET might keep them away, but you have to be desperate to rub anything that poisonous on your skin. A loose, lightweight, long-sleeve shirt is preferable. Better yet, check out bug-net garments. Head covers are especially helpful.

Bandanas are effective anti-fly weapons. While hiking, you can wave one briskly around your legs, over your shoulders, and around your head. Bring an extra bandana to tuck under your hat so it will drape, Lawrence of Arabia style, over your ears, temples, cheeks and neck, keeping flies away from those otherwise exposed areas.

A folding, oriental fan is also worth a try. You can use it to whisk away flies and cool yourself at the same time. We've even seen resourceful people waving hemlock or pine boughs as they walk. This works almost as well as a fan, and has the added benefit of providing comic relief for other hikers.

Flies decrease at higher elevations. And a stiff breeze keeps them grounded, just like mosquitoes. So you can look forward to relief at most passes. But getting there requires great mental control if the flies are bad below. Try to not to focus your thoughts on them. Stay calm. Don't let them keep you from stopping to drink or rest.

Some hikers adopt a zen attitude. Refusing to be enraged by the abhorrently slow, stupid pests, they simply observe or ignore them. It's a wise approach. All of us should at least appreciate that flies in the North Cascades aren't speedy and clever. That would be a truly diabolical torture.

Battling Brush

Brush is a defining characteristic of North Cascades valleys and alpine slopes. The term "brush" refers to all the shrubs, bushes, sedges, and grasses that grow rapidly and profusely in this temperate range. "Brush" is also a verb that means to cut and clear. Some trails become choked with vegetation unless they're brushed annually by a work crew. Volunteers are critically needed in this effort. See the Volunteer Trail Maintenance section above for details.

Hiking a severely brushy trail is discouraging for all but machete-minded commandos driven by romantic images of Borneo. You'll find even mildly brushy trails make hiking less enjoyable. The plants can obscure the trail, claw at your arms and especially your legs, and make your skin itch. Stinging nettles and devil's club are downright vicious.

To combat brush, without *Battling brush on the Beaver Loop trip* wielding hedge clippers, wear long pants. It's a good solution on cool days, but too hot during warm weather. Women might want to pull a long, thin skirt over their shorts when the trail is brushy. A skirt allows more air circulation than pants. But if the brush is wet, anything you wear to cover your legs will be instantly sodden. Tall gaiters are helpful, and they repel water, but they leave your knees and thighs exposed.

In brush, we usually curse and bear it, forging ahead in shorts. But we occasionally slow down and use both hands to hold large bandanas in front of our legs as deflectors. It helps. Bandanas weigh almost nothing, dry quickly, and have a dozen other uses.

Hantavirus

Hantavirus pulmonary syndrome is related to the 1994 Ebola virus that wiped out more than 200 people in Zaire. Hanta killed 17 in the Four Corners area of the southwest U.S. in 1993, and more recently one person who had just returned from hiking in the Sierra and Cascades. Since then, another hiker became ill while on the Appalachian Trail in Virginia, but recovered after treatment.

Your chances of contracting hanta are very small, but possibly increasing. Hikers and campers are at risk because the virus is carried by rodents, especially deer mice. It's usually transmitted to people by airborne fecal matter. A microsecond of breathing infected air could do it—for example, while stepping into a trail shelter and kicking up a little dust. So never enter shelters.

Hanta-carrying rodents have been found throughout North America. The federal Centers for Disease Control and Prevention say infected rodents are in at least 20 national parks and could be in all of them. Warning signs in Stehekin, on Lake Chelan, first called our attention to the disease. Later, while camping in our van, we were alarmed by rodents scurrying inside the vehicle at night. The amount of feces they leave behind is surprising. We followed the recommended cleaning procedures: wear a face mask and rubber gloves; don't raise dust by vacuuming, sweeping or dry mopping; wipe clean with a bleach-dampened cloth.

People display symptoms within 45 days of exposure to the virus. The initial fever, coughing, headache, and muscle pain resemble the flu. Nausea follows. While victims vomit, internal bleeding begins. Fluid seeps into their lungs and suffocates them.

No antiviral drug cures hanta. Of those who contract the disease, 51% die. But early diagnosis and prompt supportive respiratory care can increase chances of recovery. The best hanta protection is to avoid rodent feces like the plague.

Cougars

You'll probably never see a cougar in the North Cascades. But they're here, and they can be dangerous, so you should know a bit about them.

Elsewhere referred to as a puma, mountain lion, or panther, the cougar is an enormous, graceful cat. An adult can reach the size of a big human: eight feet long (including a three-foot tail), 180 pounds. In the Pacific Northwest, they tend to be a tawny grey.

Nocturnal, secretive, solitary creatures, cougars come together only to mate. Each cat establishes a territory of 125 to 175 square miles. They favor dense forest that provides cover while hunting. They also hide among rock outcroppings and in steep canyons.

Habitat loss and aggressive predator-control programs have severely limited the range of this mysterious animal that once thrived across the continent. Still, cougars are not considered endangered or threatened. In Washington they're listed as a game animal and are hunted. Two other, smaller cats roam the North Cascades. Lynxes are on the sensitive-species list because their population is declining. Bobcats are maintaining a stable population.

Cougars are carnivores. They eat everything from mice to elk, but prefer deer. They occasionally stalk people, but rarely attack them. In American folklore, cougars are called ghost cats or ghost walkers, and for good reason. They're very shy and typically avoid human contact.

Cougar sightings and encounters are increasing, but it's uncertain whether that's due to a larger cougar population or the growing number of people visiting the wilderness. If you're lucky enough to see a cougar, treasure the experience. Just remember they're unpredictable. North Cascades National Park offers these suggestions to hikers:

Never hike alone in areas of known cougar sightings. Keep children close to you; pick them up if you see fresh cougar scat or tracks. Never approach a cougar, especially a feeding one. Never flee from a cougar, or even turn your back on it. Sudden movement might trigger an instinctive attack. Avert your gaze and speak to it in a calm, soothing voice. Hold your ground or back away slowly. Always give the animal a way out. If a cougar approaches, spread your arms, open your coat, do anything you can to enlarge your image. If it acts aggressively, wave your arms, shout, throw rocks or sticks. If attacked, fight back. Don't play dead.

Bears

Bears are not a problem in the North Cascades, but oblivious hikers are. Too many people are unaware that these mountains support a healthy population of bears. Unprepared for a bear encounter, and ignorant of how to prevent one, they make bears a more serious threat—to themselves and everyone else.

Backpackers who don't properly hang their food at night are inviting bears into their campsite, greatly increasing the chance of a dangerous encounter. And bears are smart. They quickly learn to associate a particular place, or people in general, with an easy meal. They become habituated and lose their fear of man. A habituated bear is a menace to any hiker within its range.

Black bears are by far the most common species here, but there are grizzly bears as well. The North Cascades Grizzly Bear Evaluation project verified 21 grizzly observations between 1964 and 1991. The project also rated another 81 grizzly reports highly reliable. Biologists estimate the U.S. part of the North Cascades is home to a small grizzly population, perhaps 20. Roughly the same number of grizzlies lives in the Canadian part of the North Cascades.

The Endangered Species Act urges recovery of threatened species, such as the grizzly. After years of study, the North Cascades were designated one of six grizzly-bear recovery areas in the U.S. As part of the recovery effort, grizzly bears from other areas might be moved to the North Cascades. Until they are, the grizzly population will not increase rapidly. They're the second slowest reproducing land animal in North America. Only the musk ox is slower. So it's highly unlikely you'll encounter a grizzly in the North Cascades. There's a better chance you'll see a black bear.

The two species can be difficult for an inexperienced observer to tell apart. Both range in color from nearly white to cinnamon to black. Full-grown grizzlies are much bigger, but a young grizzly can resemble an adult black bear, so size is not a good indicator. The most obvious differences are that grizzlies have a dished face; big, muscular shoulder humps; and long, curved front claws. Blacks have a straight face; no hump; and shorter, less visible front claws. Grizzlies are potentially more dangerous than black bears, although a black bear sow with cubs can be just as aggressive. Be wary of all bears.

Any bear might attack when surprised. If you're hiking, and forest or brush limits your visibility, you can prevent surprising a bear by making noise. Bears hear about as well as humans and are generally as anxious to avoid an encounter as you are. If you warn them of your presence before they see you, they'll usually clear out. So when you fear a bear encounter, talk to your companions, yodel, sing, make up nonsense words, practice a foreign language. Do it loudly. Shout "Bears beware! We're comin' through!" Don't be embarrassed. Be safe. The sound we've found easiest to project and sustain frequently is the two vowel combination "AY...OH!" Be especially loud near streams so your voice carries over the competing noise. Sound off more frequently when hiking into the wind. That's when bears are least able to hear or smell you coming.

Bears' strongest sense is smell. So never cook in your tent; the fabric might retain odor. Cook as far as possible from where you'll be sleeping. Afterward, hang your remaining food, cooking gear, and anything else that smells (lotion, sunscreen, bug repellent, lip balm, toothpaste, garbage) in a tree, out of reach of bears and other critters. Bring a sturdy plastic bag or extra stuff-sack to hang your food in, instead of getting your sleeping-bag stuff-sack smelly. Hoist it at least 15 feet off the ground and 5 feet from the tree trunk or other branches, which requires about 40 feet of light nylon cord. Clip the sack to the cord with an ultralight carabiner.

If you see a bear, don't look it in the eyes; it might think you're challenging it. Never run. Be still. If you must move, do it in slow motion. Bears are more likely to attack if you flee, and they're fast, much faster than humans. A grizzly can outsprint a racehorse. Climbing a tree is an option. Some people have saved their lives this way, others have been caught in the process. Despite their ungainly appearance, bears are excellent climbers. To be out of reach of an adult bear, you'd have to climb at least 33 feet, something few people are capable of. And you'd probably need to be at least 200 yards from the bear to beat it up the tree.

Several confrontations with grizzlies, and a few black-bear encounters in the North Cascades have convinced us we're unlikely to provoke an attack as long as we stay calm, retreat slowly, and make soothing sounds to convey a nonthreatening presence. Playing dead is debatable. It used to be the recommended response to a charge, but now some scientists, rangers and surviving victims say it might be better to fight back. It's your call. Every encounter involves different bears and different people, and the results vary. Even bear behavior experts cannot suggest one all-purpose defense technique. Many people who've survived a mauling had a brave companion beating on the bear. But we agree with the specialists who think victims might have lived or been less brutalized if they'd been passive. Read Steve Herrero's *Bear Attacks: Their Causes and Avoidance.* Then, if you encounter a bear, you'll have a better idea what to do.

Consider bringing a spray canister of oleoresin-capsicum, as a last line of defense. Cayenne pepper, highly irritating to a bear's sensitive nose, is the active ingredient. It's been successfully used in many cases to turn back a charging bear. Without causing permanent injury, it disables the bear for about an hour—long enough to let you escape. But remember: vigilance is your best defense. Spray only if you really think your life is at risk. Before you need to, visualize yourself calmly pointing and spraying, so you'll be able to do it effectively under threat. You can buy bear spray—possibly labeled Bearguard, Counter Assault, or OC-10— at backpacking stores.

Always call or drop by a national-park or forest-service office before hiking. You'll find phone numbers and addresses in the back of this book. They regularly post trail reports and do their best to have up-to-date back-country information. Tell them where you plan to hike and ask if there have been any recent bear sightings or problems in the area. Adjust your plans accordingly.

Merrily disregarding bears is foolish and unsafe. Worrying about them is miserable and unnecessary. Everyone occasionally feels afraid when venturing deep into the mountains, but fear of bears can be restrained by knowledge and awareness. Just take the necessary precautions and don't let your guard down. Experiencing the grandeur of the North Cascades is certainly worth risking the remote possibility of a bear encounter.

Lightning

Many of our recommendations take you to high ridges, open meadows and mountain peaks where, during a storm, you could be exposed to lightning. Your best protection is, of course, not being there. But it's difficult to always avoid hiking in threatening weather. Even if you start under a cloudless, blue sky, you might see ominous, black thunderheads marching toward you a few hours later. Upon reaching a high, thrilling vantage, you could be forced by an approaching storm to decide if and when you should retreat to safer ground. Try to reach high passes early in the day. Rain and lightning storms tend to develop in the afternoon.

The power of nature that makes wilderness so alluring often presents threats to your safety. The following is a summary of lightning precautions recommended by experts. These are not guaranteed solutions. We offer them merely as suggestions to help you make a wiser decision on your own and reduce your chance of injury.

A direct lightning strike can kill you. It can cause brain damage, heart failure or third-degree burns. Ground current, from a nearby strike, can severely injure you, causing deep burns and tissue damage. Direct strikes are worse but far less common than ground-current contact.

To avoid a direct strike, get off exposed ridges and peaks. Even a few yards off a ridge is better than right on top. Avoid isolated, tall trees. A clump of small trees or an opening in the trees is safer.

To avoid ground current, stay off crevices, lichen patches, or wet, solid rock surfaces, and away from gullies with streams in them. Loose rock, like talus, is safer.

Crouch near a high point at least 30 to 50 feet higher than you. Sit in the **low-risk area**: near the base of the high point, at least 5 feet from cliffs or walls.

If your hair is standing on end, there's electricity in the air around you. Get outa there! That's usually down the mountain, but if there's too much open expanse to traverse, look for closer protection.

Once you chose a place to wait it out, squat with your feet close together. To prevent brain or heart damage, you must stop the charge from flowing through your whole body. It helps to keep your hands and arms away from rocks. Several books say to insulate yourself by crouching on a dry sleeping pad, but we wonder, how do you do this if it's raining and you're not in a tent or cave?

Stay at least 30 feet from your companions, so if one is hit, another can give cardiopulmonary resuscitation.

Deep caves offer protection, but stay out of shallow or small caves because ground current can jump across openings. Crouch away from the opening, at least 5 feet from the walls. Also avoid rock overhangs. You're safer in the low-risk area below a high point.

Hypothermia

Many deaths outdoors involve no obvious injury. "Exposure" is usually cited as the killer, but that's a misleading term. It vaguely refers to conditions that contributed to the death. The actual cause is hypothermia: excessive loss of body heat. It can happen with startling speed, in surprisingly mild weather—often between 30 and 50°F. Guard against it vigilantly.

Cool temperatures, wetness (perspiration or rain), wind, or fatigue, usually a combination, sap the body of vital warmth. Hypothermia results when heat loss continues to exceed heat gain. Initial symptoms include chills and shivering. Poor coordination, slurred speech, sluggish thinking, and memory loss are next. Intense shivering then decreases while muscular rigidity increases, accompanied by irrationality, incoherence, even hallucinations. Stupor, blue skin, slowed pulse and respiration, and unconsciousness follow. The heartbeat finally becomes erratic until the victim dies.

Avoid becoming hypothermic by wearing synthetic clothing that wicks moisture away from your skin and insulates when wet. Polypro/lycra tights are excellent when it gets too brisk for shorts. Always have a thick, longsleeve top you can slip on during rest breaks, while your hiking shirt dries. In case of emergency, pack extra layers in a plastic bag: fleece gloves and hat, synthetic socks and underwear (top and bottom). A windproof, waterproof (preferably breathable) shell and pants are mandatory. So are matches in a waterproof container, a lighter, and fire starters. Food fuels your internal fire, so bring more than you think you'll need, including several energy bars for emergencies only. On dayhikes, also carry a heat reflecting "space" bag, maybe an ultralight tube tent, or at least a couple big garbage bags in case you're forced to bivouac.

If you can't stay warm and dry, you must escape the wind and rain. Turn back. Keep moving. Eat snacks. Seek shelter. Do it while you're still mentally and physically capable. Watch others in your party for signs of hypothermia. Victims might resist help at first. Trust the symptoms, not the person. Be insistent. Act immediately.

Create the best possible shelter for the victim. Take off his wet clothes and replace them with dry ones. Insulate him from the ground. Provide warmth. A prewarmed sleeping bag inside a tent is ideal. If necessary, add more warmth by taking off your clothes and crawling into the bag with the victim. Build a fire. Keep the victim conscious. Feed him sweets. Carbohydrates quickly convert to heat and energy. In advanced cases, victims should not drink hot liquids.

Glacier Peak, one of the prominent giants of the North Cascades

DAYHIKES

Trip 1
Skyline Divide

Location	Mt. Baker-Snoqualmie National Forest / Mt. Baker Wilderness.
Distance	6.0-mile round trip to the knoll at 6215'; 9.5-mile round trip to the 6200' saddle beneath Chowder Ridge.
Elevation gain	2150' to the knoll; 2250' to the saddle.
Maps	Green Trails No. 13–Mt. Baker; Trails Illustrated No. 223–North Cascades National Park Complex.

OPINION

If you're not already a mountain junkie, ingesting such a walloping dose of alpine elixir will have you hooked for sure.

Either that, or you'll pass out from sensory overload. So prepare yourself for the power of this glorious yet easily attained paradise.

Just 2 miles of gradual, well-engineered switchbacks deliver you to the north end of the Skyline crest. From there on, it's an easy amble, with gleaming Mt. Baker the centerpiece of an exploding panorama. On a clear day, you can see the Strait of Georgia and the mountains of Vancouver Island to the west; British Columbia's Coast Range, the Border Peaks and the Cheam Range to the north; and Mt. Shuksan to the east. Sometimes you can also see the pollution over Vancouver.

Obviously this is a popular trail, but you'll see options for wandering the bluffs, basins and ridges away from the crowd. Your best chance of contemplating the orgasmic vistas in solitude is to head up after 1 P.M. By the time you reach the end of the trail above Chowder Basin, most people will have left. Or, instead of making it a dayhike, camp up top and hope for a rosy sunrise while you enjoy breakfast with glacial garnish.

If you've been plagued by flies on other hikes in the North Cascades, you'll be relieved to know they're more tolerable here, even in August. And the resident butterfly population is booming. They will light on your hands and pose patiently for photographs.

FACT

By Car

From the Glacier Public Service Center on Highway 542, drive 1.0 mile east, then turn south onto well-signed Glacier Creek Road 39. You'll quickly come to a fork: turn left onto Dead Horse Road 37 and travel approximately 4.0 level miles along the south side of the North Fork Nooksack River. The final 8.9 miles are steep and rough, as the road switchbacks the 2900 feet you don't have to hike. It's easily passable in a low-clearance vehicle if you drive slowly. The trailhead at 4400 feet is across the road from a large parking lot.

On Foot

Bring plenty of water; after the snow melts, there's no convenient source on the divide. Start by switchbacking 1.0 mile through hemlock and fir. The next mile of forest is interspersed with meadows—flower filled in late July and early August. After gaining 1400 feet in 2.25 miles, you attain the Skyline Divide crest, mostly above treeline from here on. Walk 0.75 mile along the ridge to the obvious knoll (6215 feet) just left of the main trail. There you'll gain a better view of Mt. Baker, and you can survey the route you might want to wander south on for an even closer inspection. At 3.5 miles you can go left (southeast) to a water source and campsites in Chowder Basin, near the headwaters of Deadhorse Creek. If you stay right at the 3.5-mile point, a boot-beaten path undulates south to about 5 miles. There's an obvious route to the 6200' saddle at the base of Chowder Ridge.

Skyline Divide, Mt. Baker

Trip 2

Winchester Mountain /
High Pass and Mt. Larrabee

Location	Mt. Baker Wilderness.
Distance	3.4-mile round trip up Winchester; 7.0-mile round trip to trail's end above High Pass.
Elevation gain	1321' for Winchester; 1460' to trail's end above High Pass.
Maps	Green Trails No. 14–Mt. Shuksan; Trails Illustrated No. 223–North Cascades National Park Complex.

OPINION

The magnificent views awaiting you here are shockingly easy to attain. So don't be shocked when you see lots of other hikers. Start early or late if you hope to avoid some of them. When we descended Winchester at 7 P.M., there were no cars at Twin Lakes. It's also wise to delay coming here until late August or September, so you won't encounter snow patches on the trails that might block safe passage. In September the magnificent display of red and purple heather on the slope above High Pass contrasts strikingly with the dark forests below and the gleaming glaciers of Shuksan beyond.

These short hikes allow you to survey a vast expanse: Puget Sound, the British Columbia Coast Range, and the heavyweight mountains of the North Cascades. On top of Winchester, mountain magic surrounds you. From here you can see Mt. Baker, Mt. Shuksan, the Border Peaks, Silesia Creek valley, the jagged Pleiades beside Mt. Larrabee, and nearby Goat Mountain. Winchester also gives you a better view of the Pickets than you get from the side of Larrabee. Otherwise, hiking onto Larrabee's slopes opens your eyes to even more, including Artist Point on Mt. Baker at the end of Highway 542, Skyline Divide to the southwest, and Glacier Peak way south.

In a single day, strong hikers can easily walk to High Pass on Mt. Larrabee, then zoom up and down Winchester on the way back. If you have to choose only one destination, go to High Pass. The narrow tread and varied terrain on the way to Larrabee feel wonderfully wild and rugged, even though the trail is clearly defined. Larrabee's expansive vista makes for a thrilling destination. And, equally important, Winchester is a zoo. Fewer hikers set out for Larrabee.

On top of Winchester, be sure to look down on Tomyhoi Lake and see why you shouldn't spend your time hiking over Gold Run Pass only to drop deep into forest to get there.

FACT

By Car

From the Glacier Public Service Center on Highway 542, drive 12.8 miles to where you see maintenance buildings. Turn north here onto Twin Lakes Road 3065. At 2.3 miles, pass the side road to Yellow Aster Butte trailhead. At 2.8 miles stay left, passing a narrower road. At 4.5 miles you'll reach the Gold Run Pass / Tomyhoi Lake trailhead. All types of cars can make it this far, but the final 2.5 miles beyond are steep, rough and narrow, with dropoffs only a foot or so from your tires. The road crosses several ditches that might cause low-clearance vehicles to bottom out. In years of average or high snowfall, it probably won't be passable until mid-August. Check with the Glacier Ranger Station about road conditions. At Twin Lakes there are several campsites with tables. Perched in a mountain pass with a view of Mt. Baker, it's the kind of alpine setting usually accessible only by trail.

On Foot

If you have to walk from the Gold Run Pass / Tomyhoi Lake trailhead, add 2.5 miles and 1600 feet to your agenda. From the huge parking lot at road's end—5200 feet—walk to the northwest side of the isthmus between the Twin Lakes to the Winchester Mountain trailhead. Don't walk the gated road along the southeast side of the north lake.

Where the Winchester trail forks in 0.2 mile, go left for Winchester or right for Mt. Larrabee. The Winchester trail immediately switchbacks up through heather, rocks and a few trees. After 0.9 mile, the ascent eases for the last 0.6 mile. On the summit, a

Mt. Shuksan from Mt. Larrabee

former fire-lookout cabin is now open to the public. For $15 per person per night, you can sleep here. You'll find a bed, a cot, two foam pads, and a gas stove with propane. Contact the Mt. Baker Hiking Club at (360) 617-1219 for reservations. The cabin is closed at the end of September.

If you go right for Mt. Larrabee, you'll quickly reach a small saddle just before you start to descend toward Winchester Creek canyon. The view to the northwest offers a preview of High Pass, at the top of the long southern flank of Mt. Larrabee.

Continuing toward Larrabee, the trail drops 160 feet, traversing under Winchester Mountain and heading northwest above the depths of Winchester and Silesia creeks. Then the route switchbacks up a rocky landslide slope, topping out above an outcropping at Low Pass, 5600 feet—1.5 miles from the trailhead. It's 1.0 mile farther to 5900-foot High Pass. The total distance is 2.5 miles one way—not farther as indicated on the Green Trails map. There's a faint fork at High Pass: the left fork descends to Gargett Mine at 5700 feet; the right one ascends 600 feet in about 1 mile on an old miner's trail to 6500 feet on Mt. Larrabee.

Trip 3
Table Mountain

Location	Heather Meadows Recreation Area / Mt. Baker Wilderness.
Distance	1.0-to 3.0-mile round trip.
Elevation gain	600'.
Map	Green Trails No. 14–Mt. Shuksan.

OPINION

Most people who drive up Mt. Baker to Artist Point don't hike. They think the parking lot is the destination. But looming directly above is a rocky mesa offering the shortest Premier trip in the North Cascades. The 360° view on top is a head spinner. And because the summit is as flat as its namesake, you can wander.

Milk it for all it's worth. Huge rock slabs beckon in all directions. The eye-popping overlooks are as compelling as the grand vistas of the glimmer twins: Baker and Shuksan. Pick your way out to the edges of the escarpment. You can peer down at Iceberg Lake and the Galena Chain Lakes trail and decide if you want to hike there.

To avoid crowds, tackle Table Mountain before 10 A.M. Or, if sunset isn't until 9 or 10 P.M., start after 6 P.M. At dusk you can enjoy Mt. Shuksan at its visually richest, and still be back to your car before dark.

Traversing the mountain top initially looks easy. But the route eventually becomes indefinite and requires light scrambling. The obstacles include steep snowbanks. If you're not completely confident of your ability to navigate rough terrain, turn around when the route gets sketchy.

FACT

By Car

Drive Highway 542 to the Mt. Baker ski area. Go right at the large map of Mt. Baker and continue 2.6 miles to the Artist Point parking lot at road's end on Kulshan Ridge, 5100 feet. In a year of

heavy snowfall, you might not be able to drive that far until late
August.

On Foot

The trail starts from the southwest side of the parking lot.
There's an immediate choice of trails, which is not shown on
maps. Take the trail on the right, behind the large trailhead sign.
It immediately ascends the lava cliffs of Table Mountain. On top,
you'll often have different paths to choose from. Blue flags mark
the main route for about 15 minutes. Before you hike the length
of the plateau, walk out to the southeast edge for views of Shuksan. Then go back to the main route, which is fairly clear, and
follow it along the southern edge to the plateau's southwest
corner and a sheer drop overlooking the Galena Chain Lakes
trail. If you venture to the northeast edge, you can look down to
an ice-covered lake and the valley cupping Bagley Lakes.

If you keep traversing north, in about 20 minutes you'll come
to a rock band dropping 20 feet to a snowfield. This stretch is
passable, but most people won't feel comfortable attempting it. If
you do, look on the right side of the drop for the more stable,
stair-step rocks. If no rocks are exposed, and the slope is solid
snow, forget it. Before you drop to the snowfield, look across the
snow to see two choices of path on the other side.

Table Mountain view of Mt. Shuksan

Follow the right fork for about 10 minutes until it peters out. If you want to explore more, continue wandering atop the mesa until you hit the sheer edge of the cliffs. The Galena Chain Lakes trail is several hundred feet below, but don't attempt to descend to it unless you're a trained climber.

The left fork descends to the Galena Chain Lakes trail, but soon requires scrambling. There might still be flags marking the way, but don't rely on them. Proceed only if you're a capable routefinder. If you make it down, go left (southeast) when you hit the Galena Chain Lakes trail and ascend to the junction with the Ptarmigan Ridge trail. The parking lot is then a level 1.2 miles northeast. If you don't want to negotiate that descent from the top of Table Mountain, return to the parking lot the same way you came.

Trip 4
Ptarmigan Ridge

Location	Mount Baker Wilderness.
Distance	9.4-mile round trip to Coleman Pinnacle.
Elevation gain	1000'.
Maps	Green Trails No. 14–Mt. Shuksan; Trails Illustrated No. 223–North Cascades National Park Complex.

OPINION

Congratulations. You are hereby granted temporary admission to the realm of the mountaineer. That is, if it's late in the hiking season and the previous winter's snowfall has been light. Otherwise, sections of this entirely alpine trail, swinging across steep, barren slopes, could be prohibitively snowbound.

If your timing and the conditions are right, wahoo! You'll feel like an astronaut shot to another planet. The views are so vast, the sights so jolting, the beauty so raw, it's hard to believe you're still on earth. This terrain surely bears no resemblance to the tame, humdrum settings where most of us spend our days. You'll be sharing space with other astronauts, however. When the Artist Point parking lot is accessible, the paved road to it ensures all the trails in this area are busy. Most people, however, walk only a mile toward Ptarmigan Ridge. If you push on, you'll escape the crowd.

Snow-free tread permitting, hike at least to the 3.5-mile point before turning back. The view is triumphant. In addition to the postcard image of Mt. Baker and the Rainbow Glacier, you can see Mt. Blum, Mt. Hagan, Mt. Bacon, Mt. Shuksan of course, and a long list of other titans. On the way, you'll cross meltwater creeklets singing their soothing water-songs. You'll pass pockets of flourishing wildflowers. And you'll be eyed with bemusement by the resident marmots and pikas.

Beyond Coleman Pinnacle, the trail skims across talus slopes and snowpatches, winds through a bouldery moonscape, and deposits you on the Sholes Glacier, all the while offering ever more staggering scenery and an up-close-and-personal encounter with Mr. Baker. Continue as far as the weather, the snowpack, your experience and common sense will allow. The farther you go, the better it gets. Just don't cross steep snowfields without an ice axe and the know-how to self-arrest. Don't risk getting stuck on a distant ridge when cloud or fog might diminish visibility. Remember that if you walk on a glacier, you risk falling into a hidden crevasse.

FACT

By Car

Drive Highway 542 to the Mt. Baker ski area. Go right at the large map of Mt. Baker and continue 2.6 miles to the Artist Point parking lot at road's end on Kulshan Ridge, 5100 feet. In a year of heavy snowfall, you might not be able to drive that far until late August.

On Foot

The trailhead is on the southwest side of the parking lot. There is an immediate choice of trails—not shown on the maps. Don't take the trail on the right ascending the lava cliffs of Table Mountain. Instead, take Galena Chain Lakes trail 682. Contour a mostly level 1.2 miles (passing a rough side trail ascending Table Mountain at 0.2 mile) along the south side of Table Mountain until you reach a junction at 5200 feet. The Galena Chain Lakes loop goes right. Go left (south) for Ptarmigan Ridge. Descend into a basin, where the trail splits temporarily. Take your pick of forks. The paths soon rejoin to form a better-defined trail on the beginning of Ptarmigan Ridge, up to your left. Follow the ridge trail upward, then left across a steep, airy, south-facing slope of rock, scree, volcanic dust, and possibly snow. The vistas expand the farther you walk.

At 3.7 miles, 5600 feet, you'll attain a clear view of Mt. Baker's Rainbow Glacier (Trip 6). The trail then ascends southwest 1.0 mile and 500 feet to the slopes of Coleman Pinnacle. If you're staying overnight, you'll find flat, bare spots to pitch your tent beneath the pinnacle. Bring enough water or rely on snowmelt. You could descend south cross-country from beneath Coleman Pinnacle, just before the trail makes a sharp turn northwest. You'll see a mostly frozen, turquoise tarn 0.6 mile away and about 400 feet below.

Along much of the trail, and especially beyond Coleman Pinnacle, how far you can safely proceed depends on the snowpack, your level of preparation and experience, and the weather. During late summer or early autumn in years of low snowfall, it's possible to walk an obvious trail west past Coleman Pinnacle, onto the Sholes Glacier.

Ptarmigan Ridge

Trip 5

Railroad Grade /
Park Butte

Location	Mt. Baker National Recreation Area.
Distance	6.0-mile round trip up Railroad Grade; 6.6-mile round trip to Park Butte.
Elevation gain	2100' to Railroad Grade or Park Butte.
Maps	Green Trails No. 45–Hamilton, No. 46–Lake Shannon (shows Road 12); Trails Illustrated No. 223–North Cascades National Park Complex.

OPINION

Both Park Butte and Railroad Grade are veritable holy sites—as sublimely moving (and crowded) as those of any religion. If you have time for only one, choose Railroad (RR) Grade. Strong hikers can pay homage to both in a full day. If you have two days for this area, do RR Grade one day, then combine the Scott Paul trail (Trip 25) and Park Butte the next.

Most hikers will have the energy to go at least part way up the moraine of RR Grade. The raw beauty of Mt. Baker towering above lush meadows will pull you onward and upward. Suddenly, you'll peek over the moraine at the roaring chaos of Easton Glacier's gorge and Rocky Creek. It's as if Scotty had beamed you to another, much younger planet.

The track along RR Grade feels like a pilgrimage route where seekers come to witness the glories of creation. You're likely to encounter other hikers—it's a popular trail—but the atmosphere of awe and reverence makes a crowd tolerable here. Just don't be lured by the yawning chasms, even if you see others venturing onto the ice. Unless, of course, you know what you're doing.

After the RR Grade trail peters out, you can continue by wending your way upward through rock and rubble. Footprints in the sand between rocks offer hints of a route. But if you can't figure it out on your own, you shouldn't go. Fit, competent scramblers can navigate the tantalizing reaches beside Easton Glacier all the way to High Camp near 6200 feet. Beyond that, crampons and ice axes are required equipment. Gazing up at Mt. Baker from High Camp, the summit seems within close reach, but it takes climbers another five hours.

At High Camp's rocky perch next to the cascading ice, you can pitch your tent with glacier travelers. You'll have to grind to get there with a full pack, but you'll be rewarded with an astounding view not only of Easton Glacier, but of the San Juan Islands as well.

If you make it to High Camp, cross the small snowfield west to another rocky outcropping and get a staggering view of the Deming Glacier. You'll find it hard to believe any view could compete with what you've seen already, but this one does. Approach slowly. And don't stretch for photos. The rock is straining to answer the call of gravity.

Hiking to Park Butte feels like less of an adventure than ascending RR Grade, but it too offers a visual feast: Looking southwest from the butte at plunging forests reminds you it was a gasoline engine, not your legs, that enabled you to escape those depths.

From Park Butte, Mt. Baker seems to loom even larger than it did from RR Grade, and you get a great perspective of the route you just took. You also see Deming Glacier and the yawning canyon below the Black Buttes. To the west, the impressive Sisters Range vies for your attention.

Atop the butte is a former fire lookout cabin that's now maintained by the Skagit Alpine Club of Mt. Vernon. It's open to the public when members aren't using it. Please be respectful of the furniture and other equipment. Spending a stormy night here would be an experience of a lifetime.

In and above Morovitz Meadow, you'll see paths leading to points other than RR Grade or Park Butte. They're not worth pursuing. For example, the trail to Baker Pass ascends through meadows only to descend into a forested gully before reaching Mazama Park. Views diminish down there. From Mazama one trail drops to the unscenic Ridley Creek valley; another trail leads southwest to forested Bell Pass hunkering between two hills. You probably won't be tempted by these excursions when so much glory is within easy reach up high.

FACT

By Car

Drive Highway 20 east 16.5 miles from Sedro Woolley, or west 6.0 miles from Concrete. Turn north onto the Grandy-Baker Lake Road. Drive northeast 12.4 miles and, just past Rocky Creek bridge, go left (northwest) on South Fork Nooksack Road 12. Ignore the unsigned road to your right at 1.8 miles. At 3.5 miles turn right at the sign MT. BAKER NATIONAL RECREATION AREA, onto Sulphur Creek Road 13. Follow signs to Shriebers Meadow. You'll reach the trailhead parking lot at 8.7 miles, 3300 feet. There are four campsites here, a couple beside Sulphur Creek.

On Foot

You'll gain 1400 feet hiking to Morovitz Meadow, crossing glacier meltwater streams and boulder fields along the way. At 1.9 miles, just before completing the switchbacks and reaching lower Morovitz Meadow, you'll see the Scott Paul trail (Trip 25) veering off right. It makes a long loop over moraine and meadow back to the trailhead. To continue to RR Grade, stay left. When you reach a junction in the lower meadow at 2.0 miles, you'll see the Park Butte lookout cabin above you; the left trail goes there. Go right for RR Grade and you'll soon pass about eight tent sites scattered in the trees. Some offer views of the looming volcano. Beyond the tent sites, the trail ascends the crest of the RR Grade moraine. Near 5400 feet, 3.0 miles, the trail dwindles to a climbers' path. It takes you another mile or more over jumbled rock to the edge of Easton Glacier at about 6200 feet.

Turning left at the 2.0-mile junction in lower Morovitz Meadow, it's 0.3 mile northwest to another junction. Here, in the upper meadow, the left fork ascends southwest 1.0 mile to the summit of 5400-foot Park Butte. The right fork goes west under the south side of Cathedral Crag and drops to Mazama Park at 4400 feet, about 0.5 mile from the upper meadow. If the subalpine campsites just west of RR Grade are full, you might find a private spot in Mazama Park. You can also reach Mazama from RR Grade on an old trail cutting west to Baker Pass.

From Mazama, the right fork descends above Ridley Creek 2.5 miles to the Middle Fork Nooksack Road 38, which goes west to the hamlet of Welcome on Highway 542. Left from Mazama goes 2.5 miles to forested Bell Pass.

Trip 6
Rainbow Ridge

Location	Mt. Baker Wilderness.
Distance	4.5-mile round trip.
Elevation gain	1200′.
Maps	Green Trails No. 14–Mt. Shuksan,
	No. 13–Mt. Baker (to identify glaciers),
	No. 46–Lake Shannon (shows Road 1130).

OPINION

The mammoth south face of Mt. Shuksan. A gigantic, gnawed ridge vying for attention against Mt. Baker's Rainbow Glacier. A 2000-foot cascade plunging off the ridge dividing Swift Creek and Rainbow Creek. The glaciated chaos of Avalanche Gorge. And in the center of it all, a trail surges through parklands, to lonesome vistas and infinite inspiration. Be there. It will stir the wildness in you.

The Rainbow Ridge trail is not indicated on maps, but looking at the Green Trails map you can guess at the course it follows from road's end, along the southwest side of the ridge above Rainbow Creek. Because of the trail's relative obscurity, you won't feel pressed by a throng of hikers here, like at Ptarmigan Ridge or Park Butte. The first 50 yards are sketchy and rough. After that, the trail is good all the way up the ridge and a bit northwest along it. It'll make you work hard, but only briefly.

If you're familiar with the Ptarmigan Ridge trail, you'll enjoy identifying it from atop Rainbow Ridge. It's to the northwest, slicing under the base of a green knob and reddish slope to the right of a mesa.

Though Rainbow Ridge might seem too short to bother backpacking, there are wonderful campsites up here. A smart plan is to begin hiking about 6 P.M., when the cool of the evening calms the flies and keeps you from getting sweat-soaked. In late summer, you'll still have plenty of daylight to pitch your tent. Then you can sit outside and enjoy the view without flapping furiously at the flies. After witnessing Shuksan at sunset and Baker at sunrise, wander the ridge out and back, then leave by 10 A.M., before the flies rev up and regroup.

FACT

By Car

Drive Highway 20 east 16.5 miles from Sedro Woolley, or west 6.0 miles from Concrete. Turn left (north) onto the Grandy-Baker Lake Road. At 17.8 miles you'll see Boulder Creek Campground on the right. Pass it, cross the creek, and 0.2 mile farther turn left (north) onto Marten Lake Road 1130, signed BOULDER RIDGE TRAIL, RAINBOW FALLS. At 1.5 miles go right at the fork. Cross a creek at 2.1 miles. At the signed junction in 3.9 miles, go left (northwest) toward Rainbow Falls. At 4.5 miles, Rainbow Falls is on the right; stop for a peek. Arrive at a fork 9.5 miles from the Baker Lake Road. The road ends here in a clearcut, at 3600 feet. Park in the flat area to the right. The rougher road left leads to the trail.

On Foot

The rough road ends abruptly. Continue in the same direction, picking your way over deadfall and through shoulder-high brush. Then angle right, entering timber that survived the cutting. The route has been blazed with orange tape. A trail becomes apparent within 0.2 mile of the rough road. Emerge from tall trees into heather and 5-foot trees. Gain 700 feet in the first mile to arrive at a small meadow. Then resume the steep ascent—250 feet in 0.25 mile—to the ridgecrest. You're now at 1.5 miles, just above 4220 feet. Look closely and you'll find areas flat enough to pitch a tent.

The trail now wanders among rock outcroppings, through heather and blueberry bushes. When you reach big boulders and tall mountain hemlocks, there's a view 2000 feet down into Avalanche Gorge. Here the trail descends the south side of the ridge. Follow the undulating tread as far as you feel comfortable doing so; it eventually diminishes to a game path. There are many possible campsites.

The primary sights are glacier-draped Mt. Baker in front of you, directly west; the Sulphide Glacier on Mt. Shuksan, close by to the northeast; and Hagan Mountain, Anderson Butte and Mount Watson, to the southeast, in front of Bacon Glacier on Bacon Peak.

View from Rainbow Ridge

Trip 7
Hidden Lake Peaks

Location	Mt. Baker-Snoqualmie National Forest / North Cascades National Park.
Distance	9.0-mile round trip.
Elevation gain	3200'.
Maps	Green Trails No. 47–Marblemount (shows Road 15 and 1540), No. 48–Diablo Dam, No. 80–Cascade Pass; Trails Illustrated No. 223–North Cascades National Park Complex.

OPINION

Oh, what a seductive trail this is, revealing itself shyly at first, then more brazenly, until it fulfills your every desire. The panorama from Hidden Lake lookout is the kind hikers lust after. Some think they can only experience such ecstasy elsewhere, like the Swiss Alps. But you can consummate your alpine fantasies right here.

Well before the summit, you traverse through meadows and boulder fields that would themselves be a satisfying destination if the trail didn't continue. Be grateful it does. Of all the hiker-accessible lookouts in the North Cascades, only Sourdough Mountain offers a view as impressive as this one above Hidden Lake. You can see east over the Stehekin Valley, west to the ocean, north to Mt. Baker, south to Mt. Rainier. Most of the great mountains of the range are visible from this apex. You're surrounded by serrated ridges, spiky peaks, alpine slopes, steep couloirs, and hanging valleys, all inviting you to know them more intimately. Though easy to ignore amid the overwhelming beauty, you can also see ugly clearcuts west and south. Yes, it's a logging road that whisks you to the trailhead, but it would be better to hike 10 extra miles to reach premier settings like this than tolerate the continued rape of our forests.

Be sure to pack your camera and a full roll of film. Don't hike here on a rainy or even cloudy day; you need a blue sky to fully appreciate the 360° vista. And keep in mind that the upper reaches of the trail can remain snow-covered well into summer. Before setting out, ask at a ranger station if it's hikeable.

FACT

By Car

At the eastern edge of Marblemount, where Highway 20 bends north, go straight (east) onto the Cascade River road and immediately cross the Skagit River. In 0.7 mile pass the Rockport-Cascade Road on the right. Continue east on the Cascade River road (now labeled 15), which turns to gravel at 5.2 miles. At 8.3 miles, pass the entrance to Marble Creek Campground. At 9.8 miles, turn left (east) onto Road 1540. It's a steep, narrow road that has a treacherous dropoff the last 0.3 mile. A jeep leaving the trailhead rolled off the edge here because the driver thought he could pass a car coming up. If you meet another vehicle, be safe. At 4.8 miles, 3700 feet, arrive at the trailhead. Because the parking area is narrow, it's best to turn around before you park. Don't block the turnaround area near the trailhead sign at the end of the road.

On Foot

The first 0.25 mile east is through brush and over creeklets. Then walk in deep forest for 0.75 mile on moderate switchbacks. At 1.0 mile cross East Fork Sibley Creek and burst into meadows dappled with alder, cow parsnip, Indian hellebore, penstemon, monkeypod, tiger lilies, thistle, paintbrush and bluebells. There are waterfalls above. The trail ascends as it traverses to the head of the East Fork. The narrow path is on steeply slanted grass-and-dirt slopes that can be muddy and very slippery. Heavy rain has washed out this section of trail in previous years. Ask at the Marblemount ranger station about the latest conditions. At 1.7 miles you can look from meadows across to the rocky course the trail follows on a northwest-facing slope. Cross the creek at 2.2 miles. The rich meadowland changes to predominantly alpine heather as the terrain gets rockier. At 2.3 miles, 5400 feet, the trail turns sharply southwest.

Then walk 0.8 miles through bluish-green mountain hemlock, pink-flowered alpine heather, and white granite as you traverse under the ridge of Hidden Lake Peaks. Flat rock slabs in a variety of shapes are ideal for sunning. The view from here is northwest

to nearby Lookout Mountain and Monogram Peak, and to Mt.
Baker far in the distance. In the next stretch you might encounter
several broad snowfields as late as August. There's one treacherous snow gully that could be your demise if you slip. That's why
the park rangers usually say the lookout is inaccessible without
an ice axe until mid-August.

After the switchback at 3.7 miles, you can see the lookout on
the spire ahead, so you know where you're going even if you're
walking atop snow. Just below that switchback, it's also possible
to angle off the trail to the right (west), where the snow melts
earlier and where you might feel more secure continuing the
ascent. To do this, contour directly south, scrambling over dry
rock and through heather, then angle back up left (southeast) to
rejoin the trail at the 4.0-mile point.

If the trail is buried, and both options—ascending the snowfields or routefinding—make you hesitant to proceed, and you
turn back at 3.7 miles, you'll still have had a rewarding hike. Keep
in mind, snow here doesn't mean there's snow all the way to the
lookout. The final 0.2 mile melts free much earlier.

At 4.0 miles you begin the last pitch: 700 feet in 0.5 mile. At 4.2
miles the trail turns left (east), passes a tiny tarn, and enters a
narrow gully (possibly snowfilled, but not steep) directly beneath
the lookout. At 4.3 miles you reach the notch between Hidden
Lake Peak and the spire the lookout sits on. Here, too, you cross
into the National Park.

It's possible to scramble left (northeast) to 7088-foot Hidden
Lake Peak. To reach the lookout, turn right (southwest) and pick
up the narrow, steep trail ascending the northeast side of the
spire. Look for cairns marking the route, switchbacking on
packed dirt, boulders and slabs.

At 4.5 miles, 6900 feet, reach the summit, where the lookout
cabin is anchored to a jumble of huge, rectangular rock blocks.
Hidden Lake is 1140 feet below you. The pinnacles of The Triad
and the glacier-encrusted pyramid of 8868-foot Eldorado Peak
are northeast. East are Forbidden Peak, Boston Basin and Boston
Glacier, and Sahale Mountain. Johannesburg Mountain rises in
the near southeast above the Cascade River Road. Southeast,
looming above the Middle and South forks Cascade River, are the
Middle Cascade Glacier and Mount Formidable. Mount Buckindy and Snowking Mountain are in the southern foreground,
with Glacier Peak and Mount Rainier behind them. Marblemount

is below to the northwest, in the Skagit River valley. Sauk Mountain is farther west. The Easton Glacier and Railroad Grade are discernable on Mt. Baker, far north.

The Hidden Lake lookout cabin is open to the public. It sleeps four. If you hope to spend the night there, it's first come, first served, so bring a tent in case it's occupied. You'll find several good campsites 400 feet below the notch, on the way to Hidden Lake. There are more near the eastern end of the lake, where the ground is flatter. Pick your own way over talus to the lakeshore.

Hidden Lake

Trip 8
Cascade Pass / Sahale Arm

Location	North Cascades National Park.
Distance	7.4-mile round trip to Cascade Pass; 12.4-mile round trip to Sahale Glacier.
Elevation gain	1800' to Cascade Pass; 4200' to Sahale Glacier.
Maps	Green Trails No. 80–Cascade Pass; Trails Illustrated No. 223–Cascade National Park Complex.

OPINION

If you ever want to give nonhikers a sampling of what you expend your energy to see, cart them up to this trailhead. Views along the deeper reaches of the Cascade River Road are more impressive than from Highway 20 through the National Park. At the road's end parking lot, the cliffs and couloirs of 8065-foot Johannesburg Mountain are as awesome as the culminating sights on many hikes. But that's only the appetizer. The feast is high above.

You climb 1400 feet in the first 2.5 miles. It doesn't feel as steep as it sounds, though, because the trail is gently graded. After that you can relax somewhat and enjoy the walloping welcome of Johannesburg Mountain as you contour alpine slopes to Cascade Pass.

The trail to the pass is trodden by hundreds of boots each summer weekend. Having to say "hello" so often can get to be a nuisance. On our way up one afternoon, we passed more than 50 people coming down. By starting before 8 A.M. you can avoid most of the crowd and have time to wander up Sahale Arm. If you're going only as far the pass, start after 3 P.M. That way you'll have it mostly to yourself, and when you descend around 6 or 7 P.M., you won't have to engage in people-passing pleasantries. To avoid the crowds altogether, choose another hike such as nearby Boston Basin. Or just don't plop at the pass. Not many people continue to the Doubtful Lake overlook, and fewer still attempt the arduous route to Sahale Glacier.

Try to continue beyond the pass, up Sahale Arm at least to the flowery meadows above Doubtful Lake—so named, we presume, because the bone-jarring descent to its lovely shores is a dubious enterprise. Staying above the lake, on the finger of Sahale Arm, you can see Inspiration Glacier on Eldorado Peak to the west, a scene so dramatic you might feel your heart rise in your throat. Allow yourself an hour just to sit and absorb the staggering beauty of it all.

Inspired? Press on. You ain't seen nothin' yet. You eventually leave the grassy slopes, continuing the merciless ascent on a rocky moraine. As the way gets sketchier, the views just keep getting better. You can walk, albeit knees to chest, all the way to Sahale Glacier. Coming this far is tough, but not dangerous for competent, confident hikers with some scrambling experience. Your biggest worry will be dropping your camera or running out of film in the midst of so much magnificence. Range upon range of spiky mountains to the south will gradually reveal themselves to you, including distant Glacier Peak. Further exploration onto the ice requires proper equipment and training.

FACT

By Car

At the eastern edge of Marblemount, where Highway 20 bends north, go straight (east) onto the Cascade River road and immediately cross the Skagit River. In 0.7 mile pass the Rockport-Cascade Road on the right. Continue east on the Cascade River road (now labeled 15), which turns to gravel at 5.2 miles. At 16.9 miles, pass the right fork to the Cascade River trails, and curve sharply left toward Cascade Pass. Enter the National Park at 18.3 miles. At 23.5 miles arrive at the large Cascade Pass trailhead at road's end, 3600 feet.

On Foot

The trail to Cascade Pass is wide and well-maintained. Switchback through forest for 2.5 miles, then start the long, gradual traverse across alpine slopes to Cascade Pass at 3.7 miles, 5400 feet.

Ascending to Cascade Pass

For the view of Doubtful Lake and explorations up Sahale Arm, take the narrow trail that starts several feet below the east side of Cascade Pass. Don't follow the main trail into Pelton Basin. Head north (left) up the ridge. After 0.75 mile and 1000 feet you're on the crest of Sahale Arm. A minor trail descends about 800 feet to Doubtful Lake. The main trail parts the ridgecrest meadows. When the meadows end, you'll see the faint climbers' path ascending at a 45° angle atop loose rock of the moraine. Reach the campsites at the edge of Sahale Glacier about 2.5 miles from Cascade Pass. You need permits for these sites, as you do for all backcountry camping in the National Park.

Trip 9

Thornton Lakes / Trappers Peak

Location	Ross Lake National Recreation Area / North Cascades National Park.
Distance	9.4-mile round trip to ridge above Thornton Lakes.
Elevation gain	2360'; 1004' more to Trappers Peak.
Maps	Green Trails No. 47–Marblemount; Trails Illustrated No. 223–North Cascades National Park Complex.

OPINION

The cliche "you get what you pay for" must have been coined by a hiker. Here, you get a great experience if you go as far as the overlook above Thornton Lakes, and a premier one if you go all the way up Trappers Peak. The overlook is stunning, but the trail is in unimpressive forest all the way there. Beyond, the route is a fun challenge above treeline. And atop Trappers, the panorama is complete. The exultation you'll feel on Trappers will boost your spirits through the following work-week, so go for it.

The dirt road to the trailhead is a rock-and-roller. Low-clearance cars can make it with a little coaxing. Low-energy cars will have to maintain speed; it's steep. But don't let it frustrate you. Imagine having to gain all that elevation on foot.

Backpacking here will give experienced scramblers time to explore the middle and upper lakes and the tantalizing, rocky terrain northwest of the lower lake. But don't expect a great campsite; the sites at the lower lake, just across the outlet stream, are not pleasant.

If you're dayhiking, don't drop to the lakes. Find a perch on the huge boulders, high above the lower lake. From this overlook, you can see the lower two lakes in the cirque beneath looming Mt. Triumph. You can also set your sights on Trappers Peak, to the northeast above the first lake. It's not as difficult to summit as it looks. In the other direction, past the highway, you can see Tee-bone Ridge and the Newhalem Creek drainage. The Neve Glacier and Pyramid and Colonial peaks are to the east.

After you've savored that spectacle, continue up Trappers Peak. Don't let 960 feet separate you from the scenic and geographic zenith of the trip. If stupendous, airy heights turn your crank, you'll love this. The view encompasses the wild Pickct Range to the north; the secretive, uppermost Thornton Lake; and the village of Newhalem far below to the southeast.

FACT

By Car

On Highway 20, drive 11.0 miles northeast of Marblemount, or 3.0 miles southwest of Newhalem. Between mileposts 117 and 118, you'll see a wide road veering off the northwest side of the highway. A brown sign announces THORNTON CREEK ROAD. Drive this rough road 5.1 miles to the trailhead, at 2600 feet.

On Foot

The path is in good condition, with small log bridges over mucky spots. The first 2.3 miles are on a 1960s logging road—now so narrow and overgrown it looks like a trail. The next mile passes through a dry, open, reforested area. After contouring in

The Pickets, from Trappers Peak

and out of the Thornton Creek drainage, the trail climbs steadily through forest. When you reach a post marking the national-park boundary, you're about to leave the trees. You gain the ridge at 4.7 miles, 4960 feet.

Just before the ridge, you'll come to a small fork. Five minutes to your left, following a tiny trail through boulders, is the Thornton Lakes overlook. If you chose to drop to the lower lake, it's 460 feet and 0.6 mile down a rough trail. Three campsites sit near the lower lake's outlet at 4500 feet. From there, a primitive path ascends to the upper lakes.

To ascend Trappers Peak, return to the signed fork. Head straight toward the triangular rock. Climb the clearly defined route on the ridge for about 45 minutes, until you reach the top at 5964 feet. The first 10 minutes are the hardest. You might need to use your hands, but there is no precipitous exposure.

Trip 10

Easy Pass

Location	North Cascades National Park.
Distance	7.2-mile round trip.
Elevation gain	2800'.
Maps	Green Trails No. 49–Mt. Logan; Trails Illustrated No. 223–North Cascades National Park Complex.

OPINION

A lot of people say Easy Pass is misnamed, that it isn't easy. But it's certainly not difficult compared to many hikes in the North Cascades. And the scenery is worthy of applause.

Within two miles you're in alpine country with broad views. Like a theater marquee announcing the performance, a great cliff towers above you to the left. As you ascend, you can feel the show is about to begin. Continue to the far side of Easy Pass. Just before the trail descends, find a seat on the heather slope and watch the drama unfold above the emerald depths of Fisher Basin. The principal characters are, from east to west, Fisher Peak, Black Peak behind and above it, and Mt. Arriva. Standing stage right is Mt. Logan and, far west, rising above Thunder Creek Valley, Tricouni Peak and glacier-clad Klawatti Peak. Neve Glacier even makes an appearance to the northwest. Such a star-studded scene provides hours of entertainment.

Easy is one of the last passes to melt out. It cleaves Ragged Ridge in a west-to-east swath. Because the ridge blocks a lot of sun, the pass tends to hold snow. It's usually inaccessible to hikers until August. You'll be lucky if it's safe to hike without an ice axe by mid-July. If you arrive when the final 0.2 mile of trail below the pass is still snow-covered, try to skirt it on the right where there might be solid, bare rock.

FACT

By Car

On Highway 20, drive 21.5 miles southeast from Colonial Creek Campground on Diablo Lake, or 6.3 miles northwest of Rainy Pass. On the west side of the highway, a short spur road leads to trailhead parking.

On Foot

This generally good trail takes you on a bridge over Granite Creek at 0.2 mile. After ascending moderately through thin western hemlock and Pacific silver fir for 2.0 miles, you come to the first crossing of Easy Pass Creek; logs will probably be there to make it easy. Then the trail climbs more steeply.

Near 2.3 miles you exit forest and soon cross Easy Pass Creek the second time. The cleft of Easy Pass is now visible. You get views east across the valley to the dry, rugged spires of Mt. Hardy and southeast to Cutthroat Peak. Rockhop or jump across Easy Pass Creek two more times.

Approaching the pass, the trail switchbacks up the right (north) side of the gully. The final 0.5 mile is through heather and berry bushes, then talus. At 3.6 miles attain 6500-foot Easy Pass, which bisects Ragged Ridge. The Green Trails 1985 map incorrectly indicates 3.0 miles, but the National Park trailhead sign is right: it's 3.6. Larch, alpine fir, mountain hemlock and whitebark pine adorn the pass. Scramble a few hundred feet higher up the ridgeline on either side of the pass for more glory. Mosquitoes and flies are pestiferous here, from early July until fall. Hope for a stiff breeze to keep them grounded.

Camping is not allowed at Easy Pass. You have to drop 2.1 miles into Fisher Basin, to a no-fire campsite at 5200 feet. It's easiest to enjoy Easy Pass as a dayhike. From Fisher Camp, the Fisher Creek trail leads 9.2 miles west through deep forest to Junction Camp. There, you could pick up the Thunder Creek trail. You'd then have the option of continuing north 10.0 miles to Highway 20, or south 9.4 miles to Park Creek Pass. Read Trip 93 for route details in either direction. Backpacking north from Junction Camp makes for an easy shuttle trip, but it's also a forest walk the whole way. Park Creek Pass is stupendous, but getting back to your car at the Easy Pass trailhead would be a major challenge.

Fisher Basin, Fisher Peak, Black Peak seen from Easy Pass

Trip 11

Heather Pass /
Maple Pass

Location	North Cascades Scenic Highway Area.
Distance	6.5-mile round trip.
Elevation gain	2000'.
Maps	Green Trails No. 49–Mt. Logan, No. 50–Washington Pass, No. 81–McGregor Mtn, No. 82–Stehekin; Trails Illustrated No. 223–North Cascades National Park Complex.

OPINION

Heather and Maple passes are to the North Cascades what the Indiana Jones Adventure is to Disneyworld: a feature attraction. Few hikes anywhere are so instantly gratifying; the trail virtually flings you into the alpine zone. You'll find everything you could ask for—two majestic lake cirques, waterfalls, flower-filled meadows, awesome views of rugged peaks from open ridgecrests—all within a few hours. Plus it's a loop trip. Crowds can give it a theme-park atmosphere, but that's easy to forgive when you're surrounded by such grandeur.

Here you can fully appreciate the contrast between the two sides of the Pacific Crest. To the east are dry, brown, stark, rocky peaks above sparse forest. To the west are lush, green slopes and glacier-capped mountains above big timber. The scenery changes radically with a quick swivel of your head: from the yellow and rusty scree slopes along the PCT between Cutthroat and Granite passes, to the abundant greenery ringing the snowcone of Glacier Peak.

Many thrills are packed into this short hike. But getting beyond the first one, Lake Ann, can be difficult on a sunny day. After admiring the tremendous cirque, some people end the hike right here. They find a smooth log, stretch out and doze, lulled by the music of the cascade at the far shore. Resist temptation. Push on.

Soon you'll be striding atop the green slopes hugging Lake Ann. Great mountains will swirl about you. Then comes the exciting plunge into the Rainy Lake cirque. Along the way, you'll often have the pleasure of seeing far ahead to the trail you'll be walking, or way back where you came from.

Come here midweek when there's less traffic on the trail and the highway. On a typical weekend, you'll hear cars whizzing past the trailhead for the first 20 minutes and last 40 minutes of your hike. You can also escape the crowd by rambling the sketchy-but-easy to-follow route from Heather Pass to Lewis Lake and on to Wing Lake beneath compelling Black Peak. You can camp there.

Do the loop counter-clockwise. Go to Lake Ann and Heather Pass first, then drop to Rainy Lake from Maple Pass. It would be exhausting and discouraging to ascend above Rainy Lake first. But beware: it's a knee-jolter coming down. Though this descent is not shown on the Green Trails 1985 and 1987 maps, the trail is obvious and signed.

FACT

By Car

On Highway 20, drive 37.2 miles southeast of Newhalem, or 20.8 miles southwest of the Early Winters Information Center, to Rainy Pass. Turn west into the Rainy Pass picnic-area parking lot, at 4855 feet.

On Foot

Go to the south end of the parking lot, near where you drove in. The trail is signed LAKE TRAILS. Forest Service information is posted here. Take the steep, dirt trail. The level, paved walkway will be the end of your return route from Rainy Lake.

The trail gains 670 feet in 1.0 mile, switchbacking through open forest with views across the highway to Cutthroat Peak and Whistler Mountain. It then crosses meadowy slopes with a view into the Lake Ann cirque and of Frisco Mountain to the south. At 1.2 miles the trail turns west into a narrow valley cut by Lake Ann's outlet stream.

At 1.3 miles, 5400 feet, reach a signed fork. Left leads 0.5 mile through subalpine forest and marshy meadows to Lake Ann. Look for trumpet shaped, pink monkeyflower, orange and yellow columbines, and subalpine spirea, which has small, pink blossoms in a flat cluster at the top. Camping is prohibited within 0.25 mile of the lake.

From the 1.3-mile fork, the main trail goes right. Ascend a rockslide with open views of Lake Ann below. Reach 6100-foot Heather Pass at 2.25 miles. On the right just below Heather Pass, you'll see a faint spur trail descending through heather. It leads to Lewis Lake at 5702 feet, and continues to Wing Lake at 6905 feet.

From a switchback just above Heather Pass, you can see nearby Lewis Lake to the northwest. Wing Lake is visible beyond, in the cirque beneath 8970-foot Black Peak.

From Heather Pass the trail ascends 260 feet toward Corteo Peak. Copper Pass and Stiletto Peak are visible east and slightly south. The trail contours south from Heather Pass 0.5 mile, then ascends 240 feet to Maple Pass. From the ridge, Corteo Peak is directly west. South of it is Mt. Benzarino. From Maple Pass, you can see Storm King Mountain between the two. Reach 6600-foot Maple Pass at 3.1 miles. Maple Creek valley is deep below. Peering across Glacier Peak Wilderness from here you can see Glacier Peak.

To complete the loop via Rainy Lake, go east along the ridgecrest, topping out at 6850 feet on a shoulder of Frisco Mountain. Rainy Lake is 2050 feet below. Tight, steep switchbacks descend the exposed edge separating the Lake Ann and Rainy Lake

cirques. Near 4.5 miles you can see a hanging basin above Rainy Lake and a long waterfall tumbling into it. Near 6400 feet the persistent switchbacks drop below treeline. The last 1.75 miles descend northeast along the ridge through viewless forest. When you reach the paved walkway, go left 0.25 mile to the parking lot. Right leads 0.7 mile to the shore of Rainy Lake.

Lake Ann from Heather Pass

Trip 12
Green Mountain

Location	Mt. Baker-Snoqualmie National Forest / Glacier Peak Wilderness.
Distance	8.0-mile round trip.
Elevation gain	3000'.
Maps	Green Trails No. 80–Cascade Pass; US Forest Service–Glacier Peak Wilderness.

OPINION

The summit of Green Mountain is a sublime aerie. You can peer into deep, forested valleys brooding below, and gaze across at bold peaks challenging the heavens. Having perched here once, you'll want to return again and again.

Gentle switchbacks and ever-expanding scenery ease your passage to the summit. Close by to the north is an unnamed Tahitian-green pyramidal mountain. Farther north is Mount Buckindy. To the east, you can trace the courses of Downey and Bachelor creeks below you, and above see a favorite of mountaineers: the Ptarmigan Traverse from glacier-capped Dome Peak, north to Mount Formidable. Glacier Peak dominates the southeastern horizon.

If you're aching to get views from on high, yet it's only May, the first 2 miles of the Green Mountain trail will probably be snow-free. You can spy Dome and Glacier peaks from there. Abundant glacier lilies might further reward your early-season effort. Snow in the basin beneath the summit usually stops hikers until July. But don't let an early-season venture keep you from doing the whole trip later.

From mid-July to early August, you can stalk tigers here. Not the striped, aggressive variety, but the spotted, orange, docile ones: tiger lilies. These exotic-looking blossoms speckle the greenery all the way up the south-facing hillside. Other species thrive here as well. If you're a wildflower zealot, it'll take you twice as long as others to reach the top. You'll be repeatedly stopped by arnica, Sitka valerian, purple penstemon, and colum-

bine, to name a few. The resplendent display rivals any in the
North Cascades.

FACT

By Car

On Highway 530, drive 11.3 miles south from Rockport, or 7.2
miles north from the Darrington Ranger Station. Turn east on
Suiattle River Road 26. Drive 19.0 miles southeast to Green
Mountain Road 2680. Turn left here and drive 5.8 miles to the
parking area along the road, at 3500 feet. You'll see a wood sign
on the left TRAIL 782 - TIMBERLINE 1 - LOOKOUT 4. From the road you
can survey the Suiattle River valley. Downey Mountain, directly
east, splits Sulphur and Downey creeks.

On Foot

Moderate switchbacks ascend 1.0 mile through forest before
emerging into lime-green corn lilies, wildflowers, tall grass, then
blueberry bushes. Already you get views southwest to White
Chuck Mountain, south to Sloan Peak, and southeast to Glacier
Peak. At 2.0 miles, 5200 feet, you can see east to Dome Peak and
farther southeast to Plummer and Fortress mountains, which are
above Suiattle Pass.

Then the trail rounds the end of a ridge, traverses north, and
drops 150 feet to shallow tarns in fragile meadows. Erosion here
is severe. The braided trail can be slippery from snowmelt or rain.
Do your best not to initiate yet another path. You'll also find that
here on the shaded north side of the ridge, snow lingers many
weeks longer than on the south slope. If you camp near the
meadow, use an established dirt site so you don't crush more
grass.

After climbing above the tarns, the trail enters a basin—probably snow covered until mid-July—where you can see the trail
slicing toward the summit of Green Mountain. You attain the
rocky summit and nearly 360° views at 4.0 miles, 6500 feet.
Scramble around the fire-lookout cabin for better views north.
The rickety cabin has been closed to the public, but might be
repaired and re-opened when the Forest Service budget allows.
You'll want several Green Trails maps (No. 80—Cascade Pass,
No. 81—McGregor Mtn, No. 112—Glacier Peak, No. 113—

Holden) or the Forest Service Glacier Peak Wilderness map to help you identify peaks.

View from Green Mountain

Trip 13
Mt. Dickerman

Location	Mt. Baker-Snoqualmie National Forest.
Distance	8.6-mile round trip.
Elevation gain	3723'.
Maps	Green Trails No. 111–Sloan Peak, No. 110 –Silverton and No. 143–Monte Cristo (to identify peaks).

OPINION

Gazing straight up at Mt. Dickerman from the trailhead is enough to make your knees buckle. It looks like a brutally steep hike, for masochists only. So just keep your head down and go. The trail is well engineered, the switchbacks gentle. The unmolested, ancient forest is inspiring. After just 2.5 miles the views are extensive. On top, the 360° panorama is exhilarating.

On a clear day, the summit of Dickerman offers mountain connoisseurs a visual feast. (The profuse blueberries just below are a tasty hors d'oeuvre, or perhaps dessert.) You can see all the peaks rising above the Mountain Loop Highway, towering above the South Fork Stillaguamish and Sauk river valleys, plus many, many more. To the northwest are Three Fingers and Whitehorse Mountain, with Mts. Baker and Shuksan in the background. Mt. Forgotten is immediately north. White Chuck and Pugh mountains are just beyond. To the northeast, Lost Creek Ridge angles toward Glacier Peak. To the east are Sloan Peak and the Monte Cristo group. Southeast lie the snow-capped peaks of the Alpine Lakes Wilderness. Close by to the south are, from left to right, Del Campo, Morning Star, and Sperry. Big Four is close in the southwest. Way south is the bold visage of Mt. Rainier. And finally, to the southwest are Mt. Pilchuck, the waters of Puget Sound, and the Olympic Range rising abruptly from the sea.

Strong hikers can gallop up Dickerman in a little over two hours. Less fit hikers will need a breather now and then, but most will still enjoy this well-maintained, user-friendly trail. Allow at least an hour on top to gorge on the scenery. If you enjoy identifying peaks, a couple hours will pass very quickly.

Solitude is unlikely. Even on a weekday during a very rainy October, eight people paid homage to the mountain gods atop Dickerman. Mid-September to mid-October, when the blueberries are ripe and the bushes are resplendent red, is the ideal time to come. If you're lucky, you'll be here after a brief autumn snowfall has dusted the peaks.

FACT

By Car

On the Mountain Loop Highway, drive 16.7 miles southeast from the Verlot Public Service Center. Look for the trailhead 2.2 miles beyond the Big Four turnoff. If you're heading northwest from Barlow Pass, drive 3.0 miles. Roadside parking with room for about five cars is on the northeast side of the highway. A small sign marks the trailhead under trees.

On Foot

Starting at 1900 feet, you ascend through cedars and subalpine firs. The grade slackens after the first few switchbacks. The roar of unseen water accompanies you the first couple miles.

There's a trickle of water at 2.0 miles. At 2.6 miles Big Four Mountain is visible southwest across the valley. At about 3 miles, after passing under broken cliffs, you reach a small waterfall and pool. Then, after a level stretch, the trail turns sharply east for the final ascent. Before following the main trail east, look for a boot-worn path heading west to a viewpoint over the Perry Creek drainage.

Considerable effort has gone into trail maintenance. Rock chunks and log steps prevent erosion on the upper 1.5 miles of trail. The last mile is steep, but views expand with every step.

Trip 14
Spider Meadow /
Spider Gap

Location	Wenatchee National Forest / Glacier Peak Wilderness.
Distance	10.4-mile round trip to lower Spider Meadow; 16.4-mile round trip to Spider Gap.
Elevation gain	1100' to lower Spider Meadow; 3600' to Spider Gap.
Maps	Green Trails No. 113–Holden; US Forest Service–Glacier Peak Wilderness.

OPINION

The name sounds menacing, but the place is enrapturing. Once you've been to Spider Meadow, its image will serve you as a haven—anytime you're stressed, in need of a restful, comforting thought to restore your calmness and affirm your sanity. Spider Gap has staying power too, but with a very different effect. Whenever you feel jaded, mired in the commonplace, the memory of its harsh, elemental beauty will resuscitate the wildness flickering in your soul. If you've yet to hike here, do it soon. Add these potent visions to your mental landscape.

The forested trail—prettier and more open than the one to nearby Buck Creek Pass—is a pleasant approach. The creek is usually audible. The miles pass quickly. The sight you've anticipated is soon before you: a vast, sumptuous expanse of greenery bordered by soaring cliffs. Surely this is the Mother of All Meadows. If you didn't know the trail continued to Spider Gap, you might not believe it possible, and you'd be completely satisfied. But it does, so you scan the headwall. From here it looks absurdly steep and unmercifully high. Only when you're directly beneath it does the route appear feasible. On the way up, it's less intimidating. The charge you'll get from the ever-expanding view converts to instant energy.

En route to the gap, Larch Knob juts out over the meadow. This is the unlikely location of a marvelous camp—perched high above the valley floor, next to a plunging creek. Behind it is a tremendous gorge beneath the northern ridge of Red Mountain and the eastern end of Chiwawa Mountain. Pouring off the ridge, waterfalls splash over red, rust, orange, and grey rock. From here on, hikers have a rare opportunity to experience the exclusive, otherworldly domain of the mountaineer.

Technically a walk-up, the ascent to the gap might feel like too much of a scramble for some. If steep dropoffs and a continuous sense of exposure bother you, turn around at Larch Knob—where the trail ends and only boot-beaten paths forge ahead. If you're comfortable on sharp ridges, you'll be shrieking with delight. But don't get careless. You'll pass a gnawing glacier and tumbling, raw rock, then ascend steep slopes of heather surrounded by monstrous peaks. It's an adrenaline rush just looking at them. Phelps Basin is 2000 vertical feet below. When the gap comes into view, you can see it is indeed too small and rugged to be called a pass. It's a narrow cleft between Chiwawa and Dumbell mountains. As exciting as getting here is, the view north from the gap is a superb climax.

Spider Gap is within striking distance for an ambitious, athletic dayhiker. Only ice-axe wielding, experienced climbers should attempt the snowfield descent from the north side of the gap to Lyman Lakes. Others will have to hike there on another trip, via the Railroad Creek trail from Holden (Trip 92), or the Suiattle River trail over Cloudy Pass (Trip 94).

FACT

By Car

Drive Highway 2 to Coles Corner, 19.5 miles east of Stevens Pass, or 16.0 miles northwest of Leavenworth. Turn north onto Highway 207 and head toward Lake Wenatchee. Pass the state park and the road to Plain. At 4.3 miles, go right (east) toward the Chiwawa Loop Road. At 5.7 miles turn left onto Meadow Creek Road, which takes you north to Fish Lake and the Chiwawa River valley. Pavement ends at 16.8 miles. At 28.1 miles reach a fork and a sign PHELPS CR T.H. 2 ⇒, PHELPS CR CAMPGROUND ⇑. Take the right fork. From there, the road ascends to reach the Phelps Creek

trailhead at 30.4 miles, 3500 feet. Peaks, snowfields and waterfalls
are visible from the road.

On Foot

The trail initially follows an abandoned mining road. It's a
pine-needle-covered path through dense forest. In 0.2 mile pass a
trail ascending on the right to Carne Mountain. Gradually the
roadbed narrows. Enter Glacier Peak Wilderness and pass a
campsite at 2.7 miles. At 3.1 miles rockhop a creek and walk
through glades. Reach a camp in trees beside a meadow and
Leroy Creek at 3.5 miles, 4175 feet. Cross the creek on a footlog or
rockhop it in late summer. The road is now a footpath, ascending
gently to the head of Phelps Creek. At 4.6 miles is a bridged
crossing of another creek.

Spider Meadow spreads out before you at 5.2 miles, 4600.
There are good campsites here, in trees near the creek. You can see
Red Mountain high on the left. The meadow is home to a plethora
of wildflowers: pinkish-purple asters, tiny bluebells-of-Scotland,
pink monkeyflower, the compact white flowers of yarrow, pink
steeplebush, columbine, and asters that can be 2 feet high by early
August. Farther along, Indian hellebore is dominant. Commonly
known as corn lily, it has long, bright green, accordion-pleated
leaves that grow out in swirls in early summer. By late summer,
numerous, tiny, pale-green flowers appear on the 8 to 10 branches
per stalk. Corn lily is extremely poisonous.

The trail steepens near the north end of the meadow. At 6.5
miles, rockhop across Phelps Creek where there's an obvious trail
on the other side. Come to a signed fork and a campsite on the left
at 6.7 miles, 5300 feet. Right is Phelps Creek trail 1511, leading 0.5
mile into Phelps Basin. Turn left for Spider Gap and Lyman Lakes.
The narrow trail climbs short switchbacks for 0.4 mile up a cliff
band. It's then a dirt path across a grassy slope.

At 7.5 miles, 6200 feet, reach Larch Knob—a treed (larches,
obviously), rocky peninsula hanging above Spider Meadow and
beneath Red Mountain. With about 4 tent sites, the knob is sometimes referred to as Spider Glacier Camp. You can survey all of
Spider Meadow below and see the 9000-foot-plus peaks of Seven
Fingered Jack and Mt. Maude to the southeast. A glacier-fed creek
rushes past the knob and plunges into the valley.

Beyond Larch Knob, the couloir of Spider Glacier slopes 0.75
mile up to Spider Gap. It's an easy ascent for anyone with an ice

axe and the know-how to use it. Even if you don't continue that way, walk the first 20 yards into the gorge to see the red and orange cliffs of Chiwawa Mountain.

Scramblers should opt for the steeper but probably safer rock-and-heather route to the gap. From Larch Knob, take the steep, eroded, faint path signed for the toilet. This toilet-trail ascends right, across from where a path turns sharply left onto Larch Knob. At the second toilet sign, go left through more larch and heather. When the path branches, go whichever way you feel safest. There's an uncomfortably steep heather slope just above the toilet. You can see the glacier 60 yards to your left, but will soon lose sight of it. Higher now, you travel through less heather and more rock. Watch for sporadic cairns. Easier stretches are followed by more precarious ones. At one point the route seems to head right, straight to the cliff, where a lone subalpine tree clings. Stay left here, toward the ridgecrest. There's one 15-yard band of exposed rock to cross. Then the way is easier, mostly level, across dirt and rock, toward a looming, dark buttress of Dumbell Mountain. Phelps Creek valley is 2000 feet below you.

When you see Spider Gap, the scree slope below it might look too dicey to attempt. It's easier than it appears, and you don't have to cross the glacier. Keep working your way over rock, staying on the right edge of the glacier. You might have to cross 2- to 8-foot-long snow patches between boulders. Boot-beaten tread leads across scree to the 7100-foot gap, 8.2 miles from the trailhead. North of and below the gap are the Lyman Lakes; beyond and above them are Cloudy Pass, Cloudy Peak, and North Star Mountain. Sitting Bull Mountain is northwest.

Spider Meadow and headwall leading to Spider Gap

Trip 15

Holden Lake

Location	Glacier Peak Wilderness.
Distance	11.8-mile round trip.
Elevation gain	2100'.
Maps	Green Trails No. 113–Holden; US Forest Service–Glacier Peak Wilderness.

OPINION

No need to steel yourself for an arduous approach. After a brief, pleasing invocation, the scenery here is soul-rousing. As the trail penetrates the stupendous Railroad Creek valley, peaks topping 8400 feet cheer you on.

The robust facade of one of them, Copper Peak, belies its hollowness. Fifty-six miles of tunnels honeycomb it. Copper Peak supplied the life blood for the once-thriving mining town of Holden. Ten million tons of ore were extracted—enough to cover the surface of Lake Chelan. During 20 years of production, that ore was converted into $66.5 million worth of copper, gold and zinc. Now people come to Holden valley seeking spiritual inspiration—a wealth that endures.

The most wondrous visage in this mountain enclave is 9511-foot Bonanza Peak. The highest non-volcanic peak in Washington, it reigns in prominence above Holden Lake. Plan to spend several hours exploring the lake basin and reveling in its glories.

In recent winters, up to 340 inches of snow has smothered Holden valley. That's 100 inches over the average. Nevertheless, you might be able to hike to Holden Lake as early as mid-June. Flagging on the trees will enable you to follow the upper reaches of the trail even when the snow is 5 feet deep in the basin and the lake is iced over. The scenery is still thrilling, and the ascent is never so steep or precarious that falling and sliding are serious threats. So if you're in the area in June to hike the Chelan Lakeshore trail, consider tacking Holden Lake onto the end of your trip. Inquire at the Stehekin Ranger Station about trail conditions.

Holden village was the base camp for Washington's largest

copper mine and, at the height of activity, had a population of 600. When the price of copper plummeted in the 1950s, the mine closed and the village emptied. Nobody wanted to buy the village, so the buildings were donated to the Lutheran Church. It's now a retreat that anyone can pay to stay at. Non-guests are welcome to buy meals at the lodge.

FACT

By Car

See the Chelan Lakeshore description (Trip 108) for directions to the Lake Chelan boat landing.

By Boat & Bus

The *Lady of the Lake II* and the *Lady Express*, departing from Chelan or Fields Point, stop at Lucerne. Disembark at Lucerne either before or after the boat calls at Stchekin. A bus meets the boat to take people to Holden village. The round-trip bus ride costs $10 per person for those not staying at the lodge in Holden. Until mid-April, the bus leaves Holden only at 11 A.M. on Mondays, Wednesdays and Fridays to meet the boat at Lucerne. After mid-April, the bus runs daily. During summer it also leaves Holden at 1:45 P.M. to meet the afternoon boat. From Lucerne, the bus climbs 2100 feet in 12 miles to Holden at 3200 feet. For details about accommodation in Holden, write to the Registrar, Holden Village, Chelan, WA 98816. The boat purser and captain can confirm the bus schedule for you.

On Foot

Follow the dirt road west from Holden village. Pass the ranger station, mining junk, the trailhead sign GOAT TRAIL, a bridge over Railroad Creek, and the cement foundations of the long-gone miners' village. In 1.0 mile come to the village baseball field, which also serves as the Holden Campground. You can pitch your tent here for free. A trailhead sign is posted on the northeast corner. The trail to Holden Lake and Lyman Lakes continues from the northwest corner of the field, where you enter Glacier Peak Wilderness.

The trail gently gains 300 feet in 0.9 mile, through cottonwood, mixed conifer and giant willow, reaching a signed junction at 1.9 miles, 3600 feet. Go right onto the Holden Lake trail, and switchback moderately up willow-and-brush-covered slopes. At about 2.5 miles, 8966-foot Copper Peak and 8421-foot Dumbell Mountain subsume the horizon across the valley. At 3.0 miles attain optimal views up and down Railroad Creek valley. North Star Mountain and the forested headwall below Lyman Lake are visible to the west. Then the route retreats north into the ravine created by the Holden Lake outlet creek, and enters pine trees at 3.75 miles.

High, thick willows engulf the trail for a while, but the path clearly tunnels through them. The ascent continues through meadows dotted with wildflowers—glacier lilies in early summer. From openings in the forest, you can see the glacier-topped cirque you're entering. Dumbell and Copper are still visible to the south.

The last 0.6 mile through stout trees will probably be snow-covered until mid-July. If you can't see the trail, ascend the gently undulating terrain beside the cliff rising on your left, rather than the steeper slope beneath Martin Peak. The route near the cliff is marked by ribbon flagging tied to tree branches. The bright orange ones are obvious. Others are yellow-and-white- or green-and-white-striped and harder to spot.

The trail ends at 5300 feet, 5.9 miles from Holden village, on the east side of Holden Lake. 8511-foot Martin Peak forms the east wall of the cirque. 9511-foot Bonanza Peak, with Mary Green Glacier tumbling off it, forms the north and west walls.

Dumbell Mountain from the ascent to Holden Lake

Trip 16

Frosty Mountain

Location	Manning Provincial Park.
Distance	13.6-mile (22.0-km) round trip.
Elevation gain	3800' (1160 m).
Maps	the free B.C. Parks brochure–Manning Provincial Park; Manning Park and Skagit Valley Rec Area topo printed by the B.C. Ministry of Environment.

OPINION

Frosty Mountain is the ultimate viewpoint over the northern reaches of the North Cascades. Hiking elsewhere in Manning Park, aside from the Skyline trail, you see chiefly bland, rolling, forested mountains. You'd never suspect there was such a magnificent rock-and-ice panorama nearby. But hike up Frosty on a clear day and your internal spectacle-meter will red-line.

The trail was engineered so well that the elevation gain, though daunting, is surprisingly easy. Moderately graded switchbacks enable you to keep a steady pace. On the way down, your knees won't scream like they probably do on other, typically steep North Cascades trails. Most were built by miners who, desperate to strike it rich, paid little attention to physical comfort. This one was built by the park service. It's mostly on a north-facing slope. Though the mountain's lower reaches can be snow-free in early July, the summit ridge might not be safely walkable until late July.

On the way up, the forest opens several times to give you good views of Hozomeen and Silvertip mountains, Flash and Lightning lakes, and impressive, jagged peaks west above Ross Lake. You can also see the Heather trail north across the highway. It looks boring from this distant vantage, but when you're hiking it in flower season, it's not.

If you doubt your desire or ability to reach the summit of Frosty, there's a fulfilling turnaround point on a plateau at 5.6 miles. It's open and meadowy, with a beautiful larch forest. The view here is good, but it pales compared to the top. So imagine yourself gazing across the border into Washington, ogling the southern horizon crowded with peaks and glaciers. Hold that image in mind; if it spurs you beyond the plateau, you might find the rest of the way easier than it looks.

Don't hike the loop dropping to Windy Joe Mountain. After a 0.4-mile descent over talus, you'd be in trees to Windy Joe—an insignificant runt. Then it's a boring fire-road walk in forest along Little Muddy Creek back to the parking lot. The loop adds 3.4 miles to the trip and offers nothing new to warrant the extra effort. This will become apparent when you reach Frosty's summit ridge. It's better to return the way you ascended and enjoy the meadow-and-larch plateau again.

FACT

By Car

Drive B.C. Highway 3 to Manning Park. At 5.8 miles (9.3 km) southeast of Allison Pass, turn south at the signed Lightning Lake turnoff, immediately east of the Manning Park Lodge. Drive 1.8 miles (2.9 km) west to a junction. Fork left 0.5 mile (0.8 km) to the Lightning Lake Day Use area, at 4100 feet (1250 meters). Park near the start of the parking lot, close to the east end of the lake.

On Foot

From the Lightning Lake Day Use Area, start at the far east end of the lake. Cross the cement bridge over the outlet stream. Proceed over the small dam. Immediately ahead is a sign pointing left to Frosty Mountain, right to Strike and Thunder lakes. Go left and ascend switchbacks through Engelmann spruce and subalpine fir.

At 1.6 miles (2.6 km) you can see snowcapped Silvertip Mountain to the northwest and Mount Hozomeen to the southwest. At 2.8 miles (4.5 km), the grade relaxes in scrubby forest. Walk level ground 0.5 mile (0.8 km) through meadows dotted in season with lupine, arnica, and valerian, then come to a comically huge sign WILDERNESS CAMP—1 KM. Views are lost in this flat area. At 4.5 miles (7.2 km), 6070 feet (1850 meters), you arrive at dark, closed-in Frosty Creek Camp, set in thin, scraggly trees. Don't go in the old cabin. It might harbor mouse feces, which can carry a lethal disease. (See the section "Hantavirus.") There are two campsites with fire grates. If the creek is dry here, follow its bed uphill several yards/meters and you'll find a spring.

At 4.8 miles (7.7 km), where you get a view of Frosty up ahead and a severe ridge to your right across the canyon, don't follow the trail going straight and level. It will probably be blocked by a log. Turn left on the main trail to ascend switchbacks. You soon get more views west to snowy peaks beyond the ridge that bears the Skyline trail.

At 5.6 miles (9.0 km), reach the meadow-and-larch plateau. Frosty now looms before you. At the edge of the larch forest, a small side trail drops right to a campsite in a pretty basin. Snowmelt provides water here all summer. The main trail continues straight. When it starts working up through talus, a sign warns you to use extreme caution. Steep switchbacks lead 0.9 mile (1.4 km) farther to the summit ridge and a junction with the trail down to Windy Joe Mountain. Castle Creek valley is directly below to the east. An orange sign here states KM 13. That's the distance accumulated via the Windy Joe ascent. It's 6.8 miles (11.0 km) to this point if you come directly up from the Lightning Lake Day Use Area.

For the grand finale, scramble from this junction 330 feet (100 meters) over talus to the first of Frosty's two summits, at 7900 feet (2408 meters). People have built rock wind shelters here. The other summit is inaccessible to hikers.

Chuwanten Mountain is in the eastern foreground. Farther east, you can see the Cathedral Provincial Park massif breaking out of low mountains. To the north and west, counterclockwise, look for Three Brothers, Outram, Silvertip, Finlayson and Wright. The Coast Mountains are barely visible. Spiky Mount Spickard and Redoubt Glacier are far southwest. Nearby, directly south is Castle Peak, backed by range upon range of the North Cascades. The predominant lone mountain shouldering the gleaming glacier is Jack Mountain.

If you choose to descend via Windy Joe rather than return the same way, follow the trail dropping off the southeast side of the ridge from the 6.8-mile point. Then stay left at all trail junctions to loop back to the Lightning Lake Day Use Area. Returning this way makes an 18.0-mile (29.0-km) loop.

Trip 17
Skyline I and II

Location	Manning Provincial Park.
Distance	12.0-mile (19.4-km) round trip from Spruce Bay; 10.3-mile (16.6 km) shuttle trip from Strawberry Flats to Spruce Bay.
Elevation gain	3000' (915 m) from Spruce Bay; 2214' (675 m) on shuttle trip.
Maps	the free B.C. Parks brochure–Manning Provincial Park; Manning Park and Skagit Valley Recreation Area topo by the B.C. Ministry of Environment.

OPINION

Ridges have ruffles. They never seem to offer the sustained, level walking you imagine they will, especially in the rugged North Cascades. But many, like the Skyline, give hikers constant views that more than compensate for all the ups and downs. And the Skyline has the added attraction of flower-filled meadows all the way west to the Skagit River valley.

Manning Park is on the northern edge of the North Cascades. So, looking north and east from the Skyline, you see dismal little mountains melting into the Interior Plateau. Everytime you turn back south, where the land tilts dramatically skyward, your admiration for this great range is renewed.

Don't let the summer wane before you hike the Skyline. It's most enjoyable during wildflower season: usually mid-July to mid-August. If you come in September, the ridgetop will be Mongolia brown, rather than Ireland green.

Both access trails to the ridgetop are boring. The Spruce Bay access is steeper, but you get views sooner. The ascent from Strawberry Flats to Despair Pass is more gradual, but the ridgeline and views are another 574 feet (175 meters) above the pass. So it's just as well to use the Spruce Bay access, whether dayhiking or backpacking. Then you won't miss the long ridgewalk to Despair Pass. Just don't expect a between-your-knees view of Lightning Lake as you ascend from Spruce Bay. The lake is directly below, but not easily visible. Only if you have a shuttle vehicle should you start at Strawberry Flats and exit at Spruce Bay. You definitely don't want to hike the loop requiring you to walk 2.4 miles (3.8 km) on a tiresome fire road (the South Gibson trail) linking Strawberry Flats and Spruce Bay.

To extend this supreme ridgewalk, backpack to Mowich Camp—a 21.3-mile (34.4-km) round trip from Spruce Bay. If you can arrange a shuttle, the crossover trip from Spruce Bay along Skyline I and II to the Skagit River valley is a glorious 17.6-mile (28.3-km) journey.

FACT

By Car

Drive B.C. Highway 3 to Manning Park. At 5.8 miles (9.3 km) southeast of Allison Pass, turn south at the signed Lightning Lake turnoff, immediately east of the Manning Park Lodge. Drive 1.8 miles (2.9 km) west to a junction. Fork right, go 1.3 miles (2.1 km), then turn left (south) into Lightning Lake Campground. At a signed fork 150 yards farther, hang right into Spruce Bay Beach Day Use Area. Drive 0.2 mile (0.3 km) and park near the end of the lot at 4100 feet (1250 meters).

For the Strawberry Flats trailhead, don't turn left into Lightning Lake Campground. Continue straight (west) another 1.9 miles (3.1 km) to where there's a gate across the road. Park before the gate, on the left side of the road. The trailhead sign is back in the trees, at 4510 feet (1375 meters).

If you're doing a shuttle trip between trailheads at Spruce Bay

Skyline ridgewalk

in Manning Park and the Skagit River valley, leave one vehicle at the trailhead off the Silver-Skagit Road. To get there, take Exit 168, signed FLOOD-HOPE RD / SILVER HOPE CREEK, off Trans-Canada Highway 1. It's 2.0 miles (3.2 km) west of Hope. After exiting, turn south onto Silver-Skagit Road and follow signs for Silver Lake and Hozomeen Campground. From 1.6 miles (2.6 km) on, the road is well-maintained gravel. Go 33.9 miles (54.6 km) south on Silver-Skagit Road, then turn left (east) into the trailhead.

On Foot

Bring full water bottles. After the snow has melted, there's no water on the Skyline I. Mowich Camp is the only reliable water source on the Skyline II.

If you can arrange a shuttle allowing you to start a loop day-hike at the Strawberry Flats trailhead, begin hiking on the Three Falls trail, an old fire road through lodgepole pine. At 0.25 mile (0.4 km) head south (left) on the narrower trail ascending the north-facing slope. Reach a meadow at 2.3 mile (3.7 km). The Skyline I and II trail junction is at 3.7 miles (5.9 km). Turn east (left) to ascend the ridge and continue the loop to Spruce Bay. The longer hike starting from Spruce Bay is described below.

In the Spruce Bay parking area, look for a sign marking the Skyline I trail on the southwest side. The route starts on a wide, flat road (cross-country ski trail in winter). Stay straight on the road, passing side trails to the lake. At 0.3 mile (0.5 km), turn right at a sign MAIN TRAIL, onto a larger road. Soon there's another fork. Stay right at the sign STRIKE AND FLASH LAKES. Thirty yards farther, at 0.6 mile (1.0 km), come to a sign with a map SKYLINE I. Go right. One quarter mile (0.4 km) farther, the road narrows to normal trail width and curves around to the north slope as it climbs the ridge. You'll be cutting back above where you started at the parking lot. The ascent is viewless. One mile (1.6 km) up, an orange sign for skiers marks KM 13—from where, we don't know, but it's assurance you're heading the right way.

The trail now turns southwest. At 1.6 miles (2.6 km), you can look south to Frosty Mountain and north to the Brothers. Then, entering an area devastated by fire in the summer of 1994, start a steep ascent. Walk 0.6 mile (1.0 km) through charred trees and across barren ground with a sprinkling of new growth. The cleared patches were staging grounds for fire fighters; one was a helipad.

A rocky outcropping 100 meters beyond the burn marks the beginning of the ridge, at 3.9 miles (6.3 km). From here you can see snowcapped Mounts Redoubt and Spickard, and the Mox Peaks—all in the southwest.

Continuing west and slightly south, the trail undulates, generally staying about 330 feet (100 meters) below the ridgecrest on the south side, occasionally bobbing up to knolls, and reaching a high point of 6150 feet (1875 meters). You'll gain approximately 630 feet (192 meters) and lose 558 feet (170 meters) to the third major hump, near 6 miles (9.7 km). This is the logical turnaround point for a dayhike starting and ending at Spruce Bay. Otherwise, the trail drops west 574 feet (175 meters) to a junction at 6.6 miles (10.7 km), 5576 feet (1700 meters). The right fork then drops 3.7 miles (5.9 km) to Strawberry Flats, which is where you would ascend from if doing a shuttle trip.

If you're backpacking to Mowich Camp, take the Skyline II trail left (southwest), from the 6.6-mile junction, into forested Despair Pass. The trail climbs southwest out of Despair Pass to 6232 feet (1900 meters) on the ridge. It offers a good view of Thunder Lake, as well as Snow Camp and Lone Goat mountains. The trail skirts the actual summit of meadowy, 6494-foot (1980-meter) Snow Camp Mountain on its south side. It drops 575 feet (175 meters), then rises to 6573-foot (2004-meter) Lone Goat Mountain.

Mowich Camp is in subalpine forest at 5248 feet (1600 meters), 10.6 miles (17.2 km) from Spruce Bay. "Mowich" is a native word for deer. Water is available here, but can diminish to a trickle during a dry summer, forcing you to follow the streambed looking for small pools. If you're doing the crossover shuttle-trip to the Skagit River valley, continue on the Skyline II west 7.0 miles (11.3 km). Fill your water bottles at Mowich before departing. En route you'll pass a signed, narrow trail leading south. It undulates at roughly 5660 feet (1725 meters) along Hozameen (spelled with an 'a' in Canada and an 'o' in the U.S.) Ridge, toward Hozomeen Mountain. Stay right on the Skyline II as it heads northwest 0.3 mile (0.5 km) before plunging southwest 4100 feet (1250 meters) into the Skagit River valley, crossing extensive subalpine meadows and affording views west of peaks above and the valley below. The trail comes out at the western Skyline II trailhead 7.0 miles (11.3 km) from Mowich Camp.

Trip 18

Excelsior Mountain / High Divide / Welcome Pass

Location	Mt. Baker-Snoqualmie National Forest / Mt. Baker Wilderness.
Distance	6.6-mile round trip to Excelsior Mountain; 10.0-mile shuttle trip along the High Divide.
Elevation gain	1550' to Excelsior Mountain; 2020' on the shuttle trip.
Maps	Green Trails No. 13–Mt. Baker, No. 14– Mt. Shuksan; Trails Illustrated No. 223– North Cascades National Park Complex.

OPINION

Excelsior Mountain and the High Divide trail offer front-row seats to the big show starring Mt. Baker, Mt. Shuksan, and their companion ridges. If you can unglue your gaze from the white expanse of glaciers to the south, you'll see the Border Peaks immediately north and the beginning of the B.C. Coast Range far to the northwest. All this mountain majesty is even more amazing when you look west and see how abruptly it rises from coastal lowlands.

This is just one of many Mt. Baker viewpoints. What makes it special is the High Divide trail traversing alpine meadows along the ridge between Excelsior Mountain and Welcome Pass. The supreme views the ridgewalk affords are always enthralling. The optimal time to hike here depends on your color preference: bright green with a rainbow of wildflowers in summer, or gold, orange and purple-to-red berry shades in fall.

The Damfino Lakes trail to Excelsior Pass is an easy way to see the northern slopes of ever-captivating Mt. Baker. Less ambitious hikers will be happy just visiting the top of Excelsior Mountain. Adventurous, competent, off-trail explorers appreciate the quick access to the alpine zone because they can push on, devoting their energy to the challenge and thrill of high-country route finding. From Excelsior Pass it's possible to roam west toward Church Mountain. From Welcome Pass you can scramble northeast onto unnamed peaks along the ridge and look down at the lakelets beneath Yellow Aster Butte.

Usually the High Divide isn't snow-free until late July. By mid-June you might be able to ascend the south-facing slope from the highway most of the way to Excelsior Pass. But why? Unless all you want is a grueling training route, you'll be frustrated if you can't continue along the ridge. Wait until the whole trail is clear, then start with an easy ascent from the Damfino Lakes trailhead and hike west to east. After reaching Welcome Pass, return to Excelsior Pass and your car at the Damfino Lakes trailhead. Enjoy the ridgewalk twice rather than endure the knee-jouncing drop from Welcome Pass. If you decide to do a shuttle trip, the ascent to Welcome Pass from the east-end trailhead is absurdly steep and this segment is better left for the descent.

A massive flood in 1989 wiped out a bridge on the Canyon Creek Road leading to the Damfino Lakes trailhead. For six years the road was closed from the 11-mile point on. Road repairs were near completion in the fall of 1995, but floods during the winter delayed reopening for another year. The trail, unmaintained and virtually untraveled all that time, might still be horrendously brushy. Check with the Glacier Public Service Center to make sure that the road is open and that a trail crew has brushed the trail before you set out.

FACT

By Car

To reach the Damfino Lakes trailhead, start at the Glacier Public Service Center on Highway 542. Drive northeast 1.8 miles and turn left (northwest) on Canyon Creek Road 31. The one-lane road is paved for 10.0 miles. At 7.0 miles, pass the Canyon Creek Campground on the right. At 14.6 miles bear left (southeast) on Road 31 and drive another 1.0 mile to the signed trailhead at 4150 feet.

If you're doing a one-way shuttle trip, leave a vehicle at the east-end trailhead below Welcome Pass. To get there, drive Highway 542 east 12.3 miles from the Glacier Public Service Center. Between mileposts 45 and 46, look carefully on the left (north) for a small road tightly enclosed by trees. It's 0.3 mile west of the highway maintenance buildings. A small sign identifies it ROAD 3060. Turn left (north) here and drive 0.7 mile to the parking area at road's end, 2200 feet. Any car can make it if driven slowly. A wide vehicle, however, might get scratched by branches.

If you want to ascend the steep trail from Highway 542 to Excelsior Pass, the trailhead is 7.5 miles east of the Glacier Public Service Center. Watch for it on the left (north), 0.3 miles after you pass the signed Nooksack Falls-Wells Creek Road. The trailhead sign parallels the highway, so it's difficult to see unless you're looking at precisely the right moment. There's parking space for about three cars in a pullout across the road, at 1800 feet.

On Foot

From the Damfino Lakes trailhead, the forested path goes east, gaining 350 feet in 0.7 mile to a junction. The Canyon Ridge trail is left (north). Turn right (southeast). At 0.9 mile reach the small Damfino Lakes and campsites at 4500 feet. After the lakes, the trail heads south. Enter meadows at 2.2 miles. Snowmelt creeklets usually provide water here and along the High Divide until early August. At 3.0 miles reach 5350-foot Excelsior Pass and more campsites.

Trails converge at the pass. Trail 670 joins from the south, after a 4.2-mile, 3500-foot ascent from Highway 542. Continue left (east) on High Divide trail 630 toward Welcome Pass.

Reach the 5699-foot summit of Excelsior Mountain and enter Mt. Baker Wilderness at 3.3 miles from the Damfino Lakes trailhead. The trail then undulates east along the ridge, passing several spots flat enough to pitch a tent on. It ascends a 5930-foot knob, loses 500 feet, then gains 350 feet to a third knob where you can see Tomyhoi Peak to the north. From there it descends southeast to Welcome Pass at 7.5 miles, 5100 feet. The trail then drops into forest and makes a radical, 2400-foot descent via 67 switchbacks in 1.8 miles, followed by a more gradual descent of 500 feet in 0.75 mile. Reach the Welcome Pass trailhead on Road 3060 at 10.0 miles, 2200 feet.

Trip 19

Heliotrope Ridge

Location	Mt. Baker Wilderness.
Distance	6.5-mile round trip.
Elevation gain	1900'.
Maps	Green Trails No. 13–Mt. Baker; Trails Illustrated No. 223–North Cascades National Park Complex.

OPINION

It's amazing that with no skill whatsoever, without knowing how to do anything more complicated than walk, people can get to a place so otherworldly as this. Within a couple hours, you can be looking down on a living glacier from a vantage point high on a sleeping volcano. The hike is not only quick and easy, it's pleasant. The gentle ascent is through luxuriant forest cleaved by jubilant creeks.

At trail's end, the Coleman Glacier gnashes its way down the yawning abyss immediately below you. To the northeast is Chowder Ridge. Above, the summit of Mt. Baker is hidden behind its massive, gleaming white girth. Once onto the moraine, you can explore a bit. Or simply ponder existence. Just don't venture onto the ice without the knowledge and equipment to do it safely.

Though Heliotrope is tremendous, if you have to choose just one hike on Mt. Baker, and the incomparable Ptarmigan Ridge sounds too difficult for you or is still snow-covered, hike the nearby Skyline Divide. There, views of Mt. Baker glaciers are more expansive, green meadows add contrast to the scenery, clearcuts are not so readily visible, and you can roam longer at high elevation.

Mt. Baker from Heliotrope Ridge

FACT

By Car

From the Glacier Public Service Center on Highway 542, drive 0.8 mile east. Turn right on Glacier Creek Road 39. At 0.7 mile stay straight. At a fork in 7.8 miles continue straight. After crossing a creek, arrive in 8.2 miles at the shopping-mall-size parking area at the trailhead, 3700 feet. Don't drive beyond the chalet-style outhouse.

On Foot

The trail starts 30 yards left of the outhouse. It drops immediately down into forest. A bridge crosses deep, fast Grouse Creek at 0.2 mile, near the sign MT. BAKER WILDERNESS. After 0.5 mile the ascent eases and you get views north.

Be prepared for several unbridged stream crossings. Earlier than mid-July, though the trail might be snow-free, high meltwater could make fording dangerous. The first stream, below a small waterfall, should pose no difficulty. At 2.0 miles, between the first and second streams, there are two flat campsites beside the trail. The second stream is in subalpine territory with fewer trees, lots of heather, and views to the icy realm above. The trail continues southeast. You'll reach the third major stream at timberline. This one is more difficult, but you might be able to rockhop across instead of fording. Shortly after that you come to the fourth major stream, actually several braided ones. If your goal is to get as high as you can on Heliotrope Ridge, don't cross here. Instead, take the trail angling steeply up to the right. If you *do* cross here, you'll be on a side trail leading out a small gravel ridge to a point overlooking the Coleman Glacier. It's easy to explore both options in a 6- to 7-hour daytrip. Heading up Heliotrope, the boot-beaten path ends just above 5600 feet, on a moraine. A few hardy, red paintbrush and lavender sky pilot contrast vividly with the rocky rubble.

Though this trail is on the north side of the mountain and can hold snow until August, some years it's hikeable by early July. Check with the rangers at the Glacier Public Service Center.

Trip 20

Church Mountain

Location	Mt. Baker Wilderness.
Distance	8.4-mile round trip.
Elevation gain	3600'.
Maps	Green Trails No. 13–Mt. Baker; Trails Illustrated No. 223–North Cascades National Park Complex.

OPINION

The Church Mountain steeple, like those of all churches, is only accessible to climbers. But trail's end on the summit ridge is high enough to make most devotees feel quite close to the mountain gods. You can enjoy a nearly 360° view of the peak-studded horizon. Skyline and Heliotrope ridges on Mt. Baker are easily identifiable, if you've hiked them already. Mt. Sefrit and Icy Peak are to the east. To the north are the Canadian Border Peaks; to the northeast Tomyhoi Peak, and Mt. Larrabee. Below, to the north, are the Kidney Lakes. It's unfortunate that clearcuts are visible in all directions.

You'll have to work hard to get up Church Mountain. Come prepared with some deep thinking to do, plenty of evocative, stimulating questions to ask your hiking companion, or simply a need to meditate—anything to help pass the time on the steep, relentless switchbacks. There's little understory to make the forest more interesting, but at least there's no brush to tangle with. The roar of the Nooksack River in the valley below will accompany your heavy breathing on the ascent.

The heather and grass meadows cradled beneath the summit ridge are an idyllic place to prostrate yourself before the final spurt to the top. Most hikers stop here, so there's usually a congregation. If you prefer to worship in solitude, wander south toward the rim of the basin and find your own spot with a view of Baker. Or just keep walking the trail another quarter mile through the meadow. If you're a strong hiker ready to continue, save your rest break for the top. If you're questioning whether

Basin on Church Mountain

you can or should push on, just do it. The panorama at trail's end is a goal worth straining for. We saw a family with children aged three-and-a-half to ten gleefully bounding up the final stretch. So you probably can too, unless you're afraid of heights: the last 75 yards are exposed. Even if you go only a half mile beyond the creek crossing in the meadow, you'll get a greatly expanded view across to Baker and other peaks.

The runoff streams are unreliable after July, so carry plenty of water. It can be hot and humid on the way up, even in the meadows above. On a clear day, you'll welcome the thick forest cover on the taxing ascent. If the weather's threatening, go elsewhere. Poor visibility diminishes this hike to a mere training run. And the last short section could have you sliding like Michael Douglas and Kathleen Turner down that hillside in *Romancing the Stone*.

FACT

By Car

From the Glacier Public Service Center on Highway 542, drive 5.1 miles east. Turn left on signed Church Mountain Road, 3040, and continue 2.6 miles (the sign incorrectly says 4) to the trailhead at 2400 feet.

On foot

Walk the first 0.3 mile on an old logging road. After leaving an old clearcut at 0.8 mile, you'll be mostly in tall trees. The switch-backs have an easy gradient until 1.8 miles, then they get serious. Near 2.2 miles, glimpse Mt. Baker. Look for the waterfall to your left at 2.5 miles. Soon after, the trail contours northwest into a basin. At 3.2 miles, enter a broad meadow with a seasonal creek, tucked into the rugged slopes of Church Mountain.

At 3.5 miles ascend open slopes festooned with corn lilies. At 4.0 miles the trail deteriorates to almost nothing as it crosses a steep, bare, possibly muddy slope. Though the route is obvious, walking this short stretch is dicey in the rain. Just before the trail tops out at 4.2 miles, 6000 feet, you'll pass the splintered rem-nants of an outhouse. Watch out for an old, rusty cable dangling across the trail. There's only room for two couples to comfortably and safely sit on top.

Trip 21
Yellow Aster Butte / Tomyhoi Peak

Location	Mt. Baker Wilderness.
Distance	6.0-mile round trip to the first tarn.
Elevation gain	2100'.
Maps	Green Trails No. 14–Mt. Shuksan; Trails Illustrated No. 223–North Cascades National Park Complex.

OPINION

Compelling and multi-faceted as Mt. Baker and Mt. Shuksan are, after hiking several of the trails above Highway 542 you might wonder if any of them offers a different scenic climax. Yes, Yellow Aster Butte does. Although you'll see yet another striking visage of Mt. Shuksan here, you need never look in that direction to feel rewarded for your efforts. Hikers come here to revel in a vast undulating meadowland dimpled with a multiplicity of tarns. This is country made for wandering, not just picking a perch to eye the panorama. So allow a day or two for exploration. Ambling through the alpine expanse up Tomyhoi Peak would be a joy even if you couldn't see a string of Canadian peaks to the north as well as Baker and Shuksan to the south.

You do have to earn all this splendor. The rigorous trail to the tarns and on up Yellow Aster Butte is relentlessly steep. It's far worse than switchbacking up nearby Church Mountain. This one is more route than trail, hastily cut by prospectors long ago and kept in existence by pounding boots. Don't hike here if it's been raining. Wet rocks, slick roots and mud can be a pleasure-sapping vexation.

The trail's namesake, yellow asters (daisies), are abundant by late July. But the meadows have been trampled. Do your best not to crush any more of the fragile greenery. If the tread is muddy, let your boots get muddy; sidestepping only broadens the mess.

And certainly don't pitch a tent on grass. You'll find plenty of bare campsites where your impact will be minimal.

FACT

By Car

From the Glacier Public Service Center on Highway 542, drive 12.8 miles east. Just past the maintenance buildings, turn left (north) onto Twin Lakes Road 3065. A short way in, stay left at the fork. At 2.3 miles, across from a pullout, take the side road on the left (not shown on the maps) 0.2 mile to the Yellow Aster Butte trailhead, at 3100 feet. Motorhome pilots, or anyone with a big, awkward rig, should park at the pullout on Road 3065. Though there's room for about 10 vehicles at the trailhead parking area, it's so narrow that turning around can be difficult.

On Foot

The trail initially climbs 0.3 mile through a clearcut before entering cool, virgin forest. Mt. Baker and Mt. Shuksan are visible the first 50 feet. You have to ascend 1000 feet in 1.0 mile, without the aid of switchbacks. Near 2 miles reach a small creek. The rooty path continues steeply, then levels out in subalpine terrain with blueberry bushes and heather. At 2.4 miles Mt. Shuksan is again visible. You can also see Goat Mountain, nearby to the east, and to the southeast, Icy Peak, and the East Nooksack Glacier on the ridge between Seahpo Peak and Mt. Shuksan. After another steep stretch, reach the first tarn—scooped out of a meadow at 3.0 miles, 5200 feet. Yellow Aster Butte is ahead on the right (slightly northeast) and Tomyhoi Peak is a bit more distant on the left (slightly northwest).

At 3.2 miles pass a second tarn. A hard right turn takes you to a third tarn, this one with mining junk scattered about. Continuing toward the obvious butte before you, you'll descend 50 feet to the fourth tarn. If you walk past the tarns and proceed straight north to the edge of the upper basin on the west side of Yellow Aster Butte, you can see American Border Peak and Mt. Larrabee slightly northeast, and yet another, larger tarn below you.

The route up Yellow Aster Butte is difficult. Tread is minimal and very steep. You might want to use your hands on the initial assault, but there's nothing to grab. The ascent up the grassy slope gains about 550 feet to the 6145-foot summit. The panorama includes the wild Picket Range to the southeast. Far below to the north is Tomyhoi Lake. Bring a map to help you identify peaks.

The route to 7451-foot Tomyhoi Peak will be obvious to anyone with cross-country experience. It starts on the left side of the stream that flows into the fourth tarn. It ascends northwest through tussocky meadows, then up rocky ridges to the base of the peak.

Tarn below Yellow Aster Butte, with American Border Peak in distance

Trip 22

Goat Mountain

Location	Mt. Baker Wilderness.
Distance	8.0-mile round trip.
Elevation gain	3500'.
Maps	Green Trails No. 14–Mt. Shuksan; Trails Illustrated No. 223–North Cascades National Park Complex.

OPINION

Scenic grandeur quells the pain of physical exertion. That's what makes steep trails like the one up Goat Mountain so enjoyable.

Shortly after setting out, you'll be looking across the Nooksack River valley at awesome peaks that are jaw-droppingly close. Church Mountain to the west. Mt. Herman to the southwest, looming over the highway. Behind it, to the right, is the massive snowcone of Mt. Baker. To the left (southeast) towers the craggier Mt. Shuksan. Embedded in the shadows of Shuksan's steep slopes, beneath the Price Glacier, is Price Lake, accessible only to satyrs (half man, half goat). The East Nooksack Glacier swoops southeast of it. Beneath you and southeast is the deep Ruth Creek valley, with Mt. Sefrit rising above.

Shift your focus from macro to micro and you'll find Goat Mountain interesting from that perspective too. Stay alert for whirring sounds; this seems to be a hummingbird haven. In season, tiger lilies, paintbrush, rose, and valerian grace the meadowed slopes. Images of luscious grass will linger in your mind long after hiking this green mountain reminiscent of the palis of Hawaii.

FACT

By Car

From the Glacier Public Service Center on Highway 542, drive 13.1 miles east. Just before the Nooksack River bridge, turn left (east) toward Hannegan Pass on Road 32. At the junction in 1.3 miles, stay left on Ruth Creek Road 32. Arrive at the trailhead at 2.5 miles, 2500 feet. Parking space is just before or after it.

On Foot

You'll hear water on the way up, but don't count on any that's easy to reach. The trail is extremely steep, with only short respites. Well-maintained tread and good switchbacks aid your progress. You get a peek at Shuksan at 0.75 mile. After 1.0 mile, the gradient eases for 0.6 mile. You reach open slopes at about 2 miles. The view here is expansive, and because the trail is on a south-facing slope it's possible to hike this high as early as May.

After passing through vibrant pink heather, stay to your right to ascend a muddy, rocky, shallow gully with seeps. You'll see lots of eroded footpaths through here; take your pick. When you reach a large bare spot on the green slopes above, walk the side path right. Heading southeast toward Mt. Sefrit, it drops to an outcropping for a better view of the valley.

From the bare patch, the main trail continues left, climbing through more heather, berry bushes, and a few mountain hemlocks. The path is scant above 5400 feet as it heads north, traversing grassy slopes. It peters out around 6000 feet at 4.0 miles, but offers a commanding panorama well before that.

Trip 23
Hannegan Pass

Location	Mt. Baker Wilderness / Mt. Baker-Snoqualmie National Forest.
Distance	8.0-mile round trip.
Elevation gain	1966'.
Maps	Green Trails No. 14–Mt. Shuksan; Trails Illustrated No. 223–North Cascades National Park Complex.

OPINION

Most of the way to Hannegan Pass seems about as level as this sentence. Yet the scenery's gee-whiz quotient is surprisingly high. Long before the ascent becomes noticeable, you'll enjoy constant views of the engaging Ruth Creek valley.

At the trailhead, you'll see a cliff (on an unnamed peak to the north) bolting out of the forest. That's the beginning of a skyscape that entertains you all the way to the pass. To the south, rocky, icy, cascade-riddled Nooksack Ridge is the life of the party. Proud Mt. Sefrit on the northwest end is the host. Ruth Mountain on the southeast end is the ever-attentive hostess. After a mile, her ostentatious glaciers ensure you are never bored. Even the trail disports you as it amiably winds beneath mountainsides, across avalanche swaths, toward the Ruth Mountain cirque, then into subalpine forest.

Hannegan Pass is clutched between buttresses of Hannegan Peak to the north and Ruth Mountain to the south. It is small, treed, and offers only a view east into the headwaters of the Chilliwack River. As a destination, it's a letdown, especially after such an exceptional approach. So push on. Continue up Hannegan Peak. From the pass, an obvious route climbs to the broad summit, where you can treasure the peak-studded horizon. Baker, Shuksan and Ruth are obvious. Triumph, Challenger, Redoubt, Slesse and many more are also within sight.

Read Trip 88 for details about the extended backpack trip continuing northeast to Copper Ridge.

FACT

By Car

From the Glacier Public Service Center on Highway 542, drive 13.1 miles east. Just before the Nooksack River bridge, turn left (east) toward Hannegan Pass on Road 32. At the junction in 1.3 miles, stay left on Ruth Creek Road 32. At 5.4 miles reach the Hannegan Campground and trailhead at road's end, 3100 feet. On weekends, expect to see dozens of vehicles in the parking lot.

On Foot

The well-maintained trail stays on the northeast side of Ruth Creek, traversing under 6688-foot Granite Mountain and 6138-foot Hannegan Peak. 7191-foot Mt. Sefrit and slightly lower Nooksack Ridge form the southwest wall of Ruth Creek valley. Elevation gain is negligible the first 1.3 miles. After 1.0 mile, glaciers on Ruth Mountain are visible. Cross a water source at 1.4 miles, where the trail begins a 320-foot ascent over the next 0.6 mile. It's then mostly level for 0.7 mile, before rising 1100 feet the last 1.4 miles to Hannegan Pass. A sign at 3.7 miles points to the Hannegan campsites—bare spots in subalpine meadow on a bench overlooking Ruth Creek valley. Water is available near the camp. There's a lone campsite at 3.8 miles.

Arrive at 5066-foot Hannegan Pass in 4.1 miles. Boundary Camp is 1.0 mile and 666 feet below the pass. It's in subalpine trees, next to a corn-lily meadow, above the Chilliwack River, which at this early stage is merely a creek. It's also just inside the National Park boundary, so you need a permit to camp.

From Hannegan Pass, hikers with a bit of off-trail sense can proceed up Hannegan Peak. A path departs from the north side of the pass (on your left as you arrive). Ascend 1100 feet in 1.0 mile through open forest, steep meadow, more trees, then heather, to the rounded top. The panorama includes Ruth Mountain to the south, above the pass; Mt. Baker and Mt. Shuksan southwest; Slesse Mountain 2 miles north in Canada; Mt. Redoubt northeast; and Mt. Challenger southeast.

Another route from Hannegan Pass heads south (on your right as you arrive). This is the climbers' path leading toward Ruth Mountain. Hikers can walk it a short way to meadows and better views than are available at the pass, but the going soon gets technical, requiring mountaineering equipment and experience.

Trip 24

Lake Ann

Location	Mt. Baker Wilderness.
Distance	8.2-mile round trip.
Elevation gain	900'.
Maps	Green Trails No. 14–Mt. Shuksan; Trails Illustrated No. 223–North Cascades National Park Complex.

OPINION

Crowded? Absolutely. Worth it? Definitely. It's a short distance to a front-row seat below the Lower Curtis Glacier on Mt. Shuksan, and the route passes through a delightful variety of scenery.

It's odd to drive so high, then immediately lose elevation on the trail, but plunge in anyway. The initial descent through lush forest leads to an idyllic hanging valley—the headwaters of Swift Creek. You'll pass through grass, flowers, and more trees, then begin the ascent to the saddle above Lake Ann. The highlights: heather meadows, creeklets cascading in all directions, and graceful, small ferns softening the otherwise stark boulder field that pours down from the saddle. Though the final ascent to Lake Ann is steep, the scenery is great and there are lots of handy boulders, so you can sit, rest and spectate often.

Fast hikers can reach Lake Ann in 1.5 hours, although we feel that's not the best destination. Don't descend to the lake from the saddle. Find the faint trail veering up to the left and go feast your eyes on the glacier.

FACT

By car

Drive Highway 542 to the Mt. Baker ski area. Go right at the large map of Mt. Baker and continue 1.8 miles to the trailhead parking lot at Austin Pass, 4700 feet.

On Foot

After descending 800 feet in 2.3 miles, you pop out of the forest, into stream-fed meadows. You'll see a sign here pointing to a pit toilet. You've reached a junction. Take the left fork to Lake Ann. Right drops into the depths of the Swift Creek canyon. From the junction, ascend 1.8 miles to the saddle at 4800 feet. You'll see Lake Ann 120 feet below the other side. A rough, narrow climbers' trail leads east 0.7 mile from the saddle toward Fisher Chimney. The route gets precarious before ending at 5200 feet.

Lower Curtis Glacier on Mt. Shuksan, from above Lake Ann

Trip 25

Scott Paul

Location	Mt. Baker Wilderness.
Distance	7.9-mile loop.
Elevation gain	1800'.
Maps	1996 Green Trails No. 45–Hamilton, No. 46–Lake Shannon (shows Road 12); Trails Illustrated No. 223–North Cascades National Park Complex.

OPINION

Here's yet another way to scurry up onto the flanks of mighty Mount Baker. A relatively new trail, finished in the summer of 1994, it was named after the ranger who kept the project alive until his death in 1993. Although not as wondrous as its neighbor, Railroad Grade (Trip 5), it's well worth hiking. If you have two days for this area, do RR Grade one day, then combine the Scott Paul and Park Butte trails the next.

The path is wide, well-graded and smooth, with extensive ditches to control erosion—a veritable Yellow Brick Road. Initially it climbs through a pleasant forest with a scattering of grand trees 15 feet in circumference. Then, ta da! Suddenly you reach an open saddle and a new perspective of Mt. Baker and Mt. Shuksan. Tall grass, luscious berry patches in season, and a calming view of sweeping virgin forests below make this an excellent rest stop, or a picnic destination, especially if you have small children or aren't feeling ambitious. Moderate-paced walkers can get here in a little over an hour.

Continuing, the trail climbs a bit and then relents, providing a couple miles of level hiking. It weaves in and out of meadowed gulleys, crossing several creeklets and staying mostly in the open. Flower gardens and tiny ferns flourish in the fertile volcanic soil.

Eventually, you reach the gorge below Easton Glacier and drop, drop, drop into it. This rocky, dusty, desolate section of trail seems like northern Arizona. Even the smell is similar to that of sand and salt cedars in Southwest riparian regions. And the vast gorge itself—roaring river below, gouging ice and tumbling rubble above—could be a scene in Ladakh. The suspension bridge (thankfully, far more stable than those encountered on third-world treks) contributes to the exotic atmosphere. And you don't have to fly to the other side of the world to enjoy it. If you have time and energy, scoot up to Park Butte Lookout before completing the loop to the car park.

FACT

By Car

Drive Highway 20 east 16.5 miles from Sedro Woolley, or west 6.0 miles from Concrete. Turn north onto the Grandy-Baker Lake Road. Drive northeast 12.4 miles, and just past Rocky Creek bridge, go left (northwest) on South Fork Nooksack Road 12. Ignore the unsigned road to your right at 1.8 miles. At 3.5 miles turn right at the sign MT. BAKER NATIONAL RECREATION AREA, onto Sulphur Creek Road 13. Follow signs to Shriebers Meadow. You'll reach the trailhead parking lot at 8.7 miles, 3300 feet. There are four campsites here, a couple beside Sulphur Creek.

On Foot

This newer trail is shown on the Green Trails 1996 map. Start on the Park Butte trailhead by the large sign in the parking lot. Just beyond the picnic table, about 20 yards in, and just before the bridge, go right. A wood sign marks the trail. Ascend 1400 feet in 2.0 miles through forest to an open, grassy saddle at 4700 feet, with views: Mt. Baker up to the left (north), Mt. Shuksan far off to the right (northeast). From the saddle, ascend moderately northeast, then north to about 5000 feet. The trail then contours northwest. Shortly, cross Sulphur Creek. Near 5.25 miles, go southwest and cross Metcalf Moraine. The trail drops into the gorge below Easton Glacier. From there, cross the suspension bridge over Rocky Creek and ascend the southern end of the moraine, on top of which is the Railroad Grade trail. Join the Park Butte trail at 6.0 miles, within 0.5 mile of the bridge. The parking lot is left (southeast) 1.9 miles down. If you first detour right (northwest) on the Park Butte trail to ascend to Park Butte Lookout—a 2.8 mile out-and-back side trip—you'll increase the day's total mileage to 10.7 miles, and the total elevation gain to 3200 feet.

Trip 26

Boston Basin

Location	North Cascades National Park.
Distance	6.0-mile round trip.
Elevation gain	2600'.
Maps	Green Trails No. 47–Marblemount (shows the Cascade River road), No. 48–Diablo Dam (to identify peaks), No. 80–Cascade Pass; Trails Illustrated No. 223–North Cascades National Park Complex.

OPINION

Water and ice pouring off steep rock gave the Cascades its name, and that's what you'll find in the pinnacle-and-glacier amphitheater of Boston Basin.

Once in the basin, rock slabs and moraines bid you to wander. You can strike off in any direction, clambering over the burnt orange and red boulders that appear to have tumbled out of the forge moments ago. Maybe you'll catch a whiff of what gets climbers so high on Forbidden Peak. Across the valley to the southwest, Johannesburg Mountain is no more impressive than it was from the road, but all else is a new world. You can spend a full day exploring, or enjoy a half day of exercise and jubilation.

What's special about this basin, however, are the countless cascades from above. Here you can fully appreciate the wonder that is water. So instead of following the pull of the moraine, you might answer the call of the water. Lie down on a flat rock slab, between chattering creeklets, and tune in. While your eyes are open to the emerald slopes and gleaming glaciers, let your ears be open to the dribble and gurgle of water tumbling and frolicking all around you. This is not the sound of a voluminous river, or even a deep creek, but the light, cheerful splashing of water coursing over rock, through rock, under rock. Seemingly delicate, it's one of the great forces that shaped these mountains. Now try closing your eyes and shutting out all but the water music. At its deepest level, you might find this is yet another way your mother, Earth, speaks to your soul.

The first half of the way to Boston Basin is a vertical, rugged, slippery, rooty route; the second half is a decent though steep path through big timber. It's not difficult to follow, as long as you engage the trail with your mind and occasionally your hands, not just your feet. This isn't one you can walk on auto-pilot.

FACT

By Car

At the eastern edge of Marblemount, where Highway 20 bends north, go straight (east) onto the Cascade River road and immediately cross the Skagit River. In 0.7 mile pass the Rockport-Cascade Road on the right. Continue east on the Cascade River road (now labeled 15), which turns to gravel at 5.2 miles. At 16.9 miles, pass the road that forks right to the Cascade River trails, and curve sharply left toward Cascade Pass. Enter the National Park at 18.3 miles. After passing milepost 22, slow down and be ready to stop. At 22.8 miles, you'll see a small pullout on the left: that's the Boston Basin trailhead, at 3200 feet. If there's not enough space here, it's only 0.7 mile farther to the large Cascade Pass trailhead at road's end.

On Foot

The maps don't show a trail into Boston Basin, but it's there. From the roadside, the trail isn't always apparent. You might have to part the brush that hides the entrance. The hike begins on an old roadbed that led to the Value Mines. At 0.5 mile, where there's a big rock and a seeming fork, make a sharp right turn. Shortly, turn right up toward a rockslide. At 0.8 mile you might have to use your hands to hoist yourself over rocks and roots. Johannesburg Mountain is still behind you.

When enough snow has melted in the basin to make it accessible to hikers—usually mid- to late July—the three creek crossings on the way up should be easy to negotiate. You cross Midas and Morning Star creeks in a 0.4-mile-wide avalanche swath as you traverse northwest.

Rockhop across Boston Creek at about 3 miles. The trail continues on the other side, but you're now in wandering territory. Follow your bliss. If Boston Creek looks too high to cross, go up to your right. Scramble the moraine for even better views. Camping is prohibited in the meadows, but you can pitch your tent at the 5800-foot climbers' camp, to the north above the trail, between forks of Boston Creek.

If you face Boston Glacier (northeast), here's what you see if you turn slowly from right to left: Sahale Mountain, Forbidden Peak, Mount Torment and Eldorado Creek pouring down the avalanche slope beneath Inspiration Glacier on the east side of Eldorado Peak. Far left, directly west, are the Hidden Lake Peaks.

Boston Basin

Trip 27

Sourdough Mountain

Location	Ross Lake National Recreation Area / North Cascades National Park.
Distance	11.0-mile round trip.
Elevation gain	5100'.
Maps	Green Trails No. 16–Ross Dam, No. 48– Diablo Dam; Trails Illustrated No. 223– North Cascades National Park Complex.

OPINION

This is one of those good things in life that don't come easily. More accurately, it's one of those stupendous things that come only with excruciating difficulty. You'll have to be in Marine Corps shape to march to the top without feeling utterly depleted. On our ascent, we met hikers turning back, spent and disappointed. Only three others summitted that day: a pair of marathoners training between races, and a professional photographer/climber seeking the ultimate viewpoint for his tripod. Sourdough Mountain is the toughest dayhike in this book. The panorama at trail's end is soul awakening, but getting there is such a grueling, discouraging trudge that overall it doesn't deserve a Premier rating. Though the trail is snow-free earlier than most high-elevation options, making Sourdough your first hike of the season is unwise; build up to it.

The ascent is via short, relentless switchbacks through forest as ugly as it gets in the North Cascades. The spindly trees are just enough to obscure views most of the way up, yet insufficient to provide shade. It can get very hot here on a sunny day, so start hiking early. Heat, however, is only a possibility. Boredom is a certainty. Unless you bring along very entertaining companions, there'll be nothing to alleviate the monotony of pumping up the mountain.

Just keep telling yourself: the view will be worth it. Because the scenery *is* dazzling, and it's enhanced by the great relief and tremendous sense of accomplishment you'll feel. On a clear day (otherwise forget it!) all of North Cascades National Park will be spread out before you. You'll want a full roll of film in your camera, as well as wide-angle and zoom lenses. Big, bold, bare Jack Mountain stands high above the east shore of Ross Lake. Mt. Buckner and the Boston Glacier are way south. Northwestward loom Mount Terror and McMillan Spire, with Azure Lake clutched in an icy, rocky cirque below. Mt. Prophet is north. But there are hundreds more peaks in all directions. Anyone stationed in the fire lookout up here must have felt they'd been sent to heaven—or feared they would be when lightning jolted their perch.

Checking with the Newhalem or Marblemount park office to learn what trails are accessible in early season, you might find Sourdough is clear of snow to 5000 feet in early June. Don't go yet. That's not high enough. You need 1000 feet more for panoramic views.

Leaving the summit is painful—emotionally at first, then physically. It's probably more punishing than the ascent. Bring trekking poles, if you have them, to alleviate knee strain. Ski poles might suffice. And carry elastic kneebands for added support. Slipping one on is like wrapping an extra muscle around your knee.

It's possible, although not recommended, to make Sourdough Mountain a one-way shuttle trip. Start on the Big Beaver trail at Ross Lake Dam, then pick up the Sourdough Mountain trail and ascend Pierce Mountain. The ascent is several hundred feet less going that direction. Also, routefinding is easier (you can see your goal) going up the final mile on the east side than it is going down it. The shuttle trip is 15.1 miles and adds the burden of a full pack, without offering increased reward. If you insist on the one-way hike, park your vehicle in Diablo, where vandalism is less likely than at the Ross Dam trailhead on the highway. Then, after descending Sourdough, your car will be waiting for you.

FACT

By Car

Drive Highway 20 to the Diablo-townsite turnoff, 5.1 miles northeast from Newhalem's eastern edge, or 4.3 miles northwest from Colonial Creek Campground on Diablo Lake. At the west side of the highway bridge over Gorge Lake, turn northeast toward Diablo townsite. Continue past the homes, to the domed public swimming pool. Park on the gravel shoulder paralleling the river, at 900 feet. Look across the lawn. Near the hillside you'll see a trailhead sign. If you're hiking the shuttle trip, leave a vehicle in Diablo, and end your hike here. To start your hike, drive or hitchhike to the Ross Dam trailhead, 8.2 miles northeast of the Diablo turnoff, near milepost 134.

On Foot

Persistent switchbacks don't abate until 3.0 miles. The first mile is on the west side of a buttress—shaded until noontime. Then the trail turns northeast into the heat of the sun. The forest is dry, with only salal for understory. Shade is minimal beneath scrawny trees.

At 0.75 and 2.0 miles, at least into July, you can glimpse waterfalls on the north side of Davis Peak. At 1.5 miles you can look across to Pyramid and Colonial peaks.

Views open as you cross into the National Park at 2.7 miles. Just before the boundary, the grade relaxes a bit, then you traverse north into the Sourdough Creek drainage. Your ultimate goal is the green, alpine ridge you see ahead. Gain 900 feet in the next 1.5 miles to 5000-foot Sourdough Camp.

If you look carefully, you'll see a side trail on your left near 3 miles, just as the trail curves north around the ridge. It leads to a viewpoint near the satellite dish above Diablo. The trail is narrow, overgrown with salal, and rarely used. Skip the 800-foot climb here. Stay on the main trail to the summit—vastly more impressive.

Views expand from 3.5 miles onward. Looking southeast, you can see up Thunder Creek valley to Park Creek Pass. The trail then enters low brush and flowers and crosses meltwater creeklets (through mid-July). At 4.2 miles, Sourdough Creek is a welcome sight. Water is plentiful here. Across Highway 20, Ruby Mountain is visible to the southeast; Colonial and Snowfield peaks are close in the south; Pyramid Peak is slightly southwest.

There are campsites in trees on the ridge west of Sourdough Creek. It's another 985 vertical feet and 1.3 miles to the summit. Look for the trail continuing across the creek just below the largest grey boulder on the left. Traverse east on alpine slopes, then over a rocky, possibly muddy, slide area. If snow-covered, this stretch could be difficult. Then ascend short switchbacks north to the summit ridge.

Once on the ridge, don't go over the snowbank that will remain there until August. Go right, staying on the southwest side of the ridge, for the last 0.3 mile to the fire lookout tower. This might require you to work your way through snow and heather, but the tower marks the actual summit, at 5.5 miles, 5985 feet. That's 4777 feet above Diablo Lake directly below you, and 4381 feet higher than Ross Lake below you to the east.

If you plan to do the shuttle trip, start at the Ross Dam trailhead. Hike 0.8 mile down to the dam. Cross it and walk the Big Beaver trail 3.3 miles along the lake's northwest side to a junction. Go left (southwest) on the Sourdough Mountain trail to reach Pierce Mountain Camp at 8.3 miles, 5100 feet; it's lower than the Green Trails 1985 map indicates. The Sourdough Mountain summit is 0.7 mile farther west. This rocky stretch is almost pathless, but there are cairns.

Experienced cross-country hikers can walk northwest along Sourdough Mountain's ridgecrest. Cross-country camping is legal 0.5 mile off the trail. No fires allowed. Otherwise, Pierce Mountain Camp is the closest campground to the summit. The fire-lookout tower is closed to the public.

Diablo Lake far below Sourdough Mountain

Trip 28
Blue Lake

Location	North Cascades Scenic Highway Area.
Distance	4.4-mile round trip.
Elevation gain	1100'.
Maps	Green Trails No. 50–Washington Pass; Trails Illustrated No. 223–North Cascades National Park Complex.

OPINION

Short hikes in the North Cascades are rarely so rewarding. Blue Lake is an optimal destination for hikers of all ages and abilities. Fanatic hikers can squeeze it in on a Friday night after driving from the Coast. The ascent is mild, the switchbacks long and gentle. Even if you're just driving through the park, stop here, stretch your legs, and gain a deeper appreciation for the mountains.

Blue Lake is a charming host, making guests feel comfortable and offering them easy, varied entertainment. Beneath soaring, rose-colored cirque walls, the water is a riveting, deep turquoise. The Early Winters Spires are impressive from the highway, but more so here, where you can see the crack that earned Liberty Bell Mountain its name.

Alpine larch on the ridges surrounding the lake makes a strong case for visiting in late September when the needles have turned golden.

FACT

By Car

On Highway 20, drive 0.8 miles southwest of Washington Pass, or 4.2 miles east of Rainy Pass. Turn east off the highway to trailhead parking at 5200 feet.

On Foot

A few minutes beyond the trailhead, there's a wide bare spot where a side trail wanders off. Stay straight on the main trail. Heading northeast, it parallels the highway for 0.6 mile, so car noise can be bothersome. Long switchbacks then begin winding southward. At 1.5 miles, in a flowery avalanche meadow with cascading creeks, you attain views west and north. This is where a climbers' route turns left (east) and heads up to the cliffs of Early Winters Spires. Stay on the main trail as it curves right (southwest) and levels out in heather and trees. After crossing the outlet stream, you reach the north end of Blue Lake at 2.2 miles, 6300 feet. The trees are mostly larches and hardy whitebark pines. Camping is forbidden at this popular, fragile area. The lake is stocked with trout. Even this drier area on the east side of the Pacific Crest is plagued by mosquitoes.

Blue Lake and the Early Winters Spires

Trip 29

Grasshopper Pass

Location	Okanogan National Forest.
Distance	11.0-mile round trip.
Elevation gain	660'.
Maps	Green Trails No. 50–Washington Pass; Trails Illustrated No. 223–North Cascades National Park Complex.

OPINION

Alpine scenery attained with little effort, and a likelihood of sunny skies make the trip to Grasshopper Pass a welcome change from the steeper trails and wetter climate farther west. It's one of those rare sections of the Pacific Crest Trail where, starting at a high-elevation trailhead, you can blithely enjoy what long-distance hikers struggle to reach.

You leave the trees at the trailhead, so views are constant. Typical of the eastern Cascades, the landscape resembles the drier, more sparsely vegetated Front Range of Colorado, or even the high deserts of Arizona. The route is a long, snaking contour of rocky slopes. After rounding the first peak, you can look across a big horseshoe curve and see the path you'll follow to the pass, so there's no element of surprise. Still, the trail is a joy to walk. Looking northeast, Pasayten Wilderness stretches across the horizon. Below the pass is the upper South Fork Slate Creek drainage; across the canyon are Azurite Peak (southwest) and Mt. Ballard (northwest).

This hike is more dramatic than the one to Windy Pass (Trip 41), just north of Harts Pass. Either trail will afford you expansive vistas, but this one is closer to jagged peaks and in places has steep dropoffs on both sides.

September is the time to be here. Because there's hardly a speck of shade, it's a more pleasant hike in the cool, dreamy, fall air. If backpacking, keep in mind the trail is well above 6000 feet. You can expect chilly nights any time of year, and possibly snow in early September.

FACT

By Car

Drive Highway 20 to the signed Mazama turnoff, 13.2 miles northwest of Winthrop, or 1.5 miles southeast of the Early Winters Information Center. Turn northeast, and just after crossing the Methow River bridge turn left at a T-intersection onto Harts Pass Road 5400 (marked 54 on the Green Trails map). From Mazama, drive 9.1 miles northwest to a junction and a sign RIVER BEND CAMPGROUND ¼; METHOW TR. NO. 480 ¾; HARTS PASS 10. Go right and continue to Harts Pass at 6200 feet. From there, turn left and drive 2.0 miles south on the Meadows Campground road to where it ends at the 6400-foot trailhead. Don't count on the road being passable until mid-August. Contact the Methow Valley visitor center for road and trail conditions.

On Foot

The PCT is entirely in the open here, winding around several peaks to 6700-foot Grasshopper Pass at 5.0 miles. You first contour south on east-facing slopes, then west on south-facing slopes under an unnamed 7405-foot peak to a saddle above the headwaters of Slate Creek in Ninetynine Basin. Continue west under 7386-foot Tatie Peak to a 6880-foot saddle on its southwestern slope. Directly west is 8301-foot Mt. Ballard in clear view. From here, the trail turns south. You descend 240 feet to a basin, water source, and possible campsite at 3.8 miles, 6640 feet. Not labeled on maps, Grasshopper Pass is a small saddle at 5.5 miles, 6750 feet, just north of a 7125-foot knob. It's possible to camp near the pass. Just beyond, the PCT drops steeply to 5600-foot Glacier Pass. It continues down Brush Creek and up to Methow Pass. That 12.0-mile section is in forest.

For a broader view, hike 0.2 mile beyond Grasshopper Pass. Turn left off the trail before it starts switchbacking down to Glacier Pass. You'll see a bare spot where the side route heads off. It soon turns into a well-defined route heading south onto the ridgeline. Fifteen minutes of upward effort will enable you to peer south at distant mountains and down into the Brush Creek drainage.

Experienced scramblers can leave the trail to Grasshopper Pass almost anywhere along the way and ascend one or more of the small peaks above. It's even possible to negotiate the entire crest between the trailhead and the pass.

Ridge above Grasshopper Pass

Trip 30
Tiffany Mountain

Location	Okanogan National Forest.
Distance	6.0-mile round trip.
Elevation gain	1742'.
Map	Green Trails No. 53–Tiffany Mountain.

OPINION

Tiffany Mountain will leave with you the impression of light and space. On this bare, rocky summit, in the dry northeast corner of the range, you're almost assured of sunlight: bold and vibrant at midday, dimming to a subdued glow in evening, much like Greece. The views are grand, uneclipsed by any nearby peak. And the incredible silence, but for the occasional buzz of an insect or the swish of a breeze, is sensuous. The gentleness of Tiffany will probably be yours alone, since it's far from any sizable town.

Among the surrounding, forest-covered mountains, Tiffany's wide-open summit is unique. The main-range peaks are infinitely more dramatic, but Tiffany isn't in competition with them. It's another breed of mountain, more closely related to the Cairngorms of Scotland. If you're open to a different kind of alpine experience, you'll find this hike very rewarding.

Wildflower lovers will find plenty to excite them. Blue lupine, pastel-pink plumed avens, creamy-lime valerian, and succulent stonecrop are still healthy and ubiquitous in early August.

From the summit you look directly down on Tiffany Lake. Descending to it via the ridgeline, however, pulls you off the open slopes and into the trees, so don't bother arranging a shuttle for a one-way hike. It's also apparent from the summit why you shouldn't hike anywhere else in the immediate area. You'd have to walk many miles in forest to get above timberline.

FACT

By Car

Drive Highway 20 to Winthrop. From the center of town, follow the road north signed PEARRYGIN LAKE STATE PARK. This will lead you out the East Chewuch River Road. Pass the turnoff to the state park at 1.6 miles. At 6.6 miles, just before the road crosses the river, bear right onto Road 37 and continue north. At 7.9 miles, where Road 5010 forks left, stay right, heading northeast on Road 37 (370 on the Green Trails 1979 map). At 14.0 miles stay right toward Roger Lake on Road 37, which turns to gravel after crossing North Fork Boulder Creek. At a junction in 19.6 miles go left (northeast) onto Road 39 toward Tiffany Spring. Pass the Bernhardt Mine trail at 21.1 miles and the Roger Lake turn-in just after. At 22.8 miles, 6500 feet, arrive at Freezeout Pass and Freezeout trail 345 to Tiffany Mountain. Drive over the cattleguard and park along the right side of the road.

On Foot

The trail moderately ascends east and a bit southeast on Freezeout Ridge. The first 1.5 miles are through open forest brightened by lupine. Forest gives way to rocky meadowland scattered with granite boulders. At 2.0 miles, the trail is braided. Stay on the larger path. Don't angle left off-trail thinking that's a quicker way to the summit, which is now visible. The trail is more efficient. Generally, stay closer to the right (south) side of the ridge until the trail, sometimes a shallow trench, clearly cuts left, working upward and northward through rocks and tussock. At 2.5 miles you might notice a faint trail beginning to contour right (northeast). Ignore it. It goes to Whistler Pass. Bear left (north) now on a rough but obvious trail, and reach the former fire-lookout site atop 8242-foot Tiffany Mountain at 3.0 miles. The Green Trails map does not show a route the entire way up the summit of Tiffany.

You can see countless peaks on the distant horizon. West and a bit south you can spy Kangaroo Ridge near Washington Pass, as well as Silver Star and Gardner mountains. West are Goat Peak, Mt. Ballard, and Robinson Mountain. Southwest are the peaks rising above the Twisp River valley. North are the mountains along the Boundary Trail, west of Horseshoe Basin. East is Okanogan farmland.

Trip 31
Twisp Pass

Location	Okanogan National Forest / Lake Chelan-Sawtooth Wilderness.
Distance	8.4-mile round trip.
Elevation gain	2400'.
Maps	Green Trails No. 82–Stehekin; Trails Illustrated No. 223–North Cascades National Park Complex.

OPINION

Airy trails are thrilling. They have at least one side open to a deep expanse, because they're on a ridgetop or across cliff bands. The trail to Twisp Pass has a wonderfully long, airy stretch, reached within a couple miles. It gives you a continuous view of swooping, pinnacled peaks. The last stretch slices across a wall, for an intriguing traverse that helps you forget the climb.

From the pass, an exciting, high route continues, allowing you to roam the alpine ridge north to Stiletto Peak or even Copper Pass. Meadows, creeklets, rock gardens, larches, and glimpses of a dozen major peaks make this a magical exploration. Stiletto is an out-and-back hike; Copper can be a loop. Allow 9 hours to reach either destination and return to the trailhead in a single day. If you hike only to Twisp Pass and back, 5 hours should suffice.

The most impressive peaks and glaciers are far away, so this hike isn't premier. But the comfortable, gravelly trail surface, its predominantly open course, and the options for adventurous side trips place it solidly in the outstanding category.

We don't recommend dropping off Twisp Pass to Dagger Lake and continuing out to Bridge Creek (Trip 103) because it's terribly boring—through dry, unappealing forest.

FACT

By Car
On the east side of the North Cascades, drive Highway 20 to

Twisp. Turn west onto the paved road signed TWISP RIVER RECREA-
TION AREA. At 11.0 miles reach a junction. Continue straight
(northwest) on Twisp River Road 44. At 14.6 miles the road forks.
Proceed straight. Pass the official North Creek / Twisp Pass trailhead on the right at 25.0 miles. Reach Roads End Campground at
25.6 miles, 3700 feet. This isn't the official trailhead, but by starting here you can shorten your round-trip hiking distance by 0.8
mile. If you're not camping, don't park in a campsite.

On Foot

Look behind the outhouses for the steep, boot-beaten path up
the hillside. It vaults you onto the trail that leads west toward
Twisp and Copper passes. Proceed left once you attain the trail.
High above the north bank of the Twisp River, the trail's ascent is
almost unnoticeable the first mile. It passes through forest and
dense brush with a sprinkling of wildflowers. Though horses are
allowed, the narrow trail is infrequently ridden and the surface is
rocky, so dust and mud are not a problem.

After gaining 700 feet in 1.7 miles, reach a junction at 4400 feet.
Stay left for Twisp Pass. Right leads northwest 4.0 miles to Copper Pass (Trip 55). You can come down that way if you hike the
alpine route from Twisp to Copper, creating a loop. Turning left,
the trail immediately crosses the North Fork Twisp River—now
the size of a creek—on a footlog. It then darts upward, gaining
200 feet in 0.1 mile, before abruptly turning south to contour
around a ridge off Lincoln Butte. From 2.1 miles on, you're rewarded with views south across the South Fork Twisp River
valley at mountains 7500 to 7900 feet high. The smooth rock slabs
here are a comfortable, scenic place to rest. A bit farther on you
can see the head of the valley encircled by the serrated ridge of
looming Hock Mountain. Lush avalanche slopes pour off the
cliffs.

The trail ascends steadily northwest after 2.5 miles. Rocky
slopes the last mile afford open views. Carved into a cliffside, the
trail seems exposed but provides stable, secure footing. At 4.0
miles, a waterless campsite is off trail to the left—just before the
final switchback north to the pass. Reach 6100-foot Twisp Pass at
4.2 miles, on the boundary of North Cascades National Park. You
can see Dagger Lake 620 feet below the pass. Forested Bridge
Creek valley is farther west. If you intend to camp on the west
side of the pass, you'll need a National Park permit.

Dagger Lake from Twisp Pass

For better views ascend rocky meadows northeast of the pass. There you can look west to Goode Mountain and slightly northwest to Mt. Logan. You can also wander the ridgecrest southwest to the base of Twisp Mountain and a tiny lake. A faint 1.0-mile route heads northeast from the pass, then curves northwest toward Stiletto Peak. Competent off-trail hikers can easily wander another 1.3 miles northwest to the cliffs below Stiletto Peak. The route is through alpine parkland of boulders and grassy benches. Continue out Stiletto's western buttress and ascend to the 7200-foot site of an old lookout. From there you can look northeast to Liberty Bell and the Early Winters Spires, north to Tower Mountain, as well as northwest to Black Peak and Mt. Arriva. A round trip to the lookout site is feasible for a vigorous day trip.

If you're doing the cross-country trip from Twisp Pass to Copper Pass, you have to pick your own way when the aforementioned boot-beaten path fades. It's not difficult for anyone experienced in off-trail hiking, but start early and allow enough time to retrace your steps, just in case. From 6700-foot Copper Pass, follow the trail 4.0 miles down the North Fork to the junction with the Twisp Pass trail. You're then on familiar ground as you hike the 1.7 miles east to the trailhead.

Trip 32
Gothic Basin

Location	Mt. Baker-Snoqualmie National Forest / Department of Natural Resources.
Distance	9.4-mile round trip.
Elevation gain	2640'.
Maps	Green Trails No. 111–Sloan Peak, No. 143–Monte Cristo.

OPINION

Gothic Basin is a dramatic, rocky arena, conjuring images of the Scottish Highlands. The patches of greenery dotted with ferns and flowers contrast strikingly with the stark environment. Gothic is more interesting than nearby Glacier Basin (Trip 58). You can happily roam here for hours. Even the approach is enjoyable. After a stint in forest, you're on a long, high traverse, with open views, cooling breezes, plentiful water, and few flies.

Gothic Basin demands at least half a day of exploration, so start early if you're dayhiking. It's also an exceptional choice for a weekend backpack trip. Under a full pack, the ascent will seem steep, but it's not far. Once you sweep over the final slope, you'll be glad you can stay and play in this chaos of rocks. The basin's popularity almost assures you'll have to hunt for a campsite, but don't let that be your excuse for pitching your tent in the fragile grass. If you search the bouldery humps rising toward Foggy Lake, you should be able to find a vacant gravel niche.

The trail is clearly defined and only moderately difficult into the basin. From there, pick your own rocky course up to the surprisingly large Foggy Lake. Wander above, or around and beyond the lake. At the south shore, where you first arrive, you'll see a boulder slope to your left (southwest). It's well worth rambling up. You'll gain tremendous views of ragged pinnacles directly across from you, as well as the Sultan River basin below, and mountains marching south to Stevens Pass. If you scramble around the lake to the north end, you'll reach Foggy Pass, between Del Campo Peak (northeast) and Gothic Peak (southwest), where you can see Morning Star Peak close in the northwest.

FACT

By Car

From Darrington on Highway 530, drive the Mountain Loop Highway southeast 23.7 miles along the Sauk River to Barlow Pass. Or from the Verlot Public Service Center, drive southeast 19.8 miles to Barlow Pass. The 2361-foot pass is clearly signed. Park just off the highway, or in the lot on the north side.

On Foot

Walk the gated dirt road south toward Monte Cristo. At 1.2 miles, just before the bridge over the Sauk River, you'll see the signed Gothic Basin trailhead on your right. The 1995 Green Trails map doesn't show this trail, though it was forged in 1983 by members of Volunteers for Outdoor Washington. The Green Trails map shows the older trail, which starts 0.6 mile farther down the road and requires you to cross the river. Hike the newer trail. Leave the road before the Sauk River bridge, and, after a gentle stretch, ascend through deep forest.

At 2.75 miles from Barlow Pass, the trail begins a steep traverse on open slopes beneath Del Campo Peak. Soon cross a couple creeklets and a cool cascade. You can see Silvertip Peak southeast across Weden Creek. Farther east, above Glacier Basin, are Cadet, Monte Cristo, and Kyes peaks.

The ascent is gentler for 0.7 mile, but again turns steep and rough at 3.6 miles. Heather and flowers brighten the way. Reach Gothic Basin, beneath and southeast of 6213-foot Gothic Peak, at 4.7 miles, 5000 feet. A few campsites are scattered about. To reach Foggy Lake, proceed northwest up either side of the creekbed. Gain another 250 feet to the lake. Several campsites are spread out above the south shore. Reach 5500-foot Foggy Pass via talus slopes on the west side of the lake.

Trip 33
Monte Cristo / Twin Lakes

Location	Henry M. Jackson Wilderness.
Distance	16.8-mile round trip to ridge above Twin Lakes.
Elevation gain	2640'.
Map	Green Trails No. 143–Monte Cristo.

OPINION

If you're up for a rugged scamper to appreciate ragged peaks, this is an excellent choice. The climax is between Poodle Dog Pass and Twin Lakes. Though distinct, the trail here is little more than a boot-beaten route—gnarly and airy enough to provide a muscle-testing, soul-expanding adventure. The farther you go, the better the views and the fewer the people. Because it's a demanding goal, Twin Lakes is less popular than nearby Glacier and Gothic basins.

Monte Cristo, for reasons explained in the Glacier Basin review (Trip 58), adds nothing of interest to the trip. The ascent from Monte Cristo is steep and entirely in trees. And . . . Poodle Dog? Did some lonely, depraved miner bring a poodle up here? It's certainly no place for an effete, pampered pet. Offering only a limited view of Silver Lake, it's not even a worthy goal for hikers. But beyond Poodle Dog, on the way to Twin Lakes, the fun begins, starting with gourmet trail service. Bushes lining the path are loaded with plump, juicy berries in September. Gorge as you go.

Views are constant. The tread narrows, becoming uneven, steep, rough. It's merciless with a full pack, but a romp for experienced dayhikers who have good balance and are comfortable in precarious spots. Near the top, you get so close to the cliffs of Columbia Peak that the gouging glaciers and wispy waterfalls seem to be there for you alone—an intimate, thrilling gift of nature. Warning: a 12-foot section of the route requires a bit of scrambling. There are solid hand- and footholds, but it feels

Twin Lakes beneath Columbia Peak

exposed. A fall would be dangerous. Maybe that's where the poodle dog passed away.

The ridge above the Twin Lakes is a good place to rest before restarting your engine for the return trip. The deep blue lakes are clearly visible below, clutched in the cirque of Columbia Peak. You only need descend if you're spending the night. To the south and west, look over a sea of mountains stretching to Highway 2 and beyond. It's everything a hiker could want. Except water. Bring all you'll need. You don't cross any streams. Monte Cristo is the last source, unless you detour to Silver Lake or drop to the Twins.

FACT

By Car

From Darrington on Highway 530, drive the Mountain Loop Highway southeast 23.7 miles along the Sauk River to Barlow Pass. Or from the Verlot Public Service Center, drive southeast 19.8 miles to Barlow Pass. The 2361-foot pass is clearly signed. Park just off the highway, or in the lot on the north side.

On Foot

Walk or bike the gated dirt road south toward Monte Cristo. At 1.2 miles, pass the Gothic Basin trailhead and cross the South Fork Sauk River bridge. Continue on the road. At 4.2 miles, 2800 feet, arrive at a large bridge just before the Monte Cristo townsite. The bridge is a good place to rest, especially during fly season. Sit beside the cold water and they won't bother you as much. When you cross the bridge, look on the right side of the open area in front of the buildings for the sign SILVER LAKE. The following distances are measured from there.

The trail dives into thick foliage, then lush forest. After a steep climb of 1600 feet in 1.7 miles, reach Poodle Dog Pass and a 3-way junction, at 4400 feet. The trail going downhill on your right leads 0.3 mile to Silver Lake. For Twin Lakes, go left (southeast) at the junction. Go up a bit, down 100 feet, then contour the head of Silver Creek basin to your right.

Climbing again, reach a viewpoint at 2.7 miles, 4800 feet, and look northeast into Seventysix Gulch. Then traverse above the gulch. Across it you can see glaciers and waterfalls on Wilmon and Columbia peaks. Straight ahead (southeast), you can see a round-topped mountain with grey talus; you're heading for the ridge between it and the little peak with trees on top. Those are the Twin Peaks.

At 4.2 miles from Monte Cristo, arrive at the 4900-foot ridge between the Twin Peaks and above Twin Lakes. Campsites are 0.25 mile straight down, near the lakeshore, at 4700 feet.

Trip 34

Hozomeen Lake / Willow Lake

Location	Ross Lake Recreation Area.
Distance	7.4-mile round trip to Hozomeen Lake; 10.2-mile round trip to Willow Lake.
Elevation gain	1150' to Hozomeen or Willow lakes.
Maps	Green Trails No. 16–Ross Lake; Trails Illustrated No. 223–North Cascades National Park Complex.

OPINION

Hozomeen Lake is what makes this hike worthwhile. The two pinnacles of Hozomeen Mountain spear the sky above the east bank. It's a stirring scene. The mountain is visible from other trails in the northern reaches of the North Cascades, but it's more impressive from here, directly beneath the cliffs. And, on a hot day, the beautifully clear lake will tempt you to dive in. "Yeee-owww! Damn!" was the breathless outburst we heard from one eager dipper as he emerged from the frigid water.

The forest en route is pretty, but not grand. The only open views are at Hozomeen Lake or, if you continue, at Willow Lake. Go to Willow only if you want to lengthen your hike. Willow Lake is shallow and marshy, rapidly returning to meadow. It's anticlimactic after Hozomeen, but Willow's pastoral west end is a fine place to eat lunch before turning around. Freezeout and Joker mountains are visible to the east. Hiking beyond Willow Lake requires an overnight backpack trip, and it's not worth it; the trail is through viewless forest all the way to Ross Lake.

FACT

By Car

The trailhead is 40 miles south of Trans-Canada Highway 1. Two miles (3.2 km) west of Hope, take Exit 168, signed FLOOD-HOPE RD / SILVER HOPE CREEK. After exiting, turn right (south) onto Silver-Skagit Road, following signs for Silver Lake and

Hozomeen Lake

Hozomeen Campground. From 1.6 miles on, the road is gravel but well maintained. Near the end of the road, pass the B.C. Parks Ross Lake Campground, then stay left at a fork. Right is to the International Point Day-Use area. Just beyond the fork enter the U.S. Ross Lake National Recreation Area and see the park service's A-frame ranger station. Continue south, soon passing the free Hozomeen Campground beside the lake, and a maintenance shed a bit farther. Turn left at a sign pointing to the Hozomeen Lake trailhead. Drive through another part of the campground in trees, then come to an old cabin and the trailhead parking area at 1700 feet. It's 1.8 miles from the ranger station. There are faucets with potable water here.

On Foot

Initially ascend through lodgepole forest with mossy understory. Briefly pass through a dry, sparsely treed area, then cross a small, wood bridge and suddenly enter cool, moist, cedar forest. You can glimpse Hozomeen Mountain to the east. At 3.1 miles, 2700 feet, reach a signed junction: Hozomeen Lake left, Willow Lake straight.

The undulating trail to the left crosses a brook in 40 yards, and reaches the shore of Hozomeen Lake in 0.6 mile. At the end of the small peninsula here is a campground with room for about 10 tents. All of the lakeshore is forested, except for one rocky perch just beyond the campground.

If you continue straight (southeast) at the 3.1-mile junction, lupine lines the trail near 4.5 miles. Reach the west end of Willow Lake and a campsite at 5.1 miles, 2850 feet.

If you're hiking farther, 2.8 miles southeast of Willow Lake and 700 feet lower is Nightmare Camp in a cedar grove, just above the west bank of Lightning Creek. South 2.5 miles, the Lightning Creek trail meets the Three Fools trail at 2000 feet, then gains 500 feet before the final descent to Ross Lake at 9.1 miles, 1700 feet. For a description of the trail continuing south from there, see Ross Lake East Bank (Trip 110).

Trip 35

Nooksack Cirque

Location	North Cascades National Park.
Distance	12.0-mile round trip.
Elevation gain	600'.
Maps	Green Trails No. 14–Mt. Shuksan; Trails Illustrated No. 223–North Cascades National Park Complex.

OPINION

Thrash, thwack, leap, splash and kerplunk your way into Nooksack Cirque, and you'll discover a wickedly wild and wonderful corner of the North Cascades. The experience will bring out the yaba-daba-doo-ness in you.

This is one of the few dayhikes where you're likely to encounter only a few other hikers. The rough route puts most people off. But it's the easiest, quickest way to plumb the depths of a classic "deep hole"—the local term for the immense valleys that characterize this mountain range.

The trip has other rewards, too—less grand, yet equally compelling. You'll be passing through an ancient forest where life flourishes. Take a moment to examine a moss-covered log, and you'll realize it's not just a dead tree. It's a magnificent home. You'll count at least a dozen different tiny things growing on it. And throughout the forest you can see a varied sampling of colorful, dramatically shaped fungi: flapping elephant ears, miniature frozen waterfalls (Pom Pom du Blanc), delicate pinheads. We spotted one that looked like a whirling dervish in a brown-and-white skirt (Turkey Tail).

Despite the lack of elevation gain, the rocky bed of the Nooksack River opens the forest enough to allow good views of Icy Peak and, deeper in, the hanging glaciers of East Nooksack Glacier on Mt. Shuksan. If you press on, you can eventually ogle the entire cirque and Shuksan's 5000-foot northeast wall.

Before plunging in, realize this hike is unlike others described in this book. It stays low in a valley bottom, but the path is not straightforward. The kind of powerful, rhythmic stride that makes the miles melt away just isn't possible here. After following an overgrown logging road, the trail degenerates into a trodden route—a torment of roots, logs, ferns, brambles, mush, and holes that will eat your ankles if you're lax. Once you reach the river, even the route becomes sketchy. You have to fight your way along the brushy bank, or get your feet wet, unless you come after the river has subsided enough (usually mid-September) to allow you to walk most of the way on gravel bars. Even then, expect to be in and out of the water. Repeatedly de-booting is a hassle, so it helps to wear sport sandals, allowing you to wander at will. Wear them with neoprene socks, and you'll be laughing at your frozen-toed companions.

FACT

By Car

From the Glacier Public Service Center on Highway 542, drive 13.1 miles east. Just before the Nooksack River bridge, turn left (east) onto Nooksack River Road 32. Turn right in 1.3 miles onto Road 34. Drive 1.0 mile farther to the trailhead parking, at 2200 feet, where a bridge used to cross Ruth Creek.

On Foot

From the old bridge pilings, go down to your left and find a shallow place to wade across the creek. Walk 2.0 miles on an old logging road that's now a tree-enclosed corridor. An obvious route leads you to 3.0 miles, then spits you out at the river. There's a small, rough campsite here. Your goal is now clear—proceed upstream to ever-improving views—but specifically how to achieve that is less apparent. Assess the conditions and make your way as you see fit.

If the river is low, and the gravel bars are exposed, walk on rocks as far as possible. At times, you'll still be forced to choose between wading and bushwhacking. Much of the way along the bank, however, you'll find pathways blazed by other hikers. Following these might speed your progress. You'll also see where others have camped in the forest. Near 6 miles you'll probably have to stop. Further progress is extremely difficult. But by then you'll have seen the cirque. Camping on gravel bars or moraines is possible.

Returning downstream, look for two tree trunks forming a sharp, high-reaching **V**. If you're out on the gravel bar, that **V** marks the spot where you should turn into the forest and find the route back to the old logging road.

North Fork Nooksack River

Trip 36

Galena Chain Lakes

Location	Heather Meadows Recreation Area / Mt. Baker Wilderness.
Distance	6.5-mile shuttle trip; 8.0-mile loop.
Elevation gain	900' for shuttle trip starting at Artist Point; 1540' for loop starting at Austin Pass.
Maps	Green Trails No. 14–Mt. Shuksan; Trails Illustrated No. 223–North Cascades National Park Complex.

OPINION

Like other nearby trails, this one has grand views, but you don't end up cheek-by-jowl with Baker or Shuksan. At times you also have to put up with the sight and sound of the highway. That's why we haven't ranked it higher. The attraction here is a loop trip with variety: an impressive, rocky bowl; dramatic, towering cliffs; several forested lakes; and an alpine stroll.

If you have two cars for shuttling, leave one at the Austin Pass picnic area and visitor center parking lot above the Bagley Lakes. Then drive up to Artist Point and start the hike there. After hiking around Table Mountain and the Galena Chain Lakes and back to the Austin Pass parking lot, jump in your second car and laugh at less fortunate hikers as you whiz back up to Artist Point. Better yet, take joy in offering them a ride.

If you can't arrange a shuttle, we recommend starting the loop at the Austin Pass picnic area. Though the overall elevation gain is about the same in either direction, the Austin Pass start has several advantages. You'll do most of the climbing early in the day, when you're fresh. Later, when you're more tired, you'll end the day on a descent. Also, the section of trail between Artist Point and the Austin Pass picnic area is near the road. If you hike it last, late in the afternoon, many visitors will have left, so there will be fewer cars to annoy you. Besides, you'll probably feel less bothered hiking downhill next to motorists than you would trudging uphill. Or try to spare your knees the pounding, stay on the highway, stick your thumb out, and hope an empathetic driver gives you a lift.

FACT

By Car

Drive Highway 542 to the Mt. Baker ski area. Go right at the large map of Mt. Baker. If doing a shuttle, leave one vehicle at the Austin Pass picnic area, 0.8 mile from the map. Continue 1.8 miles farther to the Artist Point parking lot at road's end on Kulshan Ridge, 5100 feet. In a heavy snowfall year, you might not be able to drive that far until late August. If you can't arrange a shuttle, park lower at the Austin Pass picnic area, 4440 feet.

On Foot

From the Austin Pass picnic area parking lot, take the Bagley Lakes trail, which leaves beside the Heather Meadows visitor center—the stone building. To the right of the trailhead sign, the trail drops through an opening in the stone wall to cross rock slabs and steps. Below the visitor center, in 0.1 mile at a directional sign, go left about 70 yards to a small pond; then go right. After another 70 yards, at 0.4 mile total after descending 200 feet, cross the stone bridge between the Bagley Lakes. Once across it, go left (southwest) on Galena Chain Lakes trail 682.

The trail climbs 1060 feet through a rocky bowl and across a grassy slope. It's a long, gradual ascent at first, then a series of switchbacks to a 5300-foot high point on Mt. Herman's southwest flank, just east of Mazama Dome. You'll get views of Shuksan, Baker, and the highway far below. Then descend southwest 500 feet to Iceberg Lake. From its northwest side, you can take a short side trail to Hayes and Arbuthnot lakes. There are campsites at the lakes. Farther south, at 4.6 miles, after rising 240 feet, pass the minor, rougher Table Mountain trail 681, which ascends steeply on your left. Stay right (southeast) to meet the Ptarmigan Ridge trail at 5.3 miles, 5200 feet. Turn left (northeast) at this junction and continue 1.2 miles—mostly level, with an unobstructed view of Shuksan—to the Artist Point parking lot.

If you're hiking back to the Austin Pass picnic area, walk below the men's side of the restroom building at the Artist Point parking lot to the road's first switchback. Angle left and pick up the Wild

Goose trail. You'll see the trail descending past the pyramid cairn, to the right of the gravel overflow parking lot. The trail descends northeast 660 feet in 1.5 miles to the Austin Pass picnic area.

If you start the hike from Artist Point, the trail begins at the southwest end of the parking lot. Take the trail left of the large trailhead sign. Don't take the Table Mountain trail on the right, which ascends behind the sign. (The Green Trails 1988 map shows it only starting 0.2 mile in.) In 0.2 mile, pass a rough trail ascending right, which is another way to ascend Table Mountain. Reach a junction at 1.2 miles, 5200 feet. Go right (northwest), staying on Galena Chain Lakes trail 682. Reach another junction at 1.9 miles. Table Mountain trail 681 ascends to the right. Continue straight, descending to the Galena Chain Lakes, then ascending northeast toward Mt. Herman. There are no more trail junctions (other than minor side paths leading to the lakes) after that, until you're down at the stone bridge between the Bagley Lakes. From there, ascend southeast to the Heather Meadows visitor center. Then walk to Terminal Lake, the pond beside the road at the Austin Pass parking lot. From here, the Wild Goose trail leads southwest up to the Artist Point parking lot.

Galena Chain Lakes Trail

Trip 37

Anderson Butte / Anderson and Watson lakes

Location	Mt. Baker-Snoqualmie National Forest / Noisy-Diobsud Wilderness.
Distance	7.0-mile round trip to all.
Elevation gain	2200' total.
Maps	Green Trails No. 46–Lake Shannon; Trails Illustrated No. 223–North Cascades National Park Complex.

OPINION

Commanding views are easy to attain on this short hike. You can see Mt. Baker, Mt. Shuksan, Twin Sisters Mountain, Bacon Peak, and the Baker River Valley. Any sense of wilderness you might feel atop Anderson Butte, however, is nullified by all the logging roads and clearcuts that are also visible. It's a reminder that only the glacier-clad peaks you behold are safe from man's rapaciousness. The irony is that it's a logging road that enables you to quickly reach this and most other higher-elevation trailheads in the North Cascades. Chances are, you'd never visit these very pleasant lakes or the grand viewpoint at Anderson Butte if loggers hadn't been there first. It's something to think about while driving the amazingly scenic road to the trailhead. From your vehicle, you can enjoy nearly the same views awaiting you at the butte. But hike anyway. From the first Anderson Lake, the sight of Mt. Baker feels like a reward, as does Bacon Peak to the east when spied from the deep-blue Watson Lakes. This is a good place to bring the kids for a slow, meandering walk among meadows and lakes. Moderately fit hikers can visit all sights in a 7.0-mile dayhike.

FACT

By Car

Drive Highway 20 east 16.5 miles from Sedro Woolley, or west 6.0 miles from Concrete. Turn north onto the Grandy-Baker Lake Road. Drive 13.9 miles and turn right (east) at the sign BAKER LAKE—KOMA KULSHAN CAMPGROUND. Go down 1.2 miles on the badly potholed road to the free Kulshan Campground and picnic area, maintained by Puget Power. Continue straight. Follow the sign EAST BANK TRAIL—WATSON LAKE directing you over the dam, to the east side of Baker Lake. In 1.0 mile from the campground, go left on Road 1107. The dirt road winds northeast uphill and has many tight switchbacks before arriving in 10.0 miles from the dam at the 4200-foot trailhead.

On Foot

The trail gently gains 600 feet, first in forest, then through meadow, to a junction at 0.9 mile. The left trail ascends east 600 feet in 0.5 mile to an outcropping at 5420 feet, beneath the true summit of Anderson Butte. From the 0.9-mile junction, the right trail crosses a meadow and in 0.6 mile reaches a second junction. Here you can go left (east) to Watson Lakes, or right (southeast) to Anderson Lakes. The left fork gains a couple hundred feet over a rocky stretch, then switchbacks 500 feet down to the western Watson Lake at 4500 feet, 2.5 miles from the trailhead. A sketchy trail follows its northern shore and leads to the eastern Watson Lake in another 0.6 mile. Camping is allowed at designated sites around the lakes. Back at the second junction, the right fork leads 0.5 mile through forest and talus to a campsite at the lower Anderson Lake, at 4500 feet, 2.0 miles from the trailhead. Two smaller lakes are 500 feet higher on the ridge to the east.

Trip 38

Sauk Mountain

Location	Mt. Baker-Snoqualmie National Forest.
Distance	4.2-mile round trip.
Elevation gain	1200'.
Maps	Green Trails No. 46–Lake Shannon,
	No. 78–Darrington (shows Road 1030);
	Trails Illustrated No. 223–North
	Cascades National Park Complex.

OPINION

More gratifying hikes await you deeper in the North Cascades. But for a quick overview, sprinting up Sauk Mountain beats driving Highway 20 through the National Park. It offers the most easily attained panorama of any destination in this book.

Sauk is an unlikely place to hike. It's hardly even a hike. Jaunt is more accurate. The mountain is tiny, logged nearly to the top, and sits far west of the main range. From a distance, the summit ridge looks like a Bart Simpson haircut. But the view up there is amazing.

Come in mid-spring to get inspired for the upcoming hiking season. Or in fall to see how many peaks you're able to identify after the summer's explorations. Bring the Trails Illustrated map to serve as your answer sheet.

Whenever you visit, you'll have company on this popular little trail, even on a weekday. Families swarm here, because the path is short and easy, and has views the whole way. Profuse wildflowers give little ones something to look at close-up. Just don't let your kids pick them.

In addition to offering superb scenery, Sauk Mountain forces you to witness the devastation of clearcuts. The valley below is a patchwork mess. The mountain itself, as you'll see on the long drive up, has been shorn. Once this was a moist, cool, magnificent forest. Now it's a hot, dusty monument to man's myopia. The pathetic regrowth is spindly, downright ugly. Beautiful fireweed does its best to hide the unnatural nakedness, but isn't up to the task. Maybe that's for the best, if it moves the rest of us to be more conservation-minded.

FACT

By Car

On Highway 20, drive 6.4 miles southeast from Concrete's eastern edge, or 1.7 miles west from the Rockport junction. Turn north onto signed Sauk Mountain Road, just west of Rockport State Park. A good gravel road switchbacks steadily to a fork at 7.6 miles. Go right and arrive at the trailhead parking lot 0.2 mile farther, at 4300 feet. From here you can see the trail zigzagging up the mountain.

On Foot

Gentle switchbacks lead you up the meadowed southwest face of Sauk Mountain. Just after rock bands, the trail swings to the east side of the summit ridge. From 1.5 miles up, by a small wood sign, a narrow trail descends to Sauk Lake, which you can see northeast cupped below Bald Mountain as you continue up the main trail. If you drop to the lake, you'll lose 1200 feet in 1.5 miles.

Proceeding to the summit, make sure you go past the flat area with clumps of trees. Head northwest, traversing up Sauk's east side. Just below the rocky summit pinnacle, the trail pops over to the west side for the final couple turns to the top. The summit, reached at 2.1 miles, 5500 feet, can be severely fly-infested from mid-July through August.

On a clear day, you can see Mt. Baker and Mt. Shuksan to the northwest, Mt. Bacon a bit closer to the northeast. The Pickets are farther northeast, looking very much like their namesake. Jack Mountain is also northeast. Colonial, Snowfield, Eldorado, Forbidden, and Boston peaks are east, above the Cascade River valley. Snowking Mountain, Glacier Peak, Mt. Buckindy, and Dome Peak are southeast. Sloan Peak and Whitehorse are south, above Darrington. Mt. Rainier is farther south. The Olympics are southwest. The river valleys below are the Skagit (east-west) and the Sauk (north-south).

Trip 39

Lookout Mountain / Monogram Lake

Location	Mt. Baker-Snoqualmie National Forest / North Cascades National Park.
Distance	9.4-mile round trip to Lookout Mtn; 9.8-mile round trip to Monogram Lake.
Elevation gain	4470' to Lookout Mtn; 3950' to Monogram Lake.
Maps	Green Trails No. 47–Marblemount, No. 48–Diablo Dam (to identify peaks); Trails Illustrated No. 223–North Cascades National Park Complex.

OPINION

The perspective from Lookout Mountain and the scenery at Monogram Lake are staggering. The elevation gain is also staggering. And it's mostly through viewless forest. For those reasons, and because nearby Hidden Lake Lookout offers an even better view at the end of a shamelessly easy yet incomparably beautiful hike, we've demoted this trail in our rankings. It barely escaped the Don't Do pile.

If Sisyphus is one of your role models, here's your chance to walk several miles in his shoes. You can even push on higher, above Monogram's great cirque walls, all the way to Little Devil Peak. But most hikers, lacking a big **S** on their chest or a set of bionic knees, should choose a less arduous destination. Try Hidden Lake first, then look west toward Monogram and see how ambitious you feel.

Only maniacs try to hit both Lookout Mountain and Monogram Lake on a dayhike, and not all of them succeed. You'd have to cover 13.6 miles and gain 6230 feet! The sane thing to do is pick one or the other. The Monogram Lake setting is more exceptional than the Lookout Mountain view.

FACT

By Car

At the eastern edge of Marblemount, where Highway 20 bends north, go straight (east) onto the Cascade River road and immediately cross the Skagit River. In 0.7 mile pass the Rockport-Cascade Road on the right. Continue east on the Cascade River road (now labeled 15), which turns to gravel at 5.2 miles. At 7.1 miles, 1250 feet, the trailhead sign is on the left. Park in the pullout along the right side of the road.

On Foot

The trail ascends steep, tight switchbacks through thick forest. It gains 2200 feet in the first 2.0 miles, offering only one brief view. Then the gradient eases. Continue upward through 0.2 mile of high brush. Reach a signed junction at 2.8 miles, 3740 feet. For Lookout Mountain, turn left (northwest) and proceed upward in trees. Enter meadow at 3.6 miles and continue switchbacking up. Then from a point northeast of the lookout, the route turns southwest to reach the ridgecrest. Attain the 5719-foot summit at 4.7 miles. The tower is open to the public. If you hope to sleep there, it's first come, first served, so bring a tent in case the tower is occupied for the night. There's a flat campsite just below the lookout. You'll find water at a spring 0.3 mile below the summit. Views are north to the distant Picket Range, west over the heavily clearcut Skagit valley, southeast over the Cascade River valley, south to Glacier Peak, and east to Eldorado Peak.

To visit Monogram Lake, go right at the 2.8-mile junction and continue switchbacking steeply north. The trail enters the National Park at 3.3 miles, so you'll need a permit to camp. Enter meadows at 4.0 miles and cross a tributary of Lookout Creek. The trail then angles southwest up a ridge, gaining 400 feet in 0.4 mile. From the 5200-foot crest, you can peer into the Monogram Lake cirque. Crossing huge angular slabs, the trail descends 300 feet, reaching the lake at 4.9 miles, 4900 feet. There are three, official, no-fire campsites around the meadowed shore. You can also camp cross-country half a mile above the lake to the south. Expect snow in the cirque until mid-August.

For further exploration, start on the south side of Monogram Lake and follow open slopes east to a 5607-foot knoll. Here you can look down into Marble Creek (southwest) and directly across at 8868-foot Eldorado Peak (east). Without climbing equipment, experienced scramblers can ascend meadows on the southern end of Teebone Ridge and work their way to the 6844-foot summit of Little Devil Peak, wedged between two small glaciers.

Trip 40
Cutthroat Pass

Location	North Cascades Scenic Highway Corridor / Okanogan National Forest
Distance	10.0-mile round trip
Elevation gain	1920'
Maps	Green Trails No. 50–Washington Pass; Trails Illustrated No. 223–North Cascades National Park Complex

OPINION

The Pacific Crest Trail's gentle grade enables you to build and maintain momentum on this easy ascent past treeline. Compared to all the old miners' routes that mercilessly leap up North Cascade mountainsides, it's a treat to be on such a tame trail. Because you won't be distracted by whimpering muscles, you can fully appreciate the pretty forest, heather fields, and rock gardens on the way to Cutthroat Pass.

The pass offers sweeping views across dry-bones country: high, arid, bleak. But the peaks are piercing and jagged. Huge, flat, lounge-lizard boulders await you at the pass. But don't linger. Ridges on either side invite exploration. And the PCT beckons. Keep going to the knoll above Granite Pass to look down into Swamp Creek valley and out at soaring mountains. Read Trip 98 about the backpack trip to Snowy Lakes.

Don't be tempted to start this hike at Cutthroat Creek. Start at Rainy Pass. From Rainy, the grade is gentler because it's the PCT. You get out of forest sooner. And your round-trip mileage will be one mile shorter. And certainly don't bother trying to hitch or arrange a shuttle in an attempt to include Cutthroat Lake on the journey. You'll see it from the pass, looking down to the southeast. Besides, the meadows and forest between Rainy and Cutthroat passes are worth seeing twice.

By Car

On Highway 20, drive 37.2 miles southeast of Newhalem, or

20.8 miles southwest of the Early Winters Information Center, to the Rainy Pass trailhead parking lot. It's on the east side of the road, at 4880 feet. Don't turn into the Rainy Pass picnic-area parking lot on the west side.

FACT

On Foot

You'll be hiking entirely on the moderately ascending Pacific Crest Trail. After the first 0.75 mile north, the trail and Highway 20 diverge, so you leave the car noise behind. The PCT ascends northeast up Porcupine Creek. There's a view of Cutthroat Pass (northeast) at approximately 2 miles. After walking through thick timber for 3.0 miles, the trees get sparser and you enter heather and meadows. At 4.0 miles, there's a campsite. The last 1.0 mile is in open, rocky, alpine terrain. You attain 6800-foot Cutthroat Pass at 5.0 miles. Scramble onto the ridge south of the pass for a view of 7865-foot Cutthroat Peak directly south and Liberty Bell Mountain southeast of it.

Beyond the pass, the PCT contours northeast over barren slopes above Cutthroat Creek canyon. From the knoll at 6.4 miles, above the switchbacks that descend to Granite Pass, you can look northwest over Swamp Creek valley.

Looking southwest from Cutthroat Pass

Trip 41

Windy Pass

Location	Okanogan National Forest.
Distance	7.4-mile round trip.
Elevation gain	300' in, 700' out.
Maps	Green Trails No. 17–Jack Mountain (shows route north of Woody Pass), No. 18–Pasayten Peak, No. 50–Washington Pass; Trails Illustrated No. 223–North Cascades National Park Complex.

OPINION

The Pacific Crest Trail between Harts Pass and Windy Pass is baby-carriage gentle. It contours high above forested valleys, across meadowed slopes. Views are constant and easily attained—just turn your head. The difficulties will come later, because an excursion here will compel you to plan long, arduous journeys to the alluring peaks and ridges on the horizon north and west. If you're an aggressive hiker, the hardest part of this trip will be reining yourself in and turning around near Windy Pass.

The distant Three Fools Peak massif to the north will tempt you to visit that lonely, wild area. Views west might spark dreams of trekking around Crater and Jack mountains and along Jackita Ridge (Trip 102). Peering south over the Pacific Crest to Tower Mountain and Golden Horn (Trip 98) will only further add to the frustrating realization that, as much as you'd like to, you can't explore it all right now.

Given an extra day here, however, the PCT south to Grasshopper Pass (Trip 29) offers a convenient opportunity to inspect the closest, most dominant formations: Mount Ballard and Azurite Peak.

Families with small children, or anyone who prefers strolling to straining, will find Windy Pass an ideal outing. The meadows and larches at the pass are a lovely, nearly effortless destination for backpackers unwilling or unable to invest a long day on a rough trail to experience mountain glory. If you're camping, expect chilly nights up here and possibly snow as early as September.

Although the views from the trail are excellent, the nearby fire lookout atop Slate Peak affords a higher and therefore more commanding vantage. Don't miss it. Drive the short distance to the end of the road, then walk the final 0.25 mile past the gate to the 7440-foot summit. Ideally, come here after your hike and watch the sun set on a sweeping North Cascades panorama, including distant Mt. Baker.

Before traipsing north on the PCT beyond the 6700-foot ridge-crest just past Windy Pass, keep in mind: the only walking above treeline will be a spurt along Devils Backbone and about 6 miles between Goat Lakes and the north end of spectacular Lakeview Ridge. Looking west from the high, open slopes of Three Fools Peak, you'll see studly peaks in the distance. After that, you'll be in forest most of the 17.7 miles to the northern terminus of the PCT on Canada's Highway 3. That's a hefty price to pay for several miles of heady scenery. There's also the logistical challenge of arranging transportation between Harts Pass and Manning Park. Unless you have a non-hiking significant other who's a willing shuttle-slave, it's a nightmare requiring public transport and hitchhiking.

FACT

By Car

Drive Highway 20 to the signed Mazama turnoff, 13.2 miles northwest of Winthrop, or 1.5 miles southeast of the Early Winters Information Center. Turn northeast, and just after crossing the Methow River bridge turn left at a T-intersection onto Harts Pass Road 5400 (marked 54 on the Green Trails map). From Mazama, drive 9.1 miles northwest to a junction and a sign RIVER BEND CAMPGROUND ¼; METHOW TR. NO. 480 ¾; HARTS PASS 10. Go right and continue to Harts Pass at 6200 feet. From there, turn right onto Slate Peak Road 600 and drive 1.5 miles northwest to the first switchback (pointing west), where there's a small, trailhead parking area at 6800 feet. Don't count on the road being passable until mid-August. Contact the Methow Valley visitor center for road and trail conditions.

On Foot

Heading northwest, this section of the PCT begins by gently climbing a bench. It then contours around Slate Peak, eases down into Benson Basin, rises to Buffalo Pass, descends above Barron Basin and Bonita Creek, and at 3.7 miles, reaches the meadows and campsites of 6300-foot Windy Pass. If you want another open view, continue a bit farther northwest. Find more campsites and water in a basin at 4.1 miles. The trail switchbacks up to reach a ridgecrest at 4.4 miles, 6700 feet. This is a good place for dayhikers to turn around.

Continuing north, the PCT descends to Foggy Pass at 6.0 miles, 6200 feet. From the northeast ridge of Devils Backbone at 8.25 miles, it drops into trees and reaches 5100-foot, forested Holman Pass at 13.2 miles. Near the 15.0-mile point, reach the meadowy basin of Goat Lakes beneath Holman Peak by wandering east 0.5 mile off-trail. Near Woody Pass, 18.4 miles from the Slate Peak Road, begin the long, high contour beneath Three Fools Peak and along Lakeview Ridge. Near 21.5 miles the PCT starts dropping from the crest and travels the remaining 17.7 miles, mostly in deep forest, to Highway 3 in Canada's Manning Park. See Trip 100 for more details.

Trip 42
Copper Glance Lake

Location	Okanogan National Forest.
Distance	7.6-mile round trip.
Elevation gain	2300'.
Maps	Green Trails No.19–Billy Goat Mtn, No. 51–Mazama; US Forest Service–Pasayten Wilderness.

OPINION

Though the lake is pretty, that's not what makes this hike worthwhile. In a region of mostly dull, rounded mountains, it's the craggy peaks of Isabella Ridge thrusting above the Copper Glance cirque that are eye-catching. Plus the trail is short, it passes through lovely meadows, and the delicious fragrance of pines in this dry climate is soothing to the senses. Usually snow-free by July, this a good place for an early summer workout.

The hike begins on a mining road. Narrow, rugged, horrendously steep, and seldom used, it seems like a wide trail. Steel yourself for a thigh-burner, no matter how light your pack. The tree cover, however, is sufficient to keep you from being fried by a sun that's rarely obscured by clouds here on the east side of the range.

The Chewuch River you drive along to the trailhead is beautiful, and free Forest Service campgrounds are plentiful, so there's more to draw you here than just the hike. The backroads to the trailhead are very good—paved a long way, then smooth, flat gravel—so don't let the 22 miles from Winthrop scare you off. Tiffany Mountain (Trip 30), not far from here, is an Outstanding hike you could do the same weekend.

FACT

By Car

Drive Highway 20 to Winthrop. From the center of town, follow the road north, signed PEARRYGIN LAKE STATE PARK. This will lead you out the East Chewuch River Road. Pass the turnoff to the state park at 1.6 miles. At 6.6 miles, go left at the junction and cross the river. Then go right (north) at the T-junction onto West Chewuch River Road. Soon entering national forest, the road is signed NO. 51. At 9.2 miles turn left (northwest) onto Eightmile Creek Road 5130. At 21.6 miles look for a gated jeep road and the trailhead sign on your left. Park on the right side of the road. Trail 519 starts on the jeep road at 3800 feet.

On Foot

Start on the jeep road. It ascends northwest 1200 feet, with only a few switchbacks, to a mine shaft and the beginning of trail at 1.5 miles. The trail ascends steeply west. At 2.0 miles enter a flower-filled meadow with rugged mountains visible beyond it. Re-entering forest, the trail is mostly level for 0.4 mile. Cross Copper Glance Creek at 3.1 miles. Reach stands of larch and a shallow pond at 3.3 miles. You can see 8470-foot Big Craggy Peak rising on the north side of the basin. Go left, veering south, to ascend scree on a low ridge separating the pond basin from Copper Glance cirque. At the trail's highest point—6300 feet—you're confronted by the bold cliffs of Isabella Ridge. Leave the trail here and traverse up to the right 20 yards for an aerial view of the turquoise lake below. From the ridge, the trail drops 200 feet through tall firs to reach Copper Glance Lake at 3.8 miles, 6100 feet. 8204-foot Sherman Peak is the highest crag on the ridge.

Sherman Peak above Copper Glance Lake

Trip 43

Louis Lake

Location	Okanogan National Forest / Lake Chelan-Sawtooth Wilderness.
Distance	11.4-mile round trip.
Elevation gain	2200'.
Maps	Green Trails No. 82–Stehekin; Trails IllustratedNo. 223–North Cascades National Park Complex.

OPINION

Like a general decorated with medals, thrusting his warrior chest into the faces of fledgling privates, Rennie Peak assumes a bold stance among lowly mountains. The saber-sharp ridge slices the sky. The gun-metal-grey cirque invites exploration. But to reach Rennie, next to Louis Lake, you have to plod through dreary scenery.

You are, after all, in a land of dry forest, and rounded, unremarkable, nearly indistinguishable mountains. So, do you live nearby? Is it pouring rain farther west? Have you already hiked throughout the North Cascades? Are you really curious about the east side of the range? If you answered no, no, no and no, pick another trail elsewhere. If any of your answers were yes, hiking to Louis Lake to see exceptional Rennie Peak is worthwhile. But hike to nearby Twisp Pass (Trip 31) first.

The first two miles are viewless. They feel like a treadmill—the tread previously milled by horses, so you'll be kicking up and choking on dust. Proceed with faith. After crossing South Creek, the trail becomes less horse-trodden and more intimate. A mile up, it holds you in suspense as you approach what appears to be a dead end. Then you recognize the cleft that will grant you entry to the lake cirque. A stretch of lush meadow softens the austere environment.

Louis Lake is shallow and muddy. The north shore, where you arrive, is choked with deadfall. The only comfortable lunch spots are beneath trees and have limited views. But if you can ignore these drawbacks and let your thoughts soar with the commanding peak, you won't be disappointed.

FACT

By Car

On the east side of the North Cascades, drive Highway 20 to Twisp. Turn west onto the paved road signed TWISP RIVER RECREATION AREA. At 11.0 miles reach a junction. Continue straight (northwest) on Twisp River Road 44. At 14.6 miles the road forks. Proceed straight toward Roads End Campground. At 22.5 miles reach South Creek Campground on the left. The South Creek trailhead, where the Louis Lake hike begins, is 200 yards farther, also on the left, at 3200 feet.

On Foot

Immediately cross the large wood bridge over the Twisp River. At 0.4 mile ignore the side trail that forks left to a horse camp. Proceed southwest. The main trail ascends moderately above South Creek. At 2.5 miles reach the junction with Louis Lake trail 428. Turn left (south) and go downhill 0.1 mile to a bridged crossing of South Creek. Gradual, well-maintained switchbacks lead upward through forest into the Louis Creek canyon. At 3.6 miles reach the first view north and west over the South Creek valley and the dry ridges above it. Continue ascending, sometimes in alder and eventually through a brushy tunnel of trees. In moist areas, look for trumpet-shaped, fuchsia monkeyflower, and dark-purple mountain monkshood.

Beyond 4.7 miles, the trail gains little elevation. At 5.0 miles pop out of forest into meadow. Here you can see your route maneuvering southwest through a rocky cleft. A bit farther, it becomes apparent the cleft is wider than it previously seemed. After ducking back into forest, the trail arrives at a campground on the north shore of Louis Lake at 5.7 miles, 5400 feet. 7742-foot Rennie Peak (southwest) and an unnamed 7278-foot peak (south) form the cirque around the lake basin. It's possible to scramble along the west side of the lake. By pushing beyond the forested southwest end, you can get deeper into the cirque.

See page 171 for a photo of Louis Lake.

Trip 44
Perry Creek / Mt. Forgotten

Location	Mt. Baker-Snoqualmie National Forest.
Distance	3.8-mile round trip to Perry Creek Falls; 7.8-mile round trip to Mt. Forgotten.
Elevation gain	1100' to the falls; 2900' to saddle on Mt. Forgotten.
Map	Green Trails No. 111–Sloan Peak.

OPINION

The scenery along the Perry Creek trail won't set your soul ablaze. Expect nothing more than a pleasant walk in a very pretty canyon. If that's what you're in the mood for, saunter to the falls and back. If you come to the Mountain Loop area frequently, keep this walk in mind for one of those many rainy days. The tread stays high above the creek, on an open, rocky slope, so it's not muddy during rainy periods. Across the canyon, on the opposite wall, waterfalls cascade off Stillaguamish Peak. Look down at moss-carpeted boulders, up at mammoth trees. In fall, swaths of brilliant red and yellow leaves fill your field of vision.

Seen from the trail, Perry Creek Falls is disappointing. It's mostly out of sight, deep in the gorge below. You'd have to down-climb for a better perspective, and that's not easy. So don't think of the falls as a significant destination. It's just a natural turnaround point for a couple-hour stroll or a short shoulder-season hike.

Wait until the spring runoff subsides before crossing un-bridged Perry Creek and forging on toward Mt. Forgotten. Beyond the creek, you'll pass through an ancient forest of fir and hemlock that exudes nobility and steadfastness. The view from trail's end, in a saddle between Mt. Forgotten and Stillaguamish Peak, won't spark much excitement. It's no surprise you can see Glacier Peak to the northeast. Big Four is to the southwest, but from here it's less impressive than when you're gazing straight up at it from the Ice Caves day-use area off the highway. Looking at Stillaguamish Peak won't make your eyes bulge, but ascending to the Stillaguamish ridgetop might. Walk up Perry Creek to the ridge above only if the Mount Dickerman trail (Trip 13) is snow-covered or Dickerman's summit is shrouded in clouds.

FACT

By Car

On the Mountain Loop Highway, drive 15.3 miles southeast from the Verlot Public Service Center. If you're heading north-west from Barlow Pass, drive 4.3 miles. Turn north onto signed Road 4063, which is just east of Perry Creek. Drive 1.0 mile to the trailhead parking at 2100 feet. There's little room, so leave turn-around space at the end of the road. Park your car near the side once you've turned around.

On foot

Within 0.2 mile you enter a forest of impressive old giants. The ascent is moderate but steady. From the rockslide at 0.3 mile, the path to the falls is rocky. Re-enter trees just before reaching a narrow gorge and Perry Creek Falls at 1.9 miles, 3200 feet. To continue to Mt. Forgotten, walk past the sign pointing right to the toilet. Forty yards upstream from the falls, you'll see another sign pointing left. Cross the creek here, possibly on the huge log or by rockhopping. To be completely safe, you might have to wade. There are campsites just across the creek.

The trail, growing rougher and steeper, ascends through an-cient forest to a meadow at 3.4 miles. An unmaintained trail branches left (northwest). It climbs to the ridge stretching south-east off Stillaguamish Peak. On the ridgetop you can wander west through flowers, grass, and heather. The views are more open than down below at trail's end.

The main trail ends at 3.9 miles in a meadow at 5000 feet. Bring enough water from the Perry Creek crossing to keep your whistle wet until you return.

Trip 45
Mount Pilchuck

Location	Pilchuck State Park.
Distance	6.0-mile round trip.
Elevation gain	2224'.
Map	Green Trails No. 109–Granite Falls.

OPINION

"Step right up. Hurry! Hurry! Hurry!" Mt. Pilchuck is often a circus. Even on a socked in, downpouring October day, there were 14 carloads of hardy hikers scuttling up Mt. Pilchuck. Why? In bad weather, there's no reason but inflexibility for not changing plans and hiking elsewhere. But on clear days, the crowds are understandable. This is a rare treat. Standing on the summit, you have a commanding mountain *and* ocean view. You can see all the way to the Olympics and almost make out Port Angeles. Looking straight down on Puget Sound, you'll feel like the Jolly Green Giant. Then you can turn your back on the bustling I-5 corridor and ogle tantalizing peaks from Mt. Baker to Mt. Rainier.

Nearby Heather Lake and Lake Twentytwo (Trips 71 and 65) are better choices on a rainy day. There, you can still appreciate the green cirque walls, even in fog, whereas Pilchuck's summit will be unrewarding. Also, much of the Pilchuck trail is on tree roots and puncheon. It's a slick, sloppy mess when wet. On any day, it seems sacrilegious to clomp on all the roots—the life source of these venerable old trees—but there's no choice. Besides, it's Pilchuck's popularity with hikers that has helped keep loggers at bay. Boot steps are preferable to chainsaws.

Though the upper portion of the Pilchuck trail was improved during the summer of 1995, the lower reaches remain in their original, rough state. Thanks to muscle, machines and dynamite, the rocky route near the top is now easier to follow.

FACT

By Car

On the Mountain Loop Highway, drive 1.0 mile southeast from the Verlot Public Service Center. Turn right (south) onto Road 42, signed HEATHER LK TR 1, MT PILCHUCK LOOKOUT TR 7. Immediately fork left and continue 6.8 miles to the huge parking area at 3100 feet.

On Foot

The trail starts to the right of the sign at the trailhead parking area. The initial 0.25 mile is a gravel road. Pass a toilet on the left and a log staircase on the right. The gravel road soon forks. Go right, immediately rockhop across a stream and you're on the trail, which is a nearly continuous tangle of roots. Side trails swarm in all directions. Branches have been placed to block most of them, but you have to pay attention to stay on the main path. The puncheon, when wet, is too slippery to help hikers. It simply prevents trail erosion.

You ascend gently and pass a clearcut. After 1.3 miles the grade steepens. After 2.0 miles you walk among heather and interesting rock slabs. The final 0.5 mile switchbacks up Pilchuck's southwest side to the 5324-foot summit at 3.0 miles. There's a lookout cabin atop the gigantic boulders.

Due to its location on the west edge of the North Cascades, it's possible to hike Mt. Pilchuck from May until early November.

Trip 46
Blanca Lake

Location	Mt. Baker-Snoqualmie National Forest / Henry M. Jackson Wilderness.
Distance	8.0-mile round trip.
Elevation gain	2700' in, 600' out.
Map	Green Trails No. 143–Monte Cristo.

OPINION

Blanca Lake is clutched in a dramatic cirque beneath Columbia Peak. Yet this isn't just a trudge to a climactic view; it's a rich experience overall. The textures and hues on this walk are as captivating as Blanca's deep bowl and awesome headwall.

Unless it's late in the hiking season, after you've developed your mountain legs, you might feel the trail is cracking its whip at you, exhorting you to keep moving. Don't count the switchbacks; it will only weaken you. And don't rely on views for inspiration; you'll catch only a sliver of Glacier Peak and forested mountainsides. Concentrate on the immediate surroundings.

Apart from different vegetation, the ascent to Virgin Lake is like climbing through a cloud forest in Costa Rica, especially when clouds waltz through the valleys or fog sifts through the forest canopy. The thriving flora seems on the verge of taking over the trail completely. In September, you can feast along the way on a bumper crop of sweet, juicy berries. The ridge is home to delightful pocket meadows.

Virgin Lake is a miniscule mud hole. You can camp here, but why? After passing Virgin Lake, you'll see Columbia Glacier as the trail drops to milky, green-blue Blanca Lake. It looks like a lake you'd have to fly into. (Be careful on the steep descent, or you just might.) The vast, seemingly bottomless chasm to your left is almost as captivating as the lake and the glacier.

The reflection of shaggy cliffs on Blanca's cloudy surface is like an impressionist painting. From the south end of the lake, near where the trail reaches the shore, look up and admire the cliff to your right. You'll see the colors of an Italian piazza: chartreuse, siena, charcoal, salmon. Concentrate on it. Glance away, then back. The hues are resplendent.

Lots of people camp at Blanca, yet there's little room. *Crampground* is more like it. Rain or shine, expect to see tents jammed into the few cleared spaces on the log-covered shore and among the boulders across the outlet stream. It's better to day-hike and, instead of trying to fit in, just pull up a log for the show. You'll have to do some earnest scrambling around the west shore to find privacy.

Even after heavy rain, the trail should be in good shape. That, and the fact that the goal isn't a sky-high perch, make this a good choice during overcast weather. And because you're always in trees, there's little danger of being hit by lightning.

FACT

By Car

From Highway 2, take the Index turnoff. Don't cross the bridge into the town. Drive the paved North Fork Skykomish River Road 63 northeast to a junction at 14.5 miles. There are several free campsites along the way. At the junction, bear left, staying on

Blanca Lake

Road 63, which is now gravel. Go 2.2 miles farther to the signed Blanca Lake trailhead, at 1900 feet.

On Foot

The trail starts at the far end of the parking lot and immediately begins switchbacking steeply up. After gaining 2700 feet in 3.0 miles, the trail attains the ridge and enters Henry M. Jackson Wilderness. It swings around tiny Virgin Lake, then descends 600 feet in 1.0 mile to the outlet stream of 0.75-mile-long Blanca Lake. The distance is closer to 4.0 miles total, not the 3.5 miles shown on the Green Trails 1991 map. Campsites are clustered at the south end of the lake. It's possible to continue along the lake's west shore to the snout of Columbia Glacier, but the route is indistinct.

Trip 47

Lake Valhalla

Location	Wenatchee National Forest / Henry M. Jackson Wilderness.
Distance	10.8-mile round trip from Stevens Pass.
Elevation gain	980' in, 210' out.
Maps	Green Trails No. 176–Stevens Pass, No. 144–Benchmark Mtn.

OPINION

The trail is gentle, the forest pretty, the meadows pleasing. Though the lake isn't dramatic or even particularly memorable, rambling there and back is enjoyable and easy.

Your escape from civilization won't be immediate. Because the trail is initially above and parallel to the highway, you'll hear the roar of traffic for the first and last 2 miles. By mid-September, red and purple splashed on slopes northeast across the canyon add contrast to the forest views and help compensate for the noise. If the lake leaves you craving more of a climax, continue to the pass just above it and gaze south at Alpine Lakes Wilderness. Or chug farther up either side of the pass for an even wider vista.

Can you arrange a shuttle? Start at the Stevens Pass trailhead and hike 8.1 miles through to the Smith Brook trailhead. That way you only have to listen to the highway traffic once. Without a shuttle, the Stevens Pass approach is preferable. It allows you to appreciate Nason Creek canyon, even if you do see the highway, and lets you savor the forest and meadows longer. It's not just the lake, after all, that makes this trip worthwhile; it's also the delightful surroundings en route.

FACT

By car

Drive US Highway 2 to Stevens Pass, at 4061 feet. Park near the buildings at the northeast end of the summit area. To reach the Smith Brook trailhead, drive 4.2 miles farther, and turn left (north) onto signed Smith Brook Road 6700. Drive 3.3 miles northwest to the trailhead at 4200 feet. Park along the road.

On foot

From Stevens Pass, set out on the Pacific Crest Trail, just east of the buildings. The first 1.5 miles of this broad, nearly level path used to be the railbed of the Great Northern Railroad. At 2.0 miles the trail turns west, away from the highway, and contours above the canyon of a Nason Creek tributary. Pass the spur trail that drops to the research station below.

At 3.75 miles, after crossing a creek, come to a meadow basin. There's a campground on the meadow's edge. The PCT now heads generally north. Continuing, Lake Valhalla is visible northeast at the base of Lichtenberg Mountain. The trail ascends to 5040 feet and swings around a ridge, where you can look down on the lake. Drop to the shore and a choice of campsites at 5.4 miles, 4830 feet.

Rounding the north end of the lake and turning east, the trail ascends 0.4 mile to an unnamed pass and a choice of excursions. You can follow a boot-beaten path northwest up the rounded 5747-foot knob. Or, for a more strenuous climb, veer off-trail southeast up steep heather slopes to the summit of 5844-foot Lichtenberg Mountain.

From the pass, the PCT descends northeast to Union Gap, 1.8 miles from the lake. From the gap, the PCT continues left (northwest) to Lake Janus and points beyond. Smith Brook Road 6700 is 0.9 mile to the right (southeast).

Trip 48

Lake Janus / Grizzly Peak

Location	Wenatchee National Forest / Henry M. Jackson Wilderness.
Distance	15.6-mile round trip.
Elevation gain	2100' in, 800' out.
Map	Green Trails No. 144–Benchmark Mtn.

OPINION

If you expect to be jolted by electrifying scenery, Lake Janus and Grizzly Peak will be disappointing. So relax. Take more of a zen approach to hiking this time. Let the gentle beauty and tranquil ambiance permeate your being. You'll find this trail very satisfying.

The mountains here are not tall, rugged, or otherwise impressive. Eject any thoughts of macrocosmic grandeur. Allow yourself to be entertained by the microcosmic trailside world: wiggling tadpoles, leaping frogs, nervous grouse, pocket meadows, and grooves in the ridge that create miniature, winding canyons.

Since the trail doesn't push you too hard, you can take pleasure in the simple joy of walking. It's an easy backpack trip for beginners. Apparently the fishing is good at Lake Janus; some hikers pack inflatable boats. The lake isn't dramatic, but it's a welcome relief from the forest.

Grizzly might qualify as a peak in the Appalachians, but in the North Cascades? Its mien was obviously exaggerated by someone with a bad memory, a great imagination, or a lack of experience. Grizzly Hump is more like it. The views, however, are gratifying. Far to the east are Chiwawa Ridge and the distant Entiat Mountains. You can also see Glacier Peak, though it's too far north to appreciate. If the glacier-draped volcano is what you're interested in, hike someplace like Kennedy Ridge (Trip 90), where you can lick the ice; *then* say you saw Glacier Peak.

If the contemplative approach doesn't suit you, and you're hiking this trail anyway, here's a challenge for you: zoom out to Grizzly Peak and back in a day. The moderate elevation gain and lenient terrain make it possible for fit hikers. Just carry plenty of water. After the snow patches melt in August, it's difficult to find water beyond Lake Janus.

FACT

By Car

On Highway 2, drive 4.2 miles east of Stevens Pass. Turn left (north) onto signed Smith Brook Road 6700. Drive 3.3 miles northwest to the trailhead at 4200 feet. It's 0.3 mile beyond a hairpin curve that has parking space for a couple cars. There's no parking lot at the trailhead, but the road is wide enough to allow about 10 vehicles to parallel park across from the trailhead sign.

On Foot

Start on Smith Brook trail 1590. The initial 0.3 mile is across an open hillside with a view of Lichtenberg Mountain to the south. After ascending 500 feet in 0.9 mile, reach a junction at Union Gap. The left trail goes 1.8 miles southwest to Lake Valhalla (Trip 47). This northern approach to Lake Valhalla is shorter than the southern approach from Stevens Pass. Right is the Pacific Crest Trail leading northwest to Lake Janus, Grizzly Peak, and beyond.

Descend moderately in cool, tall forest. At 1.7 miles cross an open boulder field punctuated with salmonberry bushes. The trail is now level for 0.8 mile as it curves northeast. At 2.6 miles rockhop over a creek, just below a small waterfall. Reach Lake Janus at 3.1 miles, 4146 feet. At the southwest end of the lake, where you arrive, you'll see fire rings and bare campsites on what used to be meadow. The 0.4-mile-long lake is bordered by forest, except for meadows on the east side. There are lily pads at the south end, and grass in the water along most of the shore.

To follow the PCT to Grizzly Peak, cross the outlet stream at the southwest corner of the lake. Ascend 680 feet northwest through forest—predominantly mountain hemlock. At 4.6 miles there are two tent sites, one in the woods beside the trail and another in the meadow. The small stream here is just deep enough to allow you to use a water filter. At 4.8 miles cross a gap. A quick detour right (northeast) up the side of the gap will improve your view. You can see grey, stone-faced Labyrinth Mountain to the northeast.

You get open views north and east for only 0.4 mile beyond the

The Pacific Crest Trail to Grizzly Peak

gap, then the trail is on the southwest side of the ridge. At 5.6 miles you can see tiny Margaret Lake below you to the left.

At 5.8 miles, 5200 feet, overlook Glasses Lake, approximately 600 feet below to the north, and clearcuts rising from the Little Wenatchee River Road. You can also glimpse Heather Lake a bit farther north. There's a rough route down to the campsites at Glasses Lake.

Continuing gently up and down, reach a campsite in a pocket meadow 0.2 mile farther. From here, the trail winds along the ridgecrest, staying fairly level, through woods and blueberry bushes. See Heather Lake again before starting up the Grizzly Peak ridge.

At 7.3 miles the trail begins switchbacking up 400 feet through meadows to the end of the ridgeline on 5597-foot Grizzly Peak, at 7.8 miles. The PCT descends and continues north.

Trip 49
Poe Mountain

Location	Wenatchee National Forest.
Distance	5.0-mile round trip.
Elevation gain	3015'.
Maps	Green Trails No. 144–Benchmark Mtn, No. 145–Wenatchee Lake (shows Road 65); US Forest Service–Glacier Peak Wilderness.

OPINION

Poe Mountain, on Wenatchee Ridge, is worthwhile for two reasons: a pleasing, raven's-eye view from the summit; and an overview of nearby forested-valley trails that you will, as a result, be tempted to hike nevermore.

This steep but short trail is on a west-facing slope, through fairly open forest, and is usually snow-free by late June. It vaults you to delectable meadows within eyeshot of nearby Longfellow Mountain and Whittier Peak. Major mountains like Monte Cristo, Kyes, and Glacier peaks, or those in the Alpine Lakes region, are visible but distant. Peering into lonely Cougar Creek basin is enticing. On the eastern horizon are the bleak, high Chiwawa and Entiat mountains.

Before planning a trip off the Little Wenatchee River Road, perhaps up the Cady Creek valley or to Cady Ridge, you should visit Poe Mountain. It could save you days of walking through viewless, fly-ridden forest, because from Poe you'll see how boring these trails are. They're popular because they're close to Puget Sound, people love loop trips, and they assume all North Cascades scenery is good. Actually, this country north of Stevens Pass and northwest of Lake Wenatchee is utterly unarousing. Overall, the mountains are rounded and forested—nearly indiscernible from one another, but for the odd peak jutting out.

From Poe's summit be sure to walk a short way southeast along the ridgeline through an intimate, grassy ravine to a point just before Wenatchee Ridge dives into dull forest. Arranging a shuttle so you can walk the whole ridge isn't worth the trouble. There's not much more to see. And driving up rough road 6504 is a pain. Though you might prefer the gentler ascent from Irving Pass, off road 6504, the views are of logging roads. Ascending from the Little Wenatchee River trailhead, you see virgin forest and distant great peaks. If you're itching to walk more of the ridgeline, head north of Poe, to Longfellow.

FACT

By Car

Drive Highway 2 to Coles Corner, 19.5 miles east of Stevens Pass, or 16.0 miles northwest of Leavenworth. Turn north onto Highway 207 and head toward Lake Wenatchee. You'll pass the state park, the road to Plain, and, at 4.3 miles, the road to Fish Lake and the Chiwawa Loop. Stay left, heading northwest along Lake Wenatchee. From the ranger station, drive 1.8 miles to the junction of the White River and Little Wenatchee River roads. Go left (southwest) on Little Wenatchee River Road 65 and cross the White River. At 8.0 miles, bear right (northwest), continuing to Little Wenatchee Ford. The road becomes rough dirt 14.4 miles from the ranger station. The last couple miles are through deep, dark forest, past many ancient cedars. At 17.2 miles, 3000 feet, reach the Little Wenatchee River trailhead at road's end. There's a small, primitive, unappealing campground here.

If you want to arrange a shuttle between the trailheads at each end of Wenatchee Ridge, drive one vehicle back 2.8 miles. Just before pavement resumes, turn left (north) onto Road 6506. Stay right at the first fork, left at the second onto Road 6504. At a third fork, turn right. The road ends at the trailhead, at 4200 feet, 4.0 miles from Road 65.

On Foot

Staying on the right (east) side of the Little Wenatchee River, start on Little Wenatchee trail 1525. In 0.2 mile, take the minor trail signed NO VEHICLES up to the right. Immediately the trail ascends through mixed forest. You'll gain 1000 feet per mile. At 1.4 miles attain a view west over Cady Creek and see Benchmark Mountain rising above it. The Monte Cristo peaks are way northwest. You can also look southwest to hilly mountains, including Grizzly Peak and Scorpion Mountain.

The trail is mostly shaded until 1.8 miles, where thinner trees allow more sun exposure. At 2.0 miles a better view opens of Monte Cristo and Kyes peaks. Little Wenatchee River valley and Indian Head Peak are slightly northwest. At 2.4 miles, once you're clearly in the open amid low shrubs, the trail forks. You can go either way to the 6015-foot summit of Poe Mountain.

The left path leads to a flat, grassy shoulder. The tread disappears here for 12 yards, but if you curve right, you'll see the tread ascending through lupine and Indian hellebore (corn lilies) a short way to the summit. The faint trail descending left (north) goes to Longfellow Mountain. You can see the route dropping off Poe, then ascending the ridgeline toward Longfellow.

Back at the 2.4-mile fork, the right path turns southeast, offering a view of snowcapped peaks in Alpine Lakes Wilderness. In 0.2 mile watch for a boot-beaten path left that goes up 6 feet to the ridgecrest. The summit of Poe is above you, northwest. Just over the crest, there's a faint overgrown route angling right, dropping east into the Cougar Creek drainage. If you're up to the challenge of exploring Cougar, you'll find the way down. On the southwest side of the crest, the main trail along Wenatchee Ridge continues southeast, entering a green, grassy ravine graced by hemlocks. There's a sign FOR HIKERS ONLY. Five to ten minutes past here, there's a campsite in grass with a fire ring and views south. Then you pass through a rock garden. Proceed southeast along the ridge 0.4 mile until just before the ridgeline trail descends into forest.

If you went right at the 2.4-mile fork, cut back northwest to the top of Poe, then descend the other side via the grassy shoulder. The view from the summit of Poe is dominated by the smooth-sided pyramid of Whittier Peak, nearby to the northeast.

Trip 50

Little Giant Pass /
Napeequa Valley

Location	Glacier Peak Wilderness / Wenatchee National Forest.
Distance	10.0-mile round trip.
Elevation gain	3800'.
Maps	Green Trails No. 113–Holden; US Forest Service–Glacier Peak Wilderness.

OPINION

This Little Giant barely made the leap into the worthwhile category. It's a stupidly steep trail. But all your sweat and strain will be justified by a single view of the exquisitely beautiful Napeequa Valley. Gazing at this isolated, lonely Shangri-La will give you hope for the salvation of wilderness. It's a sight you will not forget.

Drab mountains above the Chiwawa River valley will not inspire you to persevere on the merciless climb to the pass. Have faith. The mountains you'll see west from the pass are totally different: green slopes, glistening wet rock, brilliant glaciers. At 3 miles, entering alpine country will bolster your desire to continue. It's a good thing; there's still plenty of work ahead.

Napeequa Valley from Little Giant Pass

The crux of the ascent is the final 40 yards. Anyone afraid of exposure will hesitate to proceed across the eroded-to-nothing trail. And the Napeequa remains hidden until you're atop the pass. So if you think you won't make it, don't even start this hike; the valley will have to remain an unrealized dream. Confident hikers with light scrambling experience should have no trouble. But everyone should be cautious on this rebelliously rough route.

FACT

By Car

Drive Highway 2 to Coles Corner, 19.5 miles east of Stevens Pass, or 16.0 miles northwest of Leavenworth. Turn north onto Highway 207 and head toward Lake Wenatchee. You'll pass the state park and the road to Plain. At the junction in 4.3 miles, go right (east) for the Chiwawa Loop Road. (The ranger station is 4.0 miles to the left.) At 5.7 miles turn left onto Meadow Creek Road, which takes you north to Fish Lake and the Chiwawa River valley. Pavement ends at 16.8 miles. At 20.2 miles pass the entrance to Riverbend Campground, the first of several excellent free campgrounds in the valley. The Little Giant trailhead and parking area is on the left at 25.2 miles, 2600 feet.

On Foot

A bridge used to cross the Chiwawa River here but it is now in ruins. Go 30 yards upstream and hope a substantial logjam is still in place, providing easy passage. Without the logjam, fording this deep, swift river is dangerous and could be impossible.

On the far bank, walk straight (west) from the river through a gravel wash beneath cottonwoods and pines. You'll come to a dirt road through a campground—abandoned when the bridge collapsed. Follow the road until it fades in 30 yards. Faint tread veers right toward Maple Creek. Jump across the creek (to the north side) before you get to the metal-roofed wood cabin. Follow Maple Creek 0.25 mile upstream. Here the trail becomes more discernible as it angles right and begins a steady ascent northwest.

Good tread climbs moderately 1.5 miles through pine forest. Where the ascent steepens, well-engineered switchbacks are losing out to entropy. This is a good example of how trails can disappear if not regularly maintained. Behind you, across the valley, are forest-covered mountains.

The trail now heads straight up the fall line. It's slippery for 0.25 mile. Solid trail resumes in a flat area at 2.0 miles. Reach the south fork of Little Giant Creek at 2.5 miles, 4000 feet, with campsites on both sides. The alpine slopes (west) below the pass are visible above. Rockhop across the creek, then face another stretch of trail so steep and slippery you'll almost be crawling on your knees.

Cross a smaller stream. Tunnel through 0.2 mile of thick brush. At 3.0 miles encounter a spine of schist, on which the trail is marked by cairns for 0.2 mile. At 3.8 miles reach a flat spot above a creekside meadow. There's a fire ring at this possible tent site.

Now you're among stunted trees, heather, and berry bushes. The trail is sometimes a muddy trough, other times a low tunnel in thick brush. Watch out for slick spots. There's a fork at 4.6 miles, beneath a rock escarpment. Left (west) ascends more steeply; right (north) is a moderate, long switchback—the safer choice for coming down. Both lead to the pass.

Slicing up to the pass across an open slope, the last 0.2 mile of trail is slumping out, eroding, rapidly disappearing. The boot-beaten route that remains is steeply slanted and probably muddy. The final 40 yards feel exposed: a slip here could result in a long tumble.

At 5.0 miles, arrive at 6400-foot Little Giant Pass on Chiwawa Ridge. Ascend the ridgeline right (north) for an unobstructed view of emerald Napeequa Valley below. Part of Glacier Peak is also visible northwest. Across the valley and a bit north, below the glaciers of Clark Mountain, look for Boulder Pass: that's the other entrance to the Napeequa. Directly across the valley, snow-fields on the White Mountains spawn waterfalls tumbling into the abyss.

Considering backpacking from Little Giant Pass down into the valley? You'll have to be experienced, determined and tough. It's a 2000-foot, 2.0-mile descent on poor trail to the Napeequa River. It's another 1.3 miles northwest to where you might be able to ford the river. From there, it's a 1900-foot ascent southwest to 6300-foot Boulder Pass, then 10.1 miles down the other side to the White River Road, with a ford of Boulder Creek en route. Or, after wandering the Napeequa Valley, you could return via Little Giant Pass.

Trip 51

Boulder Ridge

Location	Mt. Baker-Snoqualmie National Forest.
Distance	8.0-mile round trip.
Elevation gain	1700'.
Maps	Green Trails No. 13–Mt. Baker, No. 14– Mt. Shuksan, No. 45–Hamilton, No. 46– Lake Shannon (No. 46 shows the roads and route; others are to identify glaciers and ridges); Trails Illustrated No. 223– North Cascades National Park Complex.

OPINION

To bash your way up this arm of Mt. Baker and enjoy it, you need to be motivated by something much greater than just a desire to hike. Leave this one for climbers launching an assault on the Boulder Glacier. It's a cantankerous, miserable trail, often only a route. Baker's icy visage isn't even that impressive here. In August, black flies are so obscenely thick they threaten your sanity. Then there's the mud. Climbers wearing high, plastic boots won't mind all the sucky quagmires. Mud wrestlers would love them. But hikers will be continually frustrated. You risk more than getting splattered. Where it's steep, you could break an arm. Even after days of hot sun, the mud persists.

There could come a time, however, when this hike is exactly what you need: If someone you despise ever asks your advice on where to hike, smile and say "Boulder Ridge!" Whatever his or her transgressions, you will be avenged.

As for yourself, STAY AWAY! Choose one of the many premier trails on Mt. Baker. All of them, except nearby Rainbow Ridge (Trip 6), are much easier.

Trip 52

South Fork Cascade River

Location	Mt. Baker-Snoqualmie National Forest / Glacier Peak Wilderness.
Distance	4.0- or 5.0-mile round trip.
Elevation gain	400'.
Maps	Green Trails No. 80–Cascade Pass; Trails Illustrated No. 223–North Cascades National Park Complex.

OPINION

Forget it. Only a snake would enjoy this trail. Should you attempt it, you'll need immense will power to keep thwacking through the dense, tall brush. Or maybe a burning curiosity about what it was like to be a foot soldier in Vietnam. This is North Cascades foliage at its wild, prolific worst and best.

If you're ornery enough to hike into these canyons, and don't have a four-wheel-drive vehicle, you'd have to walk the 1.4 miles of gnarly road through forest to the actual trailhead. Then, less than a mile from the trailhead, the green chaos wreathes you. Sloshing and slapping your way through, it's hard to appreciate the wonderful, ancient forest. Streaked cliffs and waterfalls, like those in Venezuelan jungles, might also be visible, but the scenery is never enough to take your mind off the immediate difficulty of simply walking.

A short way in you'll pass the Middle Fork trail—so rarely maintained as to be the very definition of entropy. It ultimately leads to a magnificent view beneath great peaks, but without a commando wielding a machete to lead the way, the challenge of getting there is too brutal.

Though the Cascade River valley is usually snow-free by early June, so are more enjoyable destinations. Hike elsewhere, unless the Darrington Ranger Station assures you the South Fork trail has been brushed. If you want to experience one of the North Cascades' deep holes, try Nooksack Cirque (Trip 35). That's one mere mortals find doable and enjoyable.

Trip 53

Black Lake

Location	Pasayten Wilderness / Okanogan National Forest.
Distance	8.6-mile round trip.
Elevation gain	800'.
Maps	Green Trails No. 20–Coleman Peak, No. 52–Doe Mtn. (shows Road 100); US Forest Service–Pasayten Wilderness.

OPINION

How such dull scenery can attract so many people is a mystery. Black Lake is undeservedly popular. You can generally expect to see lots of other hikers and probably a few horseback riders. Just don't expect to see any impressive mountain scenery.

Black Lake is nothing special. It's a mile-long body of water surrounded by forested slopes. The trail to the lake is unremarkable. The most pleasing aspect of the hike is its relative ease; the trail averages an elevation gain of only 186 feet per mile. Judging by the map, you might think views of Lake Creek would keep you entertained. Not so. The creek is hidden from view by trees or thick vegetation almost the whole way.

Too many people and too much monotony add up to an obvious conclusion: pick another hike. Only consider this one if you're in the area between mid-May and mid-June, and the Forest Service says the road is snow-free. Nearby Copper Glance Lake (Trip 42) is tiny and the trail is steep, but it offers a far more interesting experience. Farther away, but still in Pasayten Wilderness, Tiffany Mountain (Trip 30) and Horseshoe Basin (Trip 87) are outstanding choices.

Trip 54

North Lake

Location	Okanogan National Forest / Lake Chelan-Sawtooth Wilderness.
Distance	11.2-mile round trip.
Elevation gain	2200'.
Maps	Green Trails No. 82–Stehekin; Trails Illustrated No. 223–North Cascades National Park Complex.

OPINION

Leave this one to the cavalry. They've already claimed it. Their mounts have pulverized the trail to inches-deep dust and left it severely pitted. When it's dry, you need a face mask to keep from choking on the airborne dirt. When it's wet, hiking here is a slopfest. And the manure keeps piling up regardless of the weather.

Why should so many hikers have to tolerate the extensive damage caused by a few horses? Equestrians defending their turf always resort to the same argument, "horse travel in the wilderness has historic precedent." Well, so does clearcutting. Does that mean it should be allowed to continue?

The obnoxious trail to North Lake might be worth negotiating if it passed through or led to magnificent scenery. But it doesn't. It's in brush or scraggly forest most of the way. The lake is small and the meadow beside it has been trampled nearly to death by horses. The peaks of Gilbert Mountain on the southeast side of the lake are almost impressive, but not quite. Scree slopes, not rock walls, rise from the shore. People have obviously camped in the lakeside meadows; you shouldn't. And you won't be tempted to if you take our advice. You'll be hiking elsewhere.

One attraction of the North Lake trail is the access it provides to Abernathy Pass—a cleft in granite cliffs from which you can scramble higher for a view northwest of Snagtooth Ridge and the pinnacles of 8876-foot Silver Star Mountain. Via the North Lake trail, the pass is 5.3 miles. That's much shorter than the 9.6-mile approach from Highway 20, via Cedar Creek. But there are many other places you should go first, including nearby Twisp Pass (Trip 31) and Louis Lake (Trip 43).

Rennie Peak and Louis Lake

Trip 55

Copper Pass

Location	Okanogan National Forest / Lake Chelan-Sawtooth Wilderness.
Distance	11.4-mile round trip.
Elevation gain	3000′.
Maps	Green Trails No. 82–Stehekin; Trails Illustrated No. 223–North Cascades National Park Complex.

OPINION

The word *pass* has a powerful effect. It inspires images of alpine wonderland. Wherever there's a pass in the mountains, hikers are drawn to it like iron filings to a magnet. And rarely are they disappointed—by the pass. But that doesn't necessarily justify the hike. Copper Pass lacks the scenic oomph to make this demanding, humdrum trail worthwhile.

Twisp Pass (Trip 31), just one valley over, is a more exciting destination at the end of a more enjoyable trail. Definitely hike there instead. On the way to Copper you'd be looking at tree trunks nearly the whole way. They're big trees, but this forest will never win a beauty contest. During the entire 5.7-mile approach, a peek at a double waterfall and a glimpse of the pass are your only rewards.

In places, calling this a trail is exaggeration. It's too rough. The route drags you through a lot of brush, then drags you up a steep incline. It doesn't switchback like the Green Trails map implies. It sways a bit, then barges ahead. In places, the brush is so strong it might knock you off the narrow tread if you don't hold your ground.

If you just want to see the Copper Pass environs, you can do that from Maple Pass (Trip 11). But it's worth visiting Copper Pass if you traverse to it cross-country from Twisp Pass. Descending from Copper enables you to create a loop trip. At dusk, however, the route could be easy to lose, so start early enough to allow sufficient daylight.

In extremely hot weather, common here in summer, the trail to Copper Pass has the advantage of being shaded—by trees, as well as by the ridge to the west that blocks the afternoon sun. That might be an important consideration for you. Still, we'd prefer Twisp Pass under any conditions. Inspiration is worth sweating for.

Trip 56

Mt. Higgins

Location	Department of Natural Resources / Mt. Baker-Snoqualmie National Forest.
Distance	9.0 miles round trip.
Elevation gain	3450'.
Map	Green Trails No. 77–Oso.

OPINION

The entire area surrounding Mt. Higgins has been logged extensively. The devastation is widely visible and very disturbing. The trail even passes *through* a clearcut for a mile. The summit view is vast, but you might get sick if you look down—not from vertigo, but from the Armageddon landscape. Maybe this is what more people need to see, so they'll stop squandering precious forest products. Bring your wasteful friends here, to shock them into becoming conservationists. Or simply hike elsewhere.

Higgins is on the west edge of the range, so the peaks you see from the top are distant. Sure, Glacier Peak and Mount Baker are visible, but you can gaze at them from dozens of better perches. Whitehorse Mountain and Three Fingers across the valley to the southeast are striking, but their visage isn't worth whipping yourself up such a steep trail through such an unappealing area. Go to Mt. Pilchuck (Trip 45) instead. The trail is shorter, less steep, more beautiful, and the goal worthy of your time and effort.

Trip 57

Crystal Lake

Location	Mt. Baker-Snoqualmie National Forest / Glacier Peak Wilderness.
Distance	10.5-mile round trip.
Elevation gain	2185' in, 300' out.
Maps	Green Trails No. 111–Sloan Peak; US Forest Service–Glacier Peak Wilderness.

OPINION

You're eager for an early-season hike. You pull out your map. You scan the area near the Sauk and White Chuck rivers. And there it is. Crystal Lake. The trail follows Crystal Creek. It's on south-facing slopes. Little elevation gain. Not too far. Looks perfect!

That's mistake #1. Mistake #2 would be actually hiking it.

Stay away. The first 2 miles is on a boring road, your only compensation being glimpses of Mt. Pugh and Glacier Peak. The trail is obnoxiously brushy most of the way. It often crosses or is in view of recent clearcuts—real eyesores. Because the forest has been shorn of its soothing canopy, you're almost always in direct sunlight. Without cloud cover, even in early May, you'll feel as if someone's holding a magnifying glass over you; it's hot! And the creek? It's tantalizingly close, usually within earshot, but almost never visible. If you insist on doing this unsatisfactory hike, avoid the heat by starting before 8 A.M. or after 5 P.M.

The trail's upper reaches, near 4200 feet and half a mile short of the lake, can remain snow-covered surprisingly long—until early June. And the last stretch of trail, ascending through tall timber, can hold snowdrifts until the end of June. By the time Crystal Lake is snow-free, you should be enjoying other, far more rewarding trails. Even when you can reach the lake, it won't inspire you to break into song. It's in a ho-hum forested bowl.

Trip 58
Monte Cristo / Glacier Basin

Location	Mt. Baker-Snoqualmie National Forest / Henry M. Jackson Wilderness.
Distance	12.6 miles round trip.
Elevation gain	2140'.
Map	Green Trails No. 143–Monte Cristo.

OPINION

In a land of colossal glaciers, the ice in Glacier Basin is a mere footnote. The name is an overstatement, implying grand, sweeping expanses of white. It's really just a bowl filled with talus. The serrated peaks daubed with snow are beautiful, but they don't justify the basin's immense popularity, especially considering the dastardly, unmaintained trail. It's steep, slick, and tangled with roots—irksome to even veteran hikers. Yet on a mid-summer weekend, it's like an anthill here, with people literally crawling up and down. And when you start this trip, unless you've brought your mountain bike, you have to walk 4.2 miles of dirt road (from Barlow Pass on the Mountain Loop Highway) to the actual trail. The road offers only so-so views, and there will be cyclists zipping by while you trudge. Worse, local property owners are allowed to drive the road, so you can expect a few vehicles to pass you in a cloud of dust.

You're still reading?

Okay, we admit this trail holds a legitimate attraction to mountain bikers, because they can ride to Monte Cristo. From there, it's 2.1 miles and 1700 feet to the basin. Even if you walk the whole way, it's an easy daytrip, because 8.4 of the total 12.6 miles are on the fairly-level road. Strong hikers can march 4 m.p.h. here.

Don't expect much of Monte Cristo. Historic it is. Fascinating it's not. Because the Northwest is lacking in ghost towns, there's too much hyperbole about the remnants of this one. The few buildings still standing are only a shadow of what was here during the mining days. All the signposts stating what structure used to be where are amusing because they're ridiculous. Go to

Montana for premier ghost towns.

On the trail beyond the town, you have to clamber up a particularly rugged section. You'll be stretching like Gumby to find foot- and handholds. It could be hazardous when wet. A few sturdy alder roots allow you to hoist yourself up and control yourself on the way down.

This is an ill-advised destination during fly season: usually late July and most of August. The insects are rapacious here on hot days. Monte Cristo must be the stronghold and breeding ground from which they're launching their assault on the rest of the world. Only up in the basin near snow do the winged demons abate enough for you to rest without flailing at them.

Finally, if you're backpacking, and therefore walking the whole way, start after 3 P.M. to avoid the merciless summer sun and the worst onslaught of flies. You'll still have plenty of time to reach the basin. Other visitors will be leaving then, so it should be more peaceful when you arrive.

Glacier Basin

Trip 59
Monte Cristo / Silver Lake

Location	Mt. Baker-Snoqualmie National Forest / Henry M. Jackson Wilderness.
Distance	12.4-mile round trip.
Elevation gain	2040' in, 140' out.
Map	Green Trails No. 143–Monte Cristo.

OPINION

Silver Lake and Silvertip Peak *are* pretty. They're just not special enough to justify the first leg of the journey: 4.2 miles on a dirt road busy with hikers, bikers, and a few property owners in their vehicles. And even ghost-town nuts will likely be disappointed by the paltry remains of the mining town of Monte Cristo.

If you bike to Monte Cristo, then Silver Lake is a worthwhile excursion. From the town, it's only a short hike to the lake. But Silver Lake is best left as merely a point of interest on the way to Twin Lakes (Trip 33). Or, if you want a shorter hike in this area, choose Gothic Basin (Trip 32). Although it requires more effort than Silver Lake, it's far more rewarding, and the trail starts only 1.2 miles down the dirt road from the parking lot.

Trip 60
Ashland Lakes / Bald Mountain

Location	Mt. Baker-Snoqualmie National Forest / Department of Natural Resources.
Distance	6.0-mile round trip to ridgetop view-point; 7.4-mile round trip to Twin Falls.
Elevation gain	1500′ to ridgetop; 500′ in, 700′ out on Twin Falls round trip.
Map	Green Trails No. 110–Silverton.

OPINION

You won't use up your film on this hike. The ancient forest is grand, but the views are limited to glimpses of only a few distinguishable peaks—nothing remarkable, just a chance to stretch your eyes. The rest of the horizon is mostly rolly, tree-covered, bunny-slope ridges.

The Ashland Lakes at 1.5 miles could be a satisfactory destination for a family with small children and low expectations. But it's an unexciting 5.5-mile trudge from there to the Bald Mountain meadows. The entire trail appears to be an encroachment on a soggy landscape that resents hikers and is doing its damndest to discourage them. In early season, there's usually too much mud for enjoyable walking. Actually, anytime of the year is likely to be wet here, because Verlot is the rainiest spot in the Cascades. So all the roots and puncheon on this trail are often perilously slick. Invest your precious free time elsewhere.

Puncheon, by the way, is a boardwalk of cut logs punched into the ground. Its main purpose is to prevent trail erosion in muddy stretches, and it does that. But puncheon is also intended to make it easier for hikers to negotiate the mud, which it can, but only when the wood is dry. Wet wood is a Slip 'n Slide.

Because of its western location and low elevation, this trail can be snow-free into November, which makes it tempting despite all the drawbacks. If you go, visit Beaver Plant Lake. The quiet, sylvan setting of this marshy lake is very soothing. Lime-green scouring rushes grow profusely in the water and are especially beautiful in sunlight. There's even a plank walkway around the lake, although the inlet and outlet streams can be difficult for kids to cross.

Thinking of hiking below lower Ashland Lake to Twin Falls? It's a rough, challenging trail.

Trip 61 Shoulder Season

Thunder Creek / Fourth of July Pass / Panther Creek

Location	Ross Lake National Recreation Area.
Distance	11.4-mile shuttle trip, 9.2-mile round trip to Fourth of July Camp.
Elevation gain	2880' on the shuttle trip; 2300' to Fourth of July Camp.
Maps	Green Trails No. 48–Diablo Dam, No. 49–Mt. Logan; Trails Illustrated No. 223–North Cascades National Park Complex.

OPINION

Here's the shock therapy you need at the end of a long winter. The sense of adventure you can attain on this hike, compared to other shoulder-season options, is cathartic. In years of light snowfall it's available by early May, when the views from Fourth of July Pass of Neve Glacier, Colonial Peak and Snowfield Peak will astonish you, leaving you lusting for more. But for the summer hiking season this trip isn't so special, because the trail is mostly in trees. Whenever possible, we'd rather be high *in* the alpine country instead of just peering up at it.

You have lots of choices: dayhike up Thunder Creek to the pass, dayhike up Panther Creek to the pass, camp overnight at the pass, or dayhike all the way through starting at either end. Since it's possible for robust hikers to complete the one-way shuttle hike in five or six hours, why not see it all? And why lug a full pack? If you can't arrange a car shuttle, stick out your thumb on the highway at the other end. It's a short, easy hitch. If you choose to camp, the sites at Fourth of July Pass are superb. They're on a narrow shelf on the side of Ruby Mountain, with an unobstructed vista of the icy heights of Neve Glacier on Snowfield Peak.

We strongly urge you to start on the more inviting Thunder

The forest cathedral along Thunder Creek

Creek side, especially if you're just going up to the pass and back. The Panther Creek drainage is narrower and darker, and the trail is brushier. Panther is where Edgar Allen Poe would hang out; Thunder is Walt Whitman's kind of place. Both are worthwhile, but most people will feel more motivated to get out of Panther than into it, so it makes a better exit.

You'll find something to enjoy throughout the journey. Powerful yet peaceful Thunder Creek has a calming, reassuring, almost hypnotic effect. The ascent to Fourth of July Pass is on a well-maintained trail, through airy, light forest. The pass itself offers a surprisingly magnificent view, so try not to stop for lunch until you get there. Panther Creek snarls and roars, slashing and ripping its way down the mountain. It's a wild, rambunctious creature.

Unless the trail's been brushed, expect to encounter all manner of fanged plants clawing and scratching your legs on the Panther Creek descent. Also be prepared for a surprise: Just when you think the highway is around the next bend, and you feel the hike down Panther Creek is over, wham: the trail goes up, up, up, several hundred feet, for no apparent reason other than to wring more sweat from your brow. Don't worry—you haven't taken a wrong turn. Keep plugging uphill. The trail *does* eventually top out. Then it sends you directly downhill to the highway.

FACT

By Car

On Highway 20, drive 4.3 miles southeast from the Diablo-townsite turnoff to Colonial Creek Campground on Diablo Lake. Turn southeast into the big parking lot, but keep going through the campground to the smaller parking area at the trailhead, 1200 feet.

To arrange a shuttle, drive 8.2 miles east from Colonial Creek and park one vehicle in the East Bank trailhead parking lot on the north side of the highway. The Panther Creek trail reaches the highway 0.3 mile west of there.

On Foot

Starting at Colonial Creek Campground, the trail contours the west side of Diablo Lake's Thunder Arm for 0.8 mile. In 1.4 miles cross a bridge to the east side of Thunder Creek and continue upstream. At 1.8 miles pass a spur trail leading right to Thunder Creek Camp. At 2.1 miles reach a junction: Thunder Creek straight ahead, Fourth of July Pass left. Turn left and begin the 2100-foot, 2.5-mile climb to Fourth of July Camp and the west end of the pass. The camp is left (north), just above the trail. There's a creeklet nearby. Several sites offer views and grated fire pits, but firewood is scarce.

For the shuttle trip, proceed east through the pass, above the tiny ponds called Panther Potholes. At 5.0 miles you'll reach 3600 feet, the highest point on the broad, flat pass. From the east side of the pass, the trail drops 900 feet in 1.4 miles to Panther Creek. Continuing downstream, cross a few side creeks and at least one avalanche swath that might require you to negotiate deep snow. At 8.7 miles arrive at the Panther campground, where you cross the creek on a bridge. The final 2.7 miles include a switchbacking ascent of 480 feet—elevation that you abruptly lose before the trail ends at 1800 feet on Highway 20. When you set foot on pavement, you'll be 7.9 miles east of Colonial Creek Campground, via Highway 20.

Trip 62 Shoulder Season
Squire Creek Pass

Location	Boulder River Wilderness.
Distance	6.8-mile round trip.
Elevation gain	2250'.
Map	Green Trails 110–Silverton.

OPINION

The cliffs of Whitehorse Mountain and Three Fingers are a striking visage, especially when you realize they're only 35 miles from the Pacific Ocean. These peaks are as impressive as others deep in North Cascades National Park. They form an enticing backdrop for this excursion.

The show starts almost immediately. The 4000-foot, Yosemite-like cliffs are visible after a ten-minute walk through virgin forest. Plunging waterfalls add to the drama. But in 45 minutes, the trail asks you to pay for all the entertainment. On a hot day, the price of admission is a lot of sweat and strain. You'll be glad shade from the ancient trees accompanies you for several miles. Even in dry weather, this high-stepping, rocky, rooty, often muddy route is a struggle much of the way. If difficult terrain throws you into a tantrum, forget it. You might be on all fours in a few places.

Red-orange columbine, yellow daisies, and orange tiger lilies brighten the way. A huge boulder field just beyond 2 miles makes an excellent rest stop, where you can stare across the abyss at the oh-so-close wall of Three Fingers. If you don't want to press on, it's a good turnaround point. At the pass you'll find giant, flat rock slabs for your lounging or camping convenience. The gazing is good and the sprawling even better. Look closely for pink-striped spring beauty decorating the pass.

We consider this a shoulder-season trip because it can be accessible by early May. But the superb scenery makes it a Worthwhile even during summer.

You might hear of another approach to the pass, via Clear Creek Road. Don't be tempted. That trail is steeper, less scenic, and only a half-mile shorter.

FACT

By Car

Drive to Darrington on Highway 530. From the business district, turn south at the highway sign CITY CENTER onto Givens Avenue (the second street west of the 3-way intersection). Take Darrington Street west. It becomes Squire Creek Road 2040. Drive 5.7 miles southwest on the rough, potholed, dirt road to the trailhead at about 1750 feet.

On Foot

There's no water at the pass. And, during a hot summer, there was only one creeklet big enough for us to filter water from along the way. Bring full water bottles. From the far end of the parking area, cross the boulder-strewn creek. The trail begins heading southwest on the other side and continues to the pass without forking. The trail gets very slippery during wet weather.

At 2.2 miles start crossing a boulder field and gain an unobstructed view of Three Fingers and Whitehorse. Squire Creek Pass is at 3.4 miles, 4000 feet. For further exploration, walk the gentle slope to the south, ascending 640 feet in 0.6 mile to a ridgetop view of Mt. Shuksan (north) and Glacier Peak (east).

Three Fingers Mountain from Squire Creek Pass

Trip 63 Shoulder Season

Kennedy Hot Springs

Location	Glacier Peak Wilderness.
Distance	10.4-mile round trip.
Elevation gain	1000'.
Maps	Green Trails No. 111–Sloan Peak, No. 112–Glacier Peak; US Forest Service–Glacier Peak Wilderness.

OPINION

For early-season muscle building and mental rejuvenation, this is a delightful walk. You'll be near the White Chuck River most of the way, lovely trilliums are abundant in spring, and the ancient trees will have you exclaiming. After May, however, choose a more scenic excursion. Or consider this merely an on-ramp for long-distance backpacking options radiating from Kennedy (Trips 89 and 90)

Somehow, the words "hot springs" hold a magnetic appeal for people who otherwise wouldn't walk beyond the corner drugstore. But these springs are a disappointment, made even less attractive by the throngs who come here to poach themselves in the tepid water.

What's the big deal, anyway? Kennedy Hot Springs consists of one puny dipping hole—roughly four feet square, plus a small patch of squishy, orange, sulfurous earth. The water's not even hot. If you want to soothe tired feet, it's better to plunk them in a stream. Cold water alleviates inflammation. Hot water aggravates it. And you certainly won't find relief from the pains of civilization at this hikers' ghetto. If you're a lover of solitude, take a look to satisfy your curiosity, then go farther to find a quiet spot where you can relish nature.

Still, the hike to and from the springs is worthwhile. Just beyond the trailhead, awesome peaks across the river herald your beginning. For a couple miles, the trail saunters 200 feet above the river, close enough for you to hear its rhapsody and glimpse the rapids. Sandy riverbanks make good lounges for cloud-bathing, or if you're fortunate, sunbathing. They also provide easy-to-reach backcountry campsites. From the depths of the valley at Kennedy, you can glimpse Kennedy Peak and Scimitar Glacier to the northeast. The views will inspire you to come back in late summer and boogie up to Kennedy Ridge.

Even after a winter of heavy snowfall, the dirt road to the trailhead should be accessible by the first week of May. If you come that early, snow will probably cover the last 0.75 mile of trail to the springs, but you'll be able to mush through. There's a chance others will have broken trail, making it easy for you to follow.

FACT

By Car

From Darrington on Highway 530, drive the Mountain Loop Highway southeast 9.5 miles. Shortly after you cross the Sauk River bridge, the second road on the left is signed WHITE CHUCK TRAIL, MEADOW MOUNTAIN TRAIL. Turn left (northeast) here, onto White Chuck River Road 23, and drive 10.4 miles east to the trailhead and Owl Creek Campground at road's end, 2300 feet. In addition to plenty of flat parking space beside trees, there's one campsite with a table near the creek.

On Foot

At the trailhead, there's a large Forest Service information sign. The trail starts to the right of it. Don't start on the old road that continues straight from the parking area.

The elevation gain is gentle the whole way. At 0.3 mile enter Glacier Peak Wilderness. At 1.2 miles, cross a log bridge over Fire Creek with its heaving waterfall just above. Reach a junction at 1.4 miles. Meadow Mountain trail 657 forks left. Stay right (southeast) on trail 643. The first possible campsite is on your right, beside the river, just after the footlog stream crossing at 1.8 miles. Five minutes past this forested site, you'll come to a big, sandy bench where you can camp in the open beside the river.

In early May, large trilliums decorate the slope you switchback up beginning at 2.1 miles. Don't continue along the river into the landslide area; that's where the old trail went, but it's wiped out now.

Near 4.4 miles, the trail passes through a narrow, rocky gorge.

At 4.9 miles, reach a signed junction where the Pacific Crest Trail ascends left (northeast) over Kennedy Ridge to Fire Creek Pass. For Kennedy Hot Springs continue straight (southeast), into the widening valley. You'll quickly reach Kennedy Creek. Cross the creek on a log bridge with a wobbly handrail.

Upon your arrival at Kennedy Campground at 5.2 miles, 3300 feet, signs point right to an outhouse and the horse camp. One minute farther, you'll see a ranger cabin signed GUARD STATION. There's an area map posted on the wall showing where the campsites are. Bears have been sighted in the area. Hang your food properly so they don't become a problem at this popular destination.

The hot springs are on the far (west) bank of the White Chuck River, across the solid footbridge and 75 yards upstream. The steep ascent to Lake Byrne also continues on the other side.

Pool at Kennedy Hot Springs

Trip 64 Shoulder Season

Goat Lake

Location	Mt. Baker-Snoqualmie National Forest / Henry M. Jackson Wilderness.
Distance	10.4-mile round trip.
Elevation gain	1300'.
Maps	Green Trails No. 111–Sloan Peak; US Forest Service–Glacier Peak Wilderness.

OPINION

Alleluia! Mountain magnificence attainable in May! Low elevation and southern exposure enable you to hike beneath sawtoothed, snow-capped peaks into awesome Goat Lake cirque, where you can safely watch avalanches crash down Foggy Peak. It's an exhilarating change from the viewless, deep-forest walks that are the usual fare in early season. The scenery here is even worth coming for in summer, although heat and crowds detract from the experience, and by then, greater, more rewarding challenges are available in the high alpine. Best to come early and feel the thrill of stealing into forbidden territory.

En route you'll pass goliath cedars that, to an open mind and appreciative eye, can be as emotionally moving as great mountains. The cedars, after all, are alive. They breathe. You encounter them intimately. By comparison, stone monoliths can seem cold, hard, distant, detached.

The trail to Goat Lake is usually hikeable by May 1, even in years of average snowfall. But until the Forest Service clears the trail each summer, you might have to negotiate significant amounts of deadfall—or perhaps "livingfall." In six places we were forced to clamber over and under toppled trees burgeoning with spring growth. The steep slopes above the trail tend to slump during constant, heavy rain, humiliating the poor trees in the process.

The trail reaches Goat Lake where its outlet stream, Elliott Creek, begins life as a plunging waterfall. Continue along the forested northeast lakeshore to find several private, rocky pocket beaches, just big enough for two or three friends to lunch and snooze beside the lapping water. On a sunny spring day, it's heavenly here. And the Goat Lake campsites are near the outlet, where you'll be lulled to sleep by the swish of the falls.

An alternate way to Goat Lake is the Elliot Creek trail, which was the main route until it severely eroded. It partly follows an old, puncheon wagon-road. It's now so sketchy, muddy, and cantankerous, we don't recommend hiking it until planned improvements are completed. But if you love scrambling beside roaring whitewater and enjoy being alone thwacking your way through brush, this is your chance to play Indiana Jones. Even the currently preferred road-trail, much of it on abandoned logging road, can present obstacles after a hard winter, so expect plenty of difficulties along Elliot Creek. Though it's a mile shorter to the lake, the crude path and boggy stretches will prevent you from saving time. And you won't get views of the surrounding topography, as you will on the main trail.

FACT

By Car

From Darrington on Highway 530, drive the Mountain Loop Highway southeast 19.8 miles toward Barlow Pass. Pavement ends at 9.5 miles. Or, from the east side of Granite Falls, drive the Mountain Loop Highway east 30.75 miles to Barlow Pass, then continue northeast 3.5 miles. From either approach, turn east onto Elliot Creek Road 4080 and drive 1.0 mile to road's end and the trailhead at 1900 feet.

On Foot

Ask at the Verlot or Darrington ranger station about the condition of the Elliot Creek trail, if you decide to brave it. This rough trail starts to the right of the trailhead sign. You'll notice a narrow trail dropping into the forest. That's it. A few feet in is a sign NO LONGER MAINTAINED. It joins the main road-trail in 3.1 miles.

Most people begin the hike straight ahead on the smooth, wide surface of an old logging road. In 0.3 mile the road veers northwest and you can see a long waterfall on Twin Peaks across the Sauk River valley. Mostly in alder, the road gently traverses above a previous clearcut, heading northeast. In 1.0 mile stay right at the fork. Follow the road as it takes a southeastward course. You'll pass many water sources—seeps, trickles, gushing spring run-off—along the way in early season, but don't count on them in summer. Pack full water bottles. Near 3.8 miles the road becomes trail. At 4.2 miles enter the Henry M. Jackson Wilderness. From this point on, you're in a lush forest that cloaks many ancient cedars. It's much cooler here than on the previous stretch through young, thin, deciduous trees.

The smooth, pine-needled trail sometimes blurs into the forest floor; watch it carefully to avoid straying off. Where the trail appears to split into a Y, and you see a sign NATIONAL FOREST PROPERTY BOUNDARY, go left on the gentle switchback, stepping over two boulders in the rocky channel. If you go right at this false junction you'll end up struggling through deadfall.

At 5.0 miles reach roaring Elliot Creek as it spills from Goat Lake. The lake is just beyond at 5.2 miles, 3200 feet. If backpacking, you'll find 10 campsites in trees just up the hill to your left. Camping is prohibited within 200 feet of the lake. A ridge of 6810-foot Foggy Peak plunges to the lake's southwest shore, and 7186-foot Cadet Peak is in plain view at the south end of the lake. You can follow the narrow, brushy path on the northeast shore past tiny beaches to a waterfall and a cove halfway up the lake.

Goat Lake in May

Trip 65 Shoulder Season
Lake Twentytwo

Location	Lake 22 Research Natural Area.
Distance	5.4-mile round trip.
Elevation gain	1300'.
Maps	Green Trails No. 109–Granite Falls, No. 110–Silverton.

OPINION

Lake 22 Research Natural Area is a 980-acre haven of virgin forest in a region of profligate logging. It was protected in 1947 for an utterly absurd reason: to see if a preserved forest would, over time, flourish more than a similar forest "under intensive management," in other words, a forest that's been plundered. We all know the answer, and the pure, raw beauty you'll experience on this hike elaborates eloquently. So chalk this up as one time we've benefitted from the government's lack of common sense.

The trail was smartly engineered and is well maintained. Thanks to the gravel surface, even during a downpour you won't be tromping in mud or sloshing through water. You'll be striding among resplendent ancient cedars and hemlocks, often beside a gorgeous creek. Several waterfalls add to the enchantment. You'll enjoy the revitalizing walk as much as the beautiful destination: an impressive glacial cirque, with ribbon waterfalls gracing luxuriant green cliffs, which rise from the lakeshore straight up the north flank of Mt. Pilchuck.

You can hike to Lake Twentytwo most of the year, since it's only at 2400 feet. It's makes an excellent rainy-day hike, because you'll still be able to fully appreciate the experience. Cloud and mist actually enhance it, creating a mysterious, primeval atmosphere. In early spring, you're likely to witness avalanches crashing into the lake. You'll be safe on the north shore, across from the cliffs. In early October, the nearly half-mile stretch of trail through maple trees is brilliantly ablaze. On summer weekends, there's a constant stream of hikers on the trail. Camping and fires are prohibited.

FACT

By Car

On the Mountain Loop Highway, drive 2.1 miles east from the Verlot Public Service Center. Turn right (south) into the large, circular, trailhead parking lot, at 1100 feet.

On Foot

You'll immediately cross Hempel Creek and head west. Cross Twentytwo Creek at 0.75 mile. The trail then maintains a moderate ascent, switchbacking through ancient forest and past waterfalls of various sizes. The third and biggest falls is a bit off the trail at 1.3 miles. When you hear a roar, look left through the trees and you'll see it. To get closer, find the rocky side-route veering off from a tight switchback where the trail doubles back from east to west. This is 0.2 mile before the trail crosses a rockslide through maples. If you miss the third falls going up, you'll probably catch it on the way down. Crossing the rockslide you can see out (north) across the heavily clearcut South Fork Stillaguamish River valley. Arrive at the north end of the lake at 2.7 miles, 2400 feet.

Trip 66 Shoulder Season

Lightning, Flash, Strike, and Thunder lakes

Location	Manning Provincial Park.
Distance	13.0-mile (21.0-km) round trip.
Elevation gain	virtually none.
Maps	the free B.C. Parks brochure–Manning Provincial Park; Manning Park and Skagit Valley Rec Area topo printed by the B.C. Ministry of Environment.

OPINION

Welcome to beginning hikers' heaven. Smooth, level, well-signed trails make neophytes feel safe and comfortable, but squelch any sense of wilderness. Experienced hikers will find no excitement at Lightning Lake. Striding along in mountaineering gear, you might feel sheepish here. But despite the tameness and the lack of soul-stirring scenery, it is pretty. Come in early season, before it gets too crowded, for a pleasant walk that will smooth your brow.

Walk is the correct word. Hiking implies an element of roughness and some degree of remoteness, neither of which applies to the first couple lakes. Because they can drive to it, visitors swarm around Lightning Lake. Families with small children love the first two miles of trail. Pine-needle soft, it's strollable in a pair of Keds. The crowd dwindles after Flash Lake. From Strike Lake on, it becomes a real hike. Thunder Lake offers a scenic departure and is worth the longer ramble. The other lakes are embedded in forest. Thunder is in a rocky, alpine-like bowl. Although it's at roughly the same elevation, it can be hot here due to the lack of forest cover.

Steep snowfields that frequently avalanche make travel beyond Flash Lake hazardous until late May. June is the best time to visit the area. The lakeshore trails should be snow-free then, while many North Cascade destinations are still buried. Proximity to water always helps compensate for a lack of dramatic topography.

The only approved backcountry campground along the trail is at Strike Lake. It's small, viewless, unappealing, yet frequently crowded. Don't go. For a gentle, early-season overnighter, backpack into a deeper, wilder valley farther south in the range. Thunder Creek, for example, in North Cascades National Park. Or the White Chuck River, in Glacier Peak Wilderness. If coming from Canada, don't let the border pose a mental block. Thunder Creek and Lightning Lake are the same distance from Vancouver. The White Chuck is only 45 minutes farther.

There are trails on both sides of Lightning and Flash lakes. Walk either side first, unless it's hot and you want more shade. In that case, stick to the south side in the morning; return on the north side in the afternoon. From the higher north-side trail you can look down at Lightning Lake and appreciate its rich green color. The trail is wider and not as aesthetically pleasing as on the south side, but might allow you to walk faster. You can also see a few more peaks from the north side.

At the start or end of your trip, be sure to cross Rainbow Bridge over the narrow stretch of Lightning Lake—unless you're staying at the Lightning Lake campground on Spruce Bay. Otherwise, to reach the parking lot, you'll have to walk a too-long stretch of dusty fire road through scrawny lodgepole forest away from the lake as you round its north end.

The Disneyesque atmosphere at these lakes, created by frequent signs, cute bridges, canoeists, and lots of other hikers, can lull you into a state of false security. Stay alert. You are in bear country.

FACT

By Car

Drive B.C. Highway 3 to Manning Park. At 5.8 miles (9.3 km) southeast of Allison Pass, turn south at the signed Lightning Lake turnoff, immediately east of the Manning Park Lodge. Drive 1.8 miles (2.9 km) west to a junction. Fork left 0.5 mile (0.8 km) to the Lightning Lake Day Use area, at 4100 feet (1250 meters). Park near the start of the parking lot, close to the east end of the lake.

Lightning Lake

On Foot

From Lightning Lake Day Use Area, start at the far east end of the lake. Cross the cement bridge over the northeast outlet stream. Proceed over the small dam. Immediately ahead is a sign pointing left to Frosty Mountain, right to Strike and Thunder lakes. Go right, staying on the level as you head west, then south to Rainbow Bridge at 0.7 mile (1.1 km). A sign here indicates you can cross the bridge, turn right and return to the parking lot in 1.5 km—not recommended for the reasons explained above. Either cross the bridge and turn left, or stay on the south-shore trail now and cross back on the bridge when returning from the north shore.

Continuing along the south shore of Lightning Lake, at 2.1 miles (3.4 km) reach the southwest outlet stream. Cross the plank bridge. Immediately turn left and go up a bit. Walk 2 minutes west to a junction with the north side of the Flash Lake Loop. Go left, recrossing the creek to stay on the south side of Flash, where there are braided brooks (until late summer), a few cedars, a rooty trail, and a few plank bridges over delicate ground. The burn you see across and above the lake is the result of the 1994 fire on Skyline Ridge. At 3.2 miles (5.2 km), cross a plank bridge over the Flash Lake outlet creek and turn left. The trail is now on the north side of Lightning Creek. A sign warns of possible avalanche danger ahead beneath steep slopes. Reach Strike Lake at 4.0 miles (6.4 km). This rocky, sunny stretch is sprinkled with flowers by late June, but the tiger lilies and columbines can take another week or so to pop open.

Strike Lake is deep, with rockslides on the north bank. In a couple places you can walk 15 yards (15 meters) down to flat, lakeshore benches. Strike Lake campsite is 5 to 7 minutes west, beyond the lake. To continue to Thunder Lake, walk through the camp, staying close to the stream. Shortly after leaving the camp, a sign warns CAUTION—BEARS IN AREA. The next 0.5 mile (0.8 km) is across a brushy avalanche slope, then it turns rough and rocky. Thunder Lake's northeast end is at 6.5 miles (10.5 km). The trail peters out 0.25 mile (0.4 km) along the north shore. The first 100 yards (100 meters) of the lake can be so choked with deadfall that you can't see the water.

The return to Lightning Lake via the north-side trail is higher, on a steeper slope than the south-side trail. A third of the way along Lightning Lake, there's a junction where the Skyline I trail angles left. Stay straight on the fire road signed MAIN TRAIL. To walk closer to the water, keep right on the side paths. Either way, you'll soon reach a map and sign SPRUCE BAY BEACH. Go right, down the stairs. This will take you to Rainbow Bridge, where you can complete your trip by walking on the north or the south side of the lake.

Trip 67 Shoulder Season

Baker Lake East Bank

Location	Mt. Baker-Snoqualmie National Forest.
Distance	9.6-mile round trip.
Elevation Loss	400'
Maps	Green Trails No. 45–Hamilton (shows Grandy-Baker Lake Road), No. 46–Lake Shannon; Trails Illustrated No. 223–North Cascades National Park Complex.

OPINION

Are you an avid hiker, eagerly waiting for the snow to melt? Stretch your legs and indulge your senses on this beautiful, well-groomed trail. It's an excellent shoulder-season or rainy-day choice and is usually snow-free all winter.

You'll be walking north, about a third of the way up the east side of Baker Lake, then retracing your steps. For most of its length, the path is not on the shore; it parallels it, well back from the lake, high on the slope, in the trees. But the forest is lush. Several marvelous, ancient Douglas firs are still standing. The moss is luxuriant. And you do catch glimpses of the lake. The trail itself is a delight. We walked it after a week of solid rain and, due to the ideal mix of pebbles and needles, encountered no mud.

Be sure to take the side route, less than 2 miles from the trailhead, out to the unnamed, walk-in campground—even if you're not camping. It's a great spot to gaze at the lake, eat a snack, and maybe catch some rays. Or, if you like the idea of a short walk to a small, pleasant campground accessible year-round, bring your tent and pitch it here.

After 3 miles, the route drops in a few places nearly to the water, enabling you to break through the brush to the rocky, stumpy beach for more expansive views of Mt. Baker and its lesser brethren. The easiest place to do this is near the Maple Grove Campground.

FACT

By Car

Drive Highway 20 east 16.5 miles from Sedro Woolley, or west 6.0 miles from Concrete. Turn north onto the Grandy-Baker Lake Road. Drive northeast 13.9 miles and turn right (east) at the sign BAKER LAKE—KOMA KULSHAN CAMPGROUND. Go down 1.2 miles on the badly potholed road to the free Kulshan Campground and picnic area, maintained by Puget Power. Continue straight. Follow the sign EAST BANK TRAIL—WATSON LAKE directing you over the dam, to the east side of Baker Lake. At 1.0 mile from the campground, go left on Road 1107. In another 0.7 mile, you'll see a pullout on the left. Park there.

On Foot

The trail starts at 1000 feet, which is 300 feet above the lake. After the initial drop, it's mostly level with a few minor ups and downs. You'll see a side trail 1.8 miles in, which descends 0.2 mile to a campground: four gravel tent pads on a ledge above the water. The main trail, indicated by a sign on a tree MAPLE GROVE, continues right. At 2.5 miles, you might notice the old East Bank trail descending from this newer, wider trail.

Maple Grove Campground is at 3.8 miles, 700 feet—just south of a broad, shallow, unbridged creek. You'll see the two campground outhouses on the slope below the trail. As of this writing, the trail was constructed only about 1 mile beyond the campground, still several miles short of the trail coming down from the north end of the lake. When the Forest Service can afford it, they'll complete the trail, creating a 14-mile hike joining the Baker River trail (Trip 68). Ask about the new trail at the Sedro Woolley ranger station.

A window of spring sunshine—Baker Lake East Bank Trail

Trip 68 Shoulder Season

Baker River

Location	Mt. Baker-Snoqualmie National Forest / North Cascades National Park.
Distance	4.8-mile round trip.
Elevation gain	100'.
Maps	Green Trails No. 14–Mt. Shuksan, No. 45–Hamilton (shows Baker Lake Road), No. 46–Lake Shannon (shows Roads 11 and 1168); Trails Illustrated No. 223–North Cascades National Park Complex.

OPINION

The ideal hike on a rainy day is short, through big timber, along a pretty river, with the possibility of views if the clouds lift. This is one. Following the Baker River, which drains glaciers on Mt. Shuksan and the Picket Range, you'll pass through ancient forest filled with magnificent cedar, hemlock, and Douglas fir—all saved by the efforts of environmentalists. The trail feels reasonably open most of the way, offering frequent glimpses of the river and the mountains above.

Even on a dreary day, the thick, lime- and lemon-green moss on the tree trunks looks so bright it's as if it were plugged in. And surprisingly, even after a week of rain, the trail isn't too muddy. We've walked it as early as the first week of March, but in some years it could still be snowed under then, even at an elevation of only 900 feet.

After you cross the log bridge and you're passing through a rocky area with big boulders on your left, be sure to look up at the cliffs. You'll see an easy-to-miss waterfall that deserves a moment of admiration.

Weather permitting, you'll see Sulphide Glacier (northwest) from trail's end at Sulphide Creek. It clings to the south side of awesome Mt. Shuksan, which rises more than 8000 stupendous feet from this valley bottom.

Stream beside Baker River Trail

FACT

By Car

Drive Highway 20 east 16.5 miles from Sedro Woolley, or west 6.0 miles from Concrete. Turn north onto the Grandy-Baker Lake Road. Continue northeast all the way to the upper end of Baker Lake. The road is paved to the Baker Lake Resort turnoff—20.0 miles from Highway 20. After it turns to gravel, drive another 5.0 miles northeast on Road 11. When the rough, dirt road comes to a T-intersection, go left 0.5 mile on Road 1168 to the trailhead parking lot beside the river.

On Foot

A sign marks the trailhead. You'll start on the remnants of a logging road, then continue on a trail. After a mile, the route climbs briefly above the river, then descends to beaver ponds. At 1.7 miles you enter North Cascades National Park, so you'll need a camping permit to stay overnight. A bit farther, you can see 7574-foot Whatcom Peak up the river valley to the northeast. The trail ends 0.7 mile farther at Sulphide Creek, where there are four campsites.

Trip 69 Shoulder Season
Driveway Butte

Location	North Cascades Scenic Highway Area / Okanogan National Forest.
Distance	9.0-mile round trip to Driveway Butte, 6.0-mile round trip to the unnamed 5545'-butte.
Elevation gain	3000' to Driveway, 2545' to the unnamed butte.
Maps	Green Trails No. 50–Washington Pass; Trails Illustrated No. 223–North Cascades National Park Complex.

OPINION

In May or June when the high trails are still unadvisable unless you're armed with an ice axe, plan a trip to Driveway Butte. If you've been slogging the low valley trails in early spring, you'll feel like a mountain goat again after getting up here.

The first half of this hike is within view of the highway. You might reject it, thinking the trail too steep and boring. But if you go, you'll be reminded that the earth is far more interesting when you travel on rubber soles instead of rubber tires. The switchbacks are gradual enough that the ascent is not grueling. And don't worry about road noise. Though you see the pavement below for a couple miles, the traffic is muted by the roar of Early Winters Creek and its tributaries.

The trail is pleasingly punctuated by ponderous ponderosa pines. The name *ponderosa* is actually from the Latin *ponderosus*, meaning *heavy*, hence the tree's name. You'll also discover that the yellow hue visible from below is a startling bounty of glowing yellow balsamroot (sunflowers) blanketing the slope. In May, you'll walk through acres of these lovely flowers. As for views, you'll see Gardner Mountain (south), the massive hulk of Silver Star Mountain (slightly southwest), and Vasiliki Ridge (southwest of Silver Star). The Needles are at the far end of Delancy Ridge (southwest). And that's just on the first half of the trail.

From Driveway Butte, you can look north at Robinson Mountain and Beauty Peak, peer southeast over the Methow Valley, and stretch your eyeballs northeast over Pasayten Wilderness.

In years of heavy snowfall, you'll probably have to wait until late June for the route all the way to Driveway Butte to be snow-free. Even when the butte is naked, the forested, shaded saddle you pass through to get there can shelter 5-foot drifts. And by June, more exciting hikes should be available elsewhere. So, unless it's been a year of abnormally light snow, we recommend hiking here in May and instead of continuing to Driveway Butte, ascending the side trail to the unnamed butte east of the saddle. This one should be easily accessible then, and you can see plenty from there, including the craggy Pacific Crest near Granite Pass (southwest). Look closely in the cindery soil and you might spot these flowers: the delicate white- and pink-striped spring beauty and the distinctive steer's head, shaped like its namesake.

While this trail is a superb early-season choice, forget it after June, when the mostly open, south-facing slopes will be sizzling. Besides, the scenery is better in early season, when all the snow, like impressive armor, makes the surrounding peaks look more formidable.

FACT

By Car

On Highway 20, drive 13.0 miles northeast of Washington Pass, or 3.0 miles west of the Early Winters Information Center. Turn north onto Road 300, signed for Klipchuck Campground, and drive 1.0 mile to the camp entrance at 3000 feet.

On Foot

Trail 481 starts from the gated road at the right of the entrance to Klipchuck Campground. After a one-minute walk on the road, you'll see a big brown sign DRIVEWAY BUTTE 4 MILES. Leave the road here, to the right, before the sign. Don't continue on the road.

The trail soon begins switchbacking north, gaining 1900 feet in 1.9 miles on mostly open slopes shaded intermittently by fir and pines. The gradient then eases as you head northwest into a tiny basin. In May, you'll cross a small runoff stream here, but don't rely on ít. Bring enough water so you won't have to grovel for snowmelt.

Just as you rise out of the basin and enter a forested saddle at 2.2 miles, notice a large, level campsite below the trail to your left. At the beginning of the saddle, a scant path branches east off the main trail and ascends the slope to your right, leading you up toward the unnamed 5545-foot butte. When this side route peters out, just pick your own way. If you hit snow, angle farther right (southeast) on the sun-exposed slopes. You'll gain 585 feet in 0.75 mile from the saddle to the summit of this butte, about 20 minutes' walk.

Continuing northwest on the main trail to Driveway Butte, your way isn't nearly as steep as the ascent to the saddle. But the forested trail eventually gets sketchier as it crosses a tributary of McGee Creek. If you look closely through the timber, you'll catch glimpses of the butte directly north. At 3.8 miles, the tread vanishes. Follow the cairns leading northeast across the butte's open slopes. If you lose them, just head for the 6000-foot summit, approximately 4.5 miles from the trailhead—not 7.0 miles, as indicated on the Green Trails 1987 map.

Trip 70 Shoulder Season
Goat Peak Lookout

Location	Okanogan National Forest.
Distance	5.0-mile round trip.
Elevation gain	1400'.
Map	Green Trails No. 51–Mazama.

OPINION

The pinnacles of Silver Star Mountain are far more jagged and numerous than you can tell from Highway 20, but you can see them clearly from Goat Peak. The site of a still-active fire lookout, Goat also offers views north and east over Pasayten Wilderness. And you won't find a better perspective of the Methow Valley, directly below.

Approximately 2,000 people visit the lookout each summer. The hike is so short you can slip it in while on your way someplace else. It's quite steep, however, so wear hiking boots. If you're seeking an escape from the rainy west side of the range, you're likely to find sunshine here.

Arriving at the lookout, you might be greeted by Lightnin' Bill. He loves being on duty during lightning storms—even when the bolts are zapping his cabin—which is how he earned his nickname among co-workers in the Forest Service. To him, no place is more thrilling than Goat Peak, so he often comes back up on his days off. See if he's finished painting the Cascade mountain panorama inside the lookout. He'll be happy to point out for you other lookouts on the horizon.

FACT

By Car

Drive Highway 20 northwest 11.8 miles from Winthrop and turn right (northwest) on the east side of the Methow River bridge, onto paved Goat Creek Road 1163. In 3.3 miles, turn right onto Road 52. Or if you're heading east on Highway 20, drive 1.5 miles southeast of the Early Winters Information Center to the

signed Mazama turnoff. Turn left (northeast), and just after crossing the Methow River bridge turn right (southeast) at the T-intersection. Drive 1.9 miles and turn left onto Road 52.

From either approach, once you're on Road 52 heading northwest, cross Goat Creek at 1.1 miles. At 2.7 miles reach a signed
fork. Go left on Road 5225. At 9.0 miles go right to head northeast
on Road (5225) 200. Arrive at the slanted parking area on the right
at 12.0 miles, 5600 feet. The trailhead sign might be missing. The
rough road continues north past the trailhead.

On Foot

There's no water en route, so bring plenty. The trail steadily
ascends southeast on a rocky ridge. It's so steep it often requires
knee-to-stomach steps. The trail is rough, but easy to follow. The
blackened hillside behind you is the result of a forest fire. At 0.6
mile the trail turns sharply west and at 1.0 mile begins tight
switchbacks. After a short way in subalpine fir, you're in open,
wind-beaten terrain. In early summer, wildflowers bloom here.
Once you attain the main ridge at 1.9 miles, the ascent is easier,
through tamarack and whitebark pine. At 2.5 miles, 7001 feet,
arrive at the lookout. It's manned, so don't plan on spending the
night inside.

Northeast is 8024-foot Sherman Peak on Isabella Ridge. Northwest are 7935-foot Beauty Peak and 8726-foot Robinson Mountain. The Lost River canyon is nearby to the northwest. The
rugged mountain with snowfields on it, rising in the southwest
above Highway 20, is 8876-foot Silver Star. 8956-foot North Gardner and 8897-foot Gardner mountains are slightly southwest.

Trip 71 Shoulder Season

Heather Lake

Location	Mt. Baker-Snoqualmie National Forest.
Distance	4.0-mile round trip.
Elevation gain	1000'.
Map	Green Trails No. 109–Granite Falls.

OPINION

Green avalanche slopes streak down cliff walls into Heather Lake. The forest is pretty after the first mile. The trail is short. Access from Verlot is quick and easy. And you can hike here nearly year-round. Don't make Heather Lake the centerpiece of your trip, but it's worth wandering up to some evening, or including in your plans the same day you go to Lake Twentytwo (Trip 65).

If you have to choose between them, hike to Lake Twentytwo. Heather is smaller than Twentytwo, and its cirque not as encircling, so it's less impressive. Also, the Heather Lake trail isn't as user-friendly. During rain, water pools on the trail in numerous depressions, rivulets stream 15 yards down the trail, and you have to rockhop a couple small creeks. If you try to dodge these obstacles instead of splashing through the water, it can be slippery. Then there's the difference between the two forests. Before entering old-growth forest, the trail to Heather Lake passes through the scene of a massacre. Here the headstones are giant stumps. Everyone should witness these sad reminders to protect our remaining ancient forests. It's moving and instructive. Compare the pathetic regrown forest on the way to Heather Lake with the virgin forest at nearby Lake Twentytwo. It starkly reveals how the results of the sin of clearcutting last decades.

FACT

By Car

On the Mountain Loop Highway, drive 1.0 mile southeast from the Verlot Public Service Center. Turn right (south) onto Road 42, signed HEATHER LK TR 1, MT PILCHUCK LOOKOUT TR 7. Immediately fork left and continue 1.3 miles to the parking area on the right by the outhouse, at 1400 feet. The trail begins across the road.

On Foot

The trail ascends southwest through second- or third-growth forest. The trees are spindly, the ground cover minimal. The trunks and branches are dark, and many trees have no needles. You'll see three or four stumps that are eight-to-ten feet in diameter. At 0.8 mile, this newer trail joins the old logging road for 50 yards. There's a wood plaque directing you to curve onto the road. Watch for where you soon leave the road and curve up left. At 1.0 mile you're in pleasant forest with large trees and healthy undergrowth. Cross a couple creeklets, and arrive at the north end of the lake at 2.0 miles, 2400 feet.

The lakeshore is forested, but there are patches of meadow. The cliffs of Mt. Pilchuck border the lake on three sides. Expect lots of company on summer weekends. For berry picking and a better chance of solitude, scramble your way to the bouldery south shore. Camping is allowed in the basin, but you must be at least 100 feet from the lake.

Trip 72 Shoulder Season

Agnes Gorge

Location	North Cascades National Park / Glacier Peak Wilderness.
Distance	5.0-mile round trip.
Elevation gain	300'.
Maps	Green Trails No. 81–McGregor Mountain; Trails Illustrated No. 223–North Cascades National Park Complex; US Forest Service–Glacier Peak Wilderness.

OPINION

Like a dramatic novel, the convulsing cataract in Agnes Gorge and the appearance of rugged peaks above have the power to roil your emotions. Like a storybook, the level approach through pretty forest dappled with wildflowers is delightful. White, three-petaled trilliums and six-petaled dogwood are abundant late-spring through mid-June. Paintbrush, red-and-yellow columbine, and orange tiger lilies abound. Also look for the scarce, timid, fuschia-colored calypso orchid.

Don't just dash in for a quick peek. Allow time to sit beside the chasm. Gorge your senses. Get comfy on a rock slab above the water's edge and let the never-ending flow mesmerize you. Close your eyes and let your imagination identify the sound. You might hear the thundering surge of a rocket blasting off. Be content with what you can safely see; it's difficult to get a full view of the longer, major falls.

You can usually hike here by late May. The short distance and minimal elevation gain make this a pleasurable walk for even inexperienced or out-of-shape hikers. It's especially worthwhile during a rainy spell. Since most of what you see here is close, poor visibility won't diminish your enjoyment.

FACT

By Car

See the Chelan Lakeshore description (Trip 108) for directions to the Lake Chelan boat landing.

By Boat & Bus

See the Chelan Lakeshore description to learn about boat travel to Stehekin and shuttle-bus connections for continuing up-valley. From Stehekin Landing, near the north end of Lake Chelan, take a shuttle bus 11 miles north to High Bridge. Cross the bridge and walk up the road. In 0.1 mile pass the signed Pacific Crest Trail, which follows Agnes Creek upstream. Just beyond is a campground on the right. It has a cooking shelter, bear poles for hanging food, tables, and pit toilets. Walk the road 0.1 mile farther to the signed Agnes Gorge trailhead, at 1700 feet. The wood sign is small, at ground level, and on the west side of the road.

On Foot

The trail generally heads southwest, initially ascending 240 feet in 0.3 mile. Near the beginning, McGregor Peak is visible behind you, to the north. The trail then contours on the north side of the gorge. Enter Glacier Peak Wilderness at 1.4 miles. At 2.0 miles Agnes Mountain becomes visible to the southwest. At 2.5 miles, 2000 feet, arrive at the chasm, waterfall, and rapids. Just before the main trail ends, there are a couple campsites and various spur paths branching off. You can see the old platform where a cable car used to carry people across the abyss. Continue on the trail angling right, dropping to the water's edge.

Trip 73 Shoulder Season

Newhalem Creek

Location	Ross Lake National Recreation Area / North Cascades National Park.
Distance	9.0-mile round trip.
Elevation gain	800'.
Maps	Green Trails No. 48–Diablo Dam; Trails Illustrated No. 223–North Cascades National Park Complex.

OPINION

Though it's inviting—there it is on the map, starting conveniently near the National Park visitor center, apparently following the creek—it's the least enjoyable of the shoulder-season trips. It follows an old logging road through thin, scraggly re-growth. You seldom see the creek. The trail has long been unmaintained, so it could be brush choked. Volunteers have been working on it, however, so ask at the visitor center how far the trail has been cleared. Meanwhile, if you're here and desperate to give your lungs and legs a mountain workout, it's another option. At least the huge, moss-covered boulders at the trailhead are impressive, conjuring images from the Tolkien trilogy and reminding you of the mystery and delight of wilderness.

Even in early spring, when there's snow on the trail after a mile or so, you can plunge in as far as the concrete bridge at 1.6 miles. There you can pause in the open, the clear water rushing beneath you, and pretend you're one of the happy green plants thriving quietly on the moist rocks.

If you crash and bash your way beyond the bridge, near 3 miles the tantalizing profiles of Big Devil Peak and Teebone Ridge appear above the east side of the drainage. Little Devil Peak is farther south. Anyone who proceeds beyond 3 miles deserves a medal for tenacity. Our advice: invest your energy elsewhere, on a worthier goal, until the trail has been re-established.

FACT

By Car

Exit Highway 20 in Newhalem, as if going to the National Park visitor center. From the bridge over the Skagit River, drive 0.6 mile then turn left onto the gravel road before reaching the visitor parking lot. You'll see a sign NEWHALEM CREEK TRAIL. The trailhead is at road's end: 2.4 miles, 1000 feet.

On Foot

After 15 minutes, the trail ventures close to the creek, then swerves back into the woods. Earlier than late May, you'll only be able to walk part way up—unless you wear snowshoes or don't mind post-holing. After crossing a cement bridge to the east side at 1.6 miles, the trail parallels the creek, about 200 feet above it, until dropping to the water's edge and a campground at trail's end, 4.5 miles, 1800 feet.

Trip 74 Shoulder Season

Stetattle Creek

Location	Ross Lake National Recreation Area / North Cascades National Park.
Distance	8.2-mile round trip.
Elevation gain	1100'.
Maps	Green Trails No. 16–Ross Lake, No. 48– Diablo Dam; Trails Illustrated No. 223– North Cascades National Park Complex.

OPINION

Come mid-October, when snow cloaks slopes above, and you're wondering "what now?" here's one answer: an enchanting trail up Stetattle Creek. The fall colors lighten this densely forested canyon. Of course, it's also a good choice in early spring. Either time of year, the deep, generous pools will make you wish for a hot summer day, when you might have the guts to plunge into the clear, frigid water. Though you soon leave the stimulation of the creek, ancient trees and lush carpets of baby ferns will continue to fill your senses.

When you finish the hike, drive farther east to the lookout above Diablo Lake for a bird's-eye look at the valley you penetrated. You'll again be reminded how minute we are in the midst of mountains.

FACT

By Car

Drive Highway 20 through the National Park to the Diablo-townsite turnoff, 5.1 miles northeast from Newhalem's eastern edge, or 4.3 miles northwest from Colonial Creek Campground on Diablo Lake. At the west side of the highway bridge over Gorge Lake, turn northeast toward Diablo townsite. Park in the pullout on the right immediately after the green bridge, at 900 feet.

On Foot

You'll see the trail across the road on the northeast side, sneaking behind a row of houses. It stays east of Stetattle Creek and generally heads northwest. The trail hugs the creek for 0.75 mile, then ascends the hillside. It reaches 1600 feet at 1.5 miles. You get a glimpse of Davis Peak, east across the canyon. The trail never returns to the creek's edge, but it does cross three tributaries before reaching what will be the final destination for most people: Dale Creek. It's the fifth drainage, if you count the one that's usually dry. You'll recognize Dale Creek by the small waterfall pouring over a striated rock wall into a pool. Beyond Dale Creek, 0.6 mile of very sketchy trail runs through deadfall and brush. Where trail peters out, blazes of pink or orange ribbons lead down to Stetattle Creek. The way is fairly steep and there's no path through the thick undergrowth.

Trip 75 Shoulder Season

Pyramid Lake

Location	Ross Lake National Recreation Area.
Distance	4.2-mile round trip.
Elevation gain	1550'.
Maps	Green Trails No. 48–Diablo Dam; Trails Illustrated No. 223–North Cascades National Park Complex.

OPINION

Strong, committed hikers should consider this walk merely an appetizer or aperitif. Even in early season, enjoy it before your major hike for the day, or after—if you still have energy and are up for a quick jaunt. It's so short and unmoving, only beginning hikers or families with young children will find it a satisfying main course.

If you want to spend time relaxing at the pond (it's too dinky to be a lake), plan to arrive early morning or late afternoon. The pond is so small you can barely spot it on the map and only a fraction of its shore provides sitting space. If two or three hikers are there, anyone else who arrives will feel like an invader. We had it to ourselves, but on the return trip passed five parties coming up. It was laughable. What were they all going to do—choose straws to see who got to stand beside the water?

The pond, however, does have its merits. It's propped in a rocky bowl with two impressively steep sides. Mighty Pyramid Peak looms above. The logs floating in the beautiful green water have micro-gardens sprouting on them. And for a pond, it's pretty deep.

A pleasant forest walk on a well-maintained trail leads you to the pond at the foot of the 7182-foot peak. If you've driven Highway 20 in clear weather, while crossing the Thunder Arm of Diablo Lake you've certainly seen Pyramid Peak. It's a sky-piercer.

Don't bother visiting the pond on a rainy day; you'll miss

seeing the peak. Instead, hike up nearby Stetattle Creek (Trip 74) for a more memorable forest experience.

FACT

By Car

From the Diablo-townsite turnoff on Highway 20, drive 0.9 mile east to a pullout on your left (north) at milepost 127.5. Or if you're heading west, drive 3.4 miles from Colonial Creek Campground on Diablo Lake. The trailhead sign is on the south side of the road, at 1100 feet.

On Foot

The trail immediately switchbacks to the left, where you can look down on the highway and north across to the Stetattle Creek drainage and glacier-clad Davis Peak. A posted description states that the lake was created by an ancient landslide. No camping is allowed along the trail or at the lake.

Climb steeply for a short way through an old burn area of lodgepole pine. Thick salal borders the trail most of its length. After 0.8 mile, the way levels somewhat in a narrow, shallow valley, where dainty Pyramid Creek glides beneath cedar giants. At 1.4 mile, the trail deposits you at a wide, flat area beside the creek. Continue 60 feet farther along the east (left) bank to where the creek narrows. Find an easy place to cross here. The way is difficult to decipher on the needly, twiggy surface, but if you now hug the west (right) bank while walking 50 feet upcreek, you'll spot the rooty trail again. It soon resumes determinedly uphill, gaining most of the elevation in the last mile. Reach the lake at 2.1 miles, 2650 feet.

Pyramid Lake

Trip 76 Shoulder Season

Ruby Creek

Location	Ross Lake National Recreation Area / Mt. Baker-Snoqualmie National Forest.
Distance	3.5 miles one way.
Elevation gain	300′ from the East Bank trailhead.
Maps	Green Trails No. 49–Mt Logan; Trails Illustrated No. 223–North Cascades National Park Complex; US Forest Service–Pasayten Wilderness.

OPINION

The Ruby Creek trail is a gem. It's beside or just above the creek nearly the whole way. When spring snowmelt turns the creek into a raging torrent, the sight and sound of wild whitewater floods your senses. It's a thrill.

Although the trail is rarely maintained and infrequently walked, it's easy to follow and presents no difficulties. It clings to the north side of the creek, which means the highway, above the opposite bank, is close and sometimes visible. Car noise, however, is obliterated by the water's roar.

Ruby is worth walking anytime, but you'll appreciate it most in early season, when runoff swells the creek. Try to squeeze it in one evening after you arrive in the mountains. Or combine it with other short trails nearby, like Stetattle Creek and Pyramid Lake, for a full day of hiking. Don't plan on fishing. That's prohibited to protect spawning, native rainbow trout.

FACT

By Car

This one-way hike links the Canyon Creek and East Bank trailheads. You can begin and end at either. Both are pullouts on the north side of Highway 20. East Bank is 8.2 miles east of the Colonial Creek Campround on Diablo Lake; Canyon Creek is 2.9 miles farther east, or 16.7 miles northwest of Rainy Pass.

On Foot

From the East Bank trailhead at 1800 feet, the trail drops 100 feet in 0.1 mile to a bridge across Ruby Creek. Turn right on the north side and follow the trail upstream beside the creek.

At 1.0 mile cross a bridged side stream and pass a sign indicating that you're leaving Ross Lake National Recreation Area and entering Okanogan National Forest. There's a small, primitive campsite here.

After clinging to the creek for a long way, the trail pulls back into the forest for 0.5 mile before returning to the creek, switchbacking up, then dropping to a big, old building on the left. Rounding a corner to the left, the trail leaves Ruby Creek and follows Canyon Creek upstream 0.1 mile. Here, at 3.3 miles, the trail to Devils Park and Jackita Ridge continues upstream; there's also an enormous footlog over Canyon Creek to the right. Cross the creek. Pass historic Beebe's cabin on the left. Pass the Canyon Creek trail, also on the left. Reach the bridge over Granite Creek 0.1 mile from the footlog. Cross the bridge, then turn right and follow the trail 0.1 mile downstream to Highway 20 and the Canyon Creek trailhead at 3.5 miles, 1900 feet.

Trip 77 Shoulder Season

Cedar Creek

Location	North Cascades Scenic Highway Area.
Distance	4.0-mile round trip to Cedar Creek falls.
Elevation gain	520'.
Maps	Green Trails No. 50–Washington Pass (shows trail beyond 2.8 miles); No. 51–Mazama; Trails Illustrated No. 223–North Cascades National Park Complex.

OPINION

Unmemorable lodgepole-and-deciduous forest is the predominant feature on this hike, until you get near the head of the valley, where larch abounds. Cedar Falls, at 2 miles, is what draws people here. It's quite a torrent, but there's nothing else of note until 5 miles up the valley, where avalanche paths have cleared the way and hikers can finally see where they are, between Silver Star and North Gardner mountains. In May, you can't count on the trail being snow-free beyond 4 miles and about 4300 feet elevation, so it's not an exceptional shoulder-season option.

As for backpacking here in mid-season, some locals proudly claim this is their favorite spot. We suspect they haven't ventured deeper into the North Cascades where the scenery climaxes. True, hiking Cedar Creek eventually has its rewards. But the obvious destination, Abernathy Pass, is accessible faster and easier from the North Lake trail (Trip 54), off the Twisp River Road, where you'll also find a variety of other worthwhile trails. So there's no compelling reason to hike here. We say leave this one to the locals. It's only a handy trail to know about if you're in the area and want to stretch your legs as far as the falls.

The best view on this hike is a mere 30 feet in from the trailhead, where you can gaze northeast at Goat Peak and Pasayten Wilderness. If you proceed, you'll appreciate the cheerful orange paintbrush and lavender penstemon decorating the trail. You can expect plenty of company at the falls, but not many people continue beyond. Neither should you. For a better early-season hike in this area, choose any of our other recommendations—like Driveway Butte (Trip 69), just across the highway.

FACT

By car

On Highway 20, drive 13.2 miles northeast of Washington Pass, or 2.7 miles southwest of the Early Winters Information Center, to the signed Cedar Creek turnoff. It's 0.3 miles east of the Klipchuck Campground turnoff. Turn south on Road 200 and drive 0.9 mile to the gravel pit and the signed trailhead at 3000 feet.

On foot

The trail is well defined and easy to follow, but the trailhead sign incorrectly states the elevation gain to Cedar Falls as 960 feet. The Green Trails map shows the falls to be at 3520 feet, so the 2.0-mile hike to the falls entails only a 520-foot gain. Two small campsites with firepits are next to Cedar Falls. If you were to continue, you'd reach Abernathy Pass at 9.6 miles, 6400 feet.

Trip 78 Shoulder Season

Lost River

Location	Okanogan National Forest / Pasayten Wilderness.
Distance	8.0-mile round trip.
Elevation gain	300' in, 100' out.
Maps	Green Trails No. 50–Washington Pass, No. 51–Mazama; Trails Illustrated No. 223–North Cascades National Park Complex; US Forest Service–Pasayten Wilderness.

OPINION

If you're coming to the east side of the North Cascades for early-season hiking, the trail along Lost River is a good choice. As we explained in the West Fork Methow River description (Trip 80), the excellent free camping in the Methow River valley makes a weekend here worthwhile.

Except for a few short stretches, this hike doesn't require you to beat your way through brush. That's an important consideration when choosing an early-season trail, because only a few are cleared by trail crews, and those usually not until summer. Brush and deadfall make many hikes, like the nearby West Fork Methow River, frustrating and unpleasant.

Looking at a map, you might assume you'll see the river the whole length of the trail. Not so. As its name suggests, Lost River is rarely visible to the hiker. The trail is usually about 250 feet above and well back from this powerhouse torrent, though you'll certainly hear it and you will get at least three good views of it. Instead, the highlight on this walk is the mighty, orange-hued ponderosa pines along the way. You'll recognize these magnificent trees by their jigsaw-puzzle-bark and long needles in bundles of three. Also pause to notice the local messengers of spring: tiny, pink, fairyslipper Calypso orchids and purplish-blue larkspur.

In an average-snowfall year, Lost River is hikeable in late April.

After May, it's a furnace here. Even during May, you'll be cooler if you start later in the day. Because the trail is on an east-facing slope, by mid-afternoon it's shaded from the sun. To avoid heat and glare and still comfortably complete the round trip to Eureka Creek before sundown, start around 3 P.M.

The confluence of Eureka Creek and Lost River is the obvious destination. You can hike uphill another 15 minutes for a good view south down the Lost River valley toward Gardner Mountain, but there's no need to go farther. Few people continue the brutal ascent to Monument Creek. Few people should. It's for masochistic hermits who'll endure misery to achieve solitude.

The hillside above the confluence of Eureka Creek and Lost River is one of few places we've encountered ticks in the North Cascades. They thrive in hot, dry, brushy areas, particularly on sunny slopes scattered with rocks and deadfall, which is exactly what you'll find in areas off the Methow Valley. The insidious little beasts are generally a problem only for a few weeks in early spring, but that's the time to hike here. So check yourself for ticks occasionally along the way. And inspect your entire body, especially your scalp, after the hike. Ticks tend to crawl around for a couple hours before choosing a dark, moist spot to burrow in and commence dining. That should give you enough time to conduct a successful search-and-destroy mission.

FACT

By Car

Drive Highway 20 to the signed Mazama turnoff, 13.2 miles northwest of Winthrop, or 1.5 miles southeast of the Early Winters Information Center. Turn northeast, and just after crossing the Methow River bridge turn left (northwest) at a T-intersection onto Harts Pass Road 5400 (marked 54 on the Green Trails map). Pavement ends 6.7 miles from Mazama, just after the bridge over Lost River. In 0.2 mile farther, turn right at the sign MONUMENT TRAIL NO. 484. Drive 0.1 mile to the trailhead parking at 2400 feet.

On Foot

The first view of the river is at 0.5 mile, followed by a stand of ponderosa pines. The trail then continues northeast away from the water. You ascend 300 feet in the first mile and lose 100 feet in the second.

The tread is soft through forest for about 2 miles. Then it gets rocky as it passes close beneath the eastern wall of the canyon. At about 2.5 miles, you might encounter a narrow but tricky creek crossing. In late afternoon during spring runoff, this tributary of Lost River can be too swollen to leap over. At 3.0 miles you can see the river again. Then your trail proceeds over an extensive rockslide. At 3.25 miles you enter Pasayten Wilderness.

The confluence of Eureka Creek and Lost River is at 4.0 miles, 2600 feet. Cross the bridge over Eureka Creek to reach the campsites on the point. For a view of Gardner Mountain to the south, stay on the trail and climb 250 feet in 0.3 mile. Beyond, the trail ascends north 4400 feet up the ridge between the two drainages, reaching 7300-foot Pistol Pass in 10.75 miles, then descending northeast to Monument Creek.

West Fork Methow River valley (Trip 80)

Trip 79 Shoulder Season

Robinson Creek

Location	Okanogan National Forest / Pasayten Wilderness.
Distance	8.0-mile round trip to the second crossing of Robinson Creek.
Elevation gain	400'.
Maps	Green Trails No. 50–Washington Pass; Trails Illustrated No. 223–North Cascades National Park Complex; US Forest Service–Pasayten Wilderness.

OPINION

It's easy to appreciate the dry east side of the North Cascades in spring. While snow is still depressingly deep in the heart of the range, here you can hike. Not far, but enough to feel invigorated. The clear skies, dusty trails, sparse forest undergrowth, and moss-free rocks can be cathartically refreshing after a long, wet, cold winter. But by mid-summer, it's way too hot here. That's when you should be exploring farther west, where the temperatures are cooler and the scenery more dramatic.

It's possible to hike 4 miles to the second Robinson Creek bridge as early as mid-May. The big boulders are a good place to break for lunch and then turn around. The next stretch is through thick forest, on a rooty, viewless trail that will likely be snow-covered or muddy in early season. In fall, it can be worth continuing to the meadows and brushy avalanche paths beyond—but not during hunting season, when the gun toters are out.

Usually by early June you can hike the 9 miles to Robinson Pass. The last 3 miles wander through flower-filled meadows. But unless you're craving solitude and a long loop, don't even think about continuing beyond the pass. The 43-mile trip through the valleys of Robinson Creek, the Middle Fork Pasayten River, Monument Creek, and Lost River is dull. The few significant peaks en route—Osceola, Carru, and Lago—are the only potential adrenalin boosters. The wilting heat, interminable trees, grueling ascents, and consistently mediocre scenery would, for most people, nullify whatever pleasure they might derive from being alone. Besides, the passes on the loop are snow-free only in prime hiking season, which is your brief, precious, once-a-year opportunity to indulge in the Premier and Outstanding trips.

To survey the surrounding high country after the road is snow-free (usually August), drive over Harts Pass to the road's end parking lot at 7280 feet. Then walk the final 0.2 mile to the lookout on 7440-foot Slate Peak, where the Pasayten Wilderness panorama is vast. Gazing down into the nearby valleys—the Middle Fork Pasayten River (northeast) and Robinson Creek (southeast)—you'll understand why we recommend other trails for prime hiking-season.

FACT

By Car

Drive Highway 20 to the signed Mazama turnoff, 13.2 miles northwest of Winthrop, or 1.5 miles southeast of the Early Winters Information Center. Turn northeast, and just after crossing the Methow River bridge turn left (northwest) at a T-intersection onto Harts Pass Road 5400 (marked 54 on the Green Trails map). Pavement ends 6.7 miles from Mazama, just after the bridge over Lost River. At 8.6 miles, cross Robinson Creek, then look for the turnoff on your right for Robinson Creek trail 478 and a small Forest Service campground, at 2600 feet.

To continue to Slate Peak, drive to the fork at 9.1 miles from Mazama. Go right to Harts Pass at the sign RIVER BEND CAMPGROUND ¼ ; METHOW TR. NO. 480 ¾ ; HARTS PASS 10. From Harts Pass, continue right (northeast) on the Slate Peak road approximately 3 miles to the road's end parking lot.

On Foot

The trail ascends north in narrow Robinson Creek canyon to a creek crossing near 1.25 miles. Then the way angles northwest. In 2.7 miles the forest opens, allowing views northeast up Beauty Creek to waterfalls and 7935-foot Beauty Peak. Robinson Mountain is also visible directly north. At 4.0 miles reach the second crossing of Robinson Creek. The way continues through forest and at 6.0 miles reaches the beginning of vast meadowlands interspersed by forest. Robinson Pass is at 9.0 miles, 6200 feet.

Ridge roaming is usually easy from the pass, depending on how
much snow remains.

North end of Robinson Creek Valley

Trip 80 Shoulder Season

West Fork Methow River

Location	Okanogan National Forest.
Distance	4.6-mile round trip.
Elevation gain	negligible.
Maps	Green Trails No. 50–Washington Pass; Trails Illustrated No. 223–North Cascades National Park Complex.

OPINION

Hiking the West Fork of the Methow is worthwhile only because other shoulder-season trails and excellent, free Forest Service campgrounds are nearby. And we recommend just the first 2.3
miles of this trail, beyond which it's too brushy and boring. Such
a short round trip hardly qualifies as a hike, but if you're eager to
get out after a long winter, or if a jaunt is all your little ones are up
to, visit the area for a weekend of camping and include the West
Fork on your activity list, along with Lost River (Trip 78) or
Robinson Creek (Trip 79).

Here, on the dry, sunny, east side of the North Cascades, car
camping is a joy. Many of the sites are under pines and beside
creeks. And you'll find it pleasantly warm even in early spring.
Early May is a good time to come. By then, the first 3 or 4 miles of
this trail and others departing the Methow Valley should be
passably snow-free. If you're really eager, try them in late April
after a winter of average snowfall. Unless you're a desert rat, June
is out. Even late May can be seriously hot.

Don't expect a lot from the West Fork trail. The first mile is
away from the river, but offers views south of Delancy Ridge,
snow-covered in spring. You walk beside the river the second
mile, as you cross a broad rockslide. Watch closely for rattle-
snakes. Peaks are visible most of the way to Trout Creek. It's
tempting to assume the rest of the trail will be as pleasant, but it's
not. From this point on, you might have to battle deadfall. Since
you'll be unable to get any views out of the forest, the shin-

scratching brush and thigh-thwacking branches will have you also battling with your motivation to continue.

The trail continues, of course, but the question is, should you? No. We suggest an immediate about-face at Trout Creek. Spend more time back at your campsite, or better yet, go hike in Lost River canyon, where you'll see gigantic ponderosa pines. It's easy for fit hikers to cover 4.6 miles round trip on the West Fork and 8 miles on Lost River in a single day, since they're so close and both are nearly level.

FACT

By Car

Drive Highway 20 to the signed Mazama turnoff, 13.2 miles northwest of Winthrop, or 1.5 miles southeast of the Early Winters Information Center. Turn northeast, and just after crossing the Methow River bridge turn left (northwest) at a T-intersection onto Harts Pass Road 5400 (marked 54 on the Green Trails map). Pavement ends 6.7 miles from Mazama, just after the bridge over Lost River. After you pass Ballard Campground on your left, at 9.1 miles you'll come to a junction and a sign RIVER BEND CAMP-GROUND ¼; METHOW TR. NO. 480 ¾; HARTS PASS 10. Go straight, on the left fork. It's another 0.8 mile to the 2700-foot trailhead and free campground.

On Foot

Trail 480 immediately crosses Rattlesnake Creek on a footlog and heads southwest. After 1.0 mile, the well-defined trail hugs the riverbank and crosses rockslides for about half a mile. It then enters an area of cottonwoods, grass and flowers. At 2.3 miles a dilapidated bridge crosses Trout Creek. Lose sight, and sometimes sound, of the river if you continue. Expect deadfall; the thin, deciduous trees and small pines don't hold up under heavy snow. At 3.2 miles another rockslide offers a momentary reprieve from bushbashing through the scraggly forest. Immediately after the rockslide, the trail briefly approaches the river. There are possible campsites here. Beyond, deadfall, brush, and possible snow until June make travel tedious.

Trip 81 Shoulder Season

Boulder River

Location	Boulder River Wilderness / Mt. Baker-Snoqualmie National Forest.
Distance	8.6-mile round trip.
Elevation gain	500'.
Maps	Green Trails No. 77–Oso, No. 109–Granite Falls.

OPINION

The scenic splendor of the Boulder River gorge and waterfalls surprised us, because the trail begins by swinging across from a clearcut. Hang in there. It's well worth walking this all-year trail at least to the tremendous cascade at 1.2 miles. If it's raining, that's even better: the tumbling waters will beat at full volume, and there are no distant views to be had here even on a clear day. Just wear your most water resistant boots and expect lots of muddy stretches. Another reason to save this one for a rainy day is its popularity, especially in spring when higher trails are un-hikable. Walk in the rain and you'll have more solitude. There were 12 vehicles at the trailhead on a drizzly Sunday in early April.

FACT

By Car

Drive Highway 530 northeast 19.6 miles from the Arlington bridge, or west 8.2 miles from Darrington. Turn south at milepost 41 onto Road 2010. You'll pass the French Creek Campground at 1.0 mile. The trailhead parking area is at 3.6 miles, 900 feet.

On Foot

After initially passing a clearcut, the trail enters regrown forest at 0.25 mile and virgin forest at 0.75 mile. Directly across from the mighty waterfall and cascades at 1.2 miles, a path leads down to the river. At 1.4 miles, there's another waterfall. After these falls, dense forest separates the trail from the river until you reach the end of trail at Boulder Ford, 4.3 miles, 1400 feet. There are several campsites here along the river.

Some North Cascades trails are just roots

Trip 82 Shoulder Season

Beaver Ponds

Location	Mount Baker-Snoqualmic National Forest.
Distance	7.0-mile round trip.
Elevation gain	200'.
Map	Green Trails No. 111–Sloan Peak.

OPINION

A Forest Service sign on the roadside labels this BEAVER LAKE TRAIL. The beavers weren't *that* ambitious. There's no lake. Just ponds. Tiny, marshy ponds. But they're interesting enough while you're eagerly awaiting the summer-hiking season or bidding it adieu in fall. And the nearly level trail, following an old railroad bed, is pleasant the whole way. So we feel this shoulder-season option stands on its own merits, without the exaggerated sales hype.

The soothing, peaceful beauty here is punctuated by giant cedars, the powerful Sauk River, and stimulating glimpses of high peaks. Frogs and songbirds voice nature's paeans. You'll hear the buzz of flies too, even in spring. Yikes!—harbingers of the August plague.

In April, the bright yellow hoods of skunk cabbage flowers, resembling hungry pelicans, and pink Nootka roses brighten the forest and bayou-like bogs. After you leave the trees along the riverbank, you soon pass picturesque railroad trestles and come to an impressive beaver dam at the ponds. Be quiet and observant if you want to spot one of the critters.

Beyond the ponds, you cross a muddy, shallow slough on a double-log bridge that'll bring out the kid in you if you bounce on it. Don't turn back until you've entered the court of ancient monarchs: three magnificent cedars, rivaling those on the Olympic Peninsula. Wow! How could anyone destroy such noble beings?

FACT

By Car

From Darrington on Highway 530, drive the Mountain Loop Highway southeast 9.5 miles. Immediately past the Sauk River bridge, you'll see the sign BEAVER LAKE TRAIL on your right. Turn here, into the northwest-end trailhead parking lot, at 1000 feet.

To reach the southeast-end trailhead, drive another 2.5 miles. You'll see a sign depicting a hiker, just before a pullout on your right. There's also a small sign at the trailhead, which is just north of Lyle Falls Creek, at 1200 feet.

On Foot

You can walk this trail almost any day of the year. Within 10 minutes from the northwestern trailhead you'll see gravel bars in the river—a good place to warm away the winter blues on a sunny day. You can't reach the big ones without wading, but you can rockhop to the first sandy spit. The beaver ponds are at 1.75 miles. Near the giant cedars, at 3.0 miles, the trail turns northeast and ascends 200 feet to the Mountain Loop Highway and the southeastern trailhead. If all you want to see is the giant cedars, they are only a 1.0-mile round trip from this end.

Magnificent ancient cedar

Trip 83 Shoulder Season

White Chuck Bench

Location	Mt. Baker-Snoqualmie National Forest.
Distance	6.6-mile shuttle trip.
Elevation loss	600' starting from the east-end trailhead.
Map	Green Trails No. 111–Sloan Peak.

OPINION

On this pleasant, mostly level, year-round walk, don't expect dramatic mountain scenery. Do expect a rich rain forest, a luxuriant understory, and maybe a few of the fantasy creatures from the Disney film *Fern Gully*. Gargantuan, brilliant-green skunk cabbage thrives in the trailside bogs. Ferns adorn the moist soil. Small streams gurgle. And cedars tower overhead, eliciting "wows" of admiration.

Families with small kids will find the White Chuck Bench a good choice, as will hikers more interested in communing with nature than struggling up a peak. The trail's brief ups and downs add variety rather than challenge. Though you can fully appreciate the area even in the rain, walking here on a clear spring day with the sun's rays beaming through the forest canopy is wonderful.

Note the small signs WBT along the trail. Wilderness Buff Terrain? Or perhaps We Built This—a proud note from the Seattle Mountaineers and Volunteers for Outdoor Washington, who constructed the path. Actually it stands for White Chuck Bench trail. But walking lubricates the imagination; see what other interpretations you can think of.

If you're going only part way, definitely hike from the east end. That's where the trail stays close to the White Chuck River, and where you'll find the lush vegetation and ancient trees. The west half of the trail is less appealing—farther from the river and mostly in second-growth forest.

Two miles in from the east end, the trail is briefly swallowed in a swath of deadfall. Pick your way through and resume in the same direction on the other side. If you're not walking the whole

way, turn around here; the forest loses its magic beyond. Hiking
east, a WBT sign will help guide you through the deadfall.

FACT

By Car

From Darrington on Highway 530, drive the Mountain Loop
Highway southeast 9.5 miles. Shortly after you cross the Sauk
River bridge, the second road on the left is signed WHITE CHUCK
TRAIL, MEADOW MOUNTAIN TRAIL. Turn left (northeast) here, onto
White Chuck River Road 23, and drive 5.5 miles. Just after cross-
ing the White Chuck River on a cement bridge, turn left into the
small, primitive campground. This is the east-end trailhead, at
1600 feet. The trail is signed on the far side of the dirt lot.

To reach the west-end trailhead, after driving the Mountain
Loop Highway to the Sauk River bridge, take the first road left
and immediately cross the White Chuck River on a cement
bridge. On the other side, the White Chuck Campground is to
your right. Follow the pavement left. You'll pass the river-access
parking lot. The pavement turns to dirt in 0.25 mile. Turn right
200 feet farther on the unmarked dirt road. Follow it steeply
uphill 0.25 mile to a parking area beside a gravel pit. Or drive the
last, short steep pitch to a tiny parking area beside the signed
trailhead, at 1000 feet.

Can't muster a car shuttle? Hitching a ride is relatively easy
here and will enable you to walk the entire trail one-way. Leave
your car at the west-end trailhead. Walk back down the road,
cross the cement bridge, turn left on the highway, and stick your
thumb out at the beginning of Road 23. Tell your chauffeur you're
going 5.5 miles to the bridge over the White Chuck River. By
hitching in this direction, your car will be nearby in case you fail
to get a ride. And if you get picked up, then your car will be
waiting for you at the end of the hike. Hitching east also makes
sense because, if you start in the morning, there should be several
cars driving that way to the Kennedy Hot Springs trailhead (Trip
63).

On Foot

Starting at the east end, you'll soon notice small signs WBT
(White Chuck Bench trail) nailed high on trees. Several signs are
visible to hikers headed west. Fewer signs are posted for east-

bound hikers. And nearly all the signs are on the eastern half of the trail.

The trail is easy to follow and has no junctions. At 2.0 miles from the east-end trailhead, sort your way through 20 yards of deadfall that might still be there. At 4.0 miles, expect lots of grasping nettles for about 0.75 mile. At 5.4 miles, cross Black Oak Creek on a good footbridge. Arrive at the west end in 6.6 miles.

Mt. Pugh from White Chuck Bench Trail

Trip 84 Shoulder Season

Rainbow Loop

Location	Lake Chelan National Recreation Area / Wenatchee National Forest.
Distance	5.5 miles from Harlequin to the bakery.
Elevation gain	1000'.
Maps	Green Trails No. 82–Stehekin; Trails Illustrated No. 223–North Cascades National Park Complex; US Forest Service–Glacier Peak Wilderness.

OPINION

Adventure doesn't end with the boat trip up Lake Chelan. Stehekin is only the beginning. Even in early season, a short hike could amplify your experience. This one provides overlooks of the fiord-like lake and the lower Stehekin River. Valley fields 800 feet below are squeezed between soaring mountains.

One vantage is on a rock outcropping just south of the junction with the Boulder Creek trail. Another, better yet, requires a short, steep side trip up the Rainbow Creek trail. What you won't see anywhere along the Rainbow Loop trail is Rainbow Falls, because the trail crosses the creek too high. To visit the falls, walk in from the picnic area just off the Stehekin Road.

Though known as the Rainbow Loop, it's only a loop if you walk a couple miles on gravel road. The trail portion is above and roughly parallel to the road. You can hike in either direction. For a quick up-and-back, start at the south-end trailhead and reach a viewpoint sooner. If you're doing the whole loop, begin at the north end. The ascent is more gradual this way, and it builds to a scenic climax. From the south end of the trail, walk the road 15 minutes farther south to the Stehekin Bakery. They serve pizza and other lunch items, as well as delicious baked goods. From there it's only a $1 bus ride south to Stehekin Landing. The bus heading north can drop you back at Harlequin Campground. Or you can pretend you're a Luddite and walk the road 2.7 miles from the bakery to the campground.

The loop is usually snow-free from March through November. By June it can be blasted hot. With all the deciduous trees here, October can be vibrantly colorful and therefore just as enjoyable as early season. Nearby Harlequin Campground is a good base of operations. The tent sites are beneath cedar and hemlock, and many are beside the Stehekin River.

FACT

By Car

See the Chelan Lakeshore description (Trip 108) for directions to the Lake Chelan boat landing.

By Boat & Bus

See the Chelan Lakeshore description to learn about boat travel to Stehekin and shuttle-bus connections for continuing up-valley. From Stehekin Landing, on the north end of Lake Chelan, catch a shuttle bus north. The bakery (Stehekin Pastry Company) is at 2.0 miles, the south end of the Rainbow Loop is at 2.5 miles, Harlequin Campground is at 4.7 miles, and the north end of the Rainbow Loop is at 5.3 miles. The bus can drop you at any of these points. If you want to camp nearby, get off at Harlequin, then walk the road to the north end of the trail, at 1200 feet, where this description starts.

On Foot

Just before the road goes downhill, the Rainbow Loop north-end trailhead sign is on the right (east). It states that the distance to the south end of the loop is 5.0 miles. The trailhead sign at the south end claims this same distance is 4.6 miles. According to the Green Trails map, it's 4.4 miles. We think the shortest distance is more accurate.

The trail moderately switchbacks up through scraggly, mixed coniferous and deciduous forest. Views are minimal. You can hear Company Creek roaring and glimpse its gorge across the valley. At 2.2 miles the trail breaks into open meadow. You can hear Rainbow Falls, about 600 feet below. At 2.4 miles, 2200 feet, reach a signed junction on the east edge of the meadow. The Rainbow Creek trail goes left, later branching west (to Rainbow Lake, 7.8 miles from the junction) and north (to McAlester Pass at 7.9 miles). If you turn left at the meadow junction, a 0.5-mile,

400-foot ascent will earn you a view southeast to Lake Chelan and southwest across the valley to Tupshin and Devore peaks. This perch is slightly off-trail to the left where a switchback heads right.

To complete the Rainbow Loop, stay right at the meadow junction. You'll soon cross a bridge over Rainbow Creek. Fifteen yards beyond, a side trail on the right drops 50 yards to a campsite.

Reach another signed junction at 2.8 miles. The Boulder Creek trail goes left (west) to War Creek Pass. The Rainbow Loop continues right (south). Shortly after this junction come to a rock outcropping that affords views over the Stehekin Valley and southwest to Lake Chelan. The trail then descends 900 feet, reaching the Stehekin Road and the south end of the Rainbow Loop, at 4.4 miles.

Surveying Stehekin Valley

Trip 85 Shoulder Season
Company Creek

Location	Lake Chelan National Recreation Area.
Distance	4.4-mile round trip to view of Dark and Bonanza peaks.
Elevation gain	2000'.
Maps	Green Trails No. 81–McGregor Mtn, No. 82–Stehekin; US Forest Service–Glacier Peak Wilderness.

OPINION

One of your dayhike options near Stehekin, on Lake Chelan, is this no-nonsense trail. It quickly provides a lofty perspective of the Stehekin Valley—from Purple Mountain in the southeast, across to Rainbow Falls, northwest to craggy McGregor Mountain and beyond to Goode Mountain. Soon you'll reach a meadow bordered by a tremendous cliff plummeting into a deep gorge. For a short jaunt, turn around here. If spying distant peaks turns you on more than cozying up to a wild river, you'll prefer this mini-hike to the one into Agnes Creek Gorge. The Company Creek trail is steeper and rougher but leaves you with a much more complete feeling for the valley. You won't, however, achieve any sense of closure here, since you'll probably about-face long before the trail ends.

Looking southwest up Company Creek canyon from 2.2 miles in, you can see Company Glacier, 8504-foot Dark Peak, and 9511-foot Bonanza Peak, all about 8.5 miles distant. They look like one peak until you examine the massif closely enough to distinguish the ridgelines. Sable Ridge, dividing Company and Hilgard creeks, and Tupshin Peak, are impressive too, especially when snow-covered in early season. From this vantage, the contrast between the settled, cheerful little valley behind you and the vast, harsh, lonely wilderness before you, is striking.

The Company Creek trail is rarely traveled and almost never maintained. Past the wilderness boundary at 1.8 miles, the tread narrows, the canyon walls steepen, the brush takes over, and the

plot thickens. Clambering over all the deadfall is sometimes precarious. If solitude is your goal and difficulty no obstacle, carry
on. Intrepid, ambitious explorers can hike, scramble and bush-
bash to 6600-foot Hilgard Pass—a demanding 11.3 miles from the
trailhead.

FACT

By Car

See the Chelan Lakeshore description (Trip 108) for directions
to the Lake Chelan boat landing.

By Boat & Bus

See the Chelan Lakeshore description to learn about boat travel
to Stehekin and shuttle-bus connections for continuing up-valley.
From Stehekin Landing, on the north end of Lake Chelan, catch a
shuttle bus 4.7 miles north to Harlequin Campground. It's on the
west side of the Stehekin River, at 1200 feet.

On Foot

From Harlequin Campground, walk the gravel road northwest
0.6 mile. You'll pass several homes before reaching Company
Creek and the Stehekin powerhouse. Cross the bridge and continue on the road another 100 yards to the signed trailhead on
your left (west).

The trail undulates southwest in rocky, open forest for 0.25
mile, then ascends steeply through open forest broken by grassy
slopes. At 0.75 mile attain a view south over Stehekin Valley and
Company Creek gorge. At 1.0 mile reach a meadow on the edge
of the gorge.

Enter Glacier Peak Wilderness at 1.8 miles. Proceed 0.4 mile
farther southwest across steep, open slopes, to a view of jagged
Dark Peak and, a bit east and behind it, Bonanza Peak. Beyond 2.3
miles expect to contend with deadfall.

Reach Cedar Camp at 3.5 miles. An unnamed camp is at 5.0
miles, near where you must ford Company Creek if you want to
continue to Hilgard Pass. But that's not a shoulder-season trip,
and in prime hiking season there are many superior options.

BACKPACK TRIPS

Extensive meadows along the Heather Trail

Trip 86
Heather Trail

Location	Manning Provincial Park.
Distance	26.0-mile (42.0-km) round trip to Nicomen Ridge; 16.8-mile (27.0-km) round trip to Kicking Horse Camp.
Elevation gain	2130' (650 m) going in, 1443' (440 m) going out; 1150' (350 m) going in, 705' (215 m) going out.
Maps	The free B.C. Parks brochure–Manning Provincial Park; Manning Park and Skagit Valley Rec Area topo printed by the B.C. Ministry of Environment.

OPINION

Glorious meadows thick with flowers keep going and going, like the Energizer bunny. The challenge of the Heather trail isn't steepness; it's identifying all the blossoms you'll see if you're here mid-July to mid-August. Though not spectacular, the scenery is grand, similar to the Beartooth Wilderness, near Yellowstone. In clear weather you can see vast distances across rolling terrain with snowcapped peaks far to the west and south. Frequent stops to gaze at the sweeping horizon and appreciate the kaleidoscopic flora will slow your progress on what would otherwise be a speedy trip.

Prepare to dodge people on this heavily used trail. Only two-and-a-half hours' drive from Vancouver, these highland meadows are a popular weekend destination. You'll leave many hikers behind after Buckhorn Camp and still more after First Brother Mountain. Try to come mid-week.

B.C. Parks maintains this trail meticulously, trying to forestall further erosion. Wood chips cover the tread part way. You'll also find wood tent platforms, trenches and pipes diverting water, and heavy-duty slat bridges over minor drainages that anywhere else would seem ridiculous. The enormous signs WILDERNESS CAMP are oxymorons. With the hubbub of so many people, the area feels more like a city park than wilderness, until you're past Kicking Horse Camp—at least a five-hour walk. But just beyond the rather civilized trail, it is wild, and there could be bears—even grizzlies—so take all the standard precautions. And bring a stove. Fires are not permitted anywhere on the Heather trail.

First Brother is a good destination for a dayhike, but an overnight backpack trip is the way to savor the area and enjoy the subalpine meadows beyond Kicking Horse Camp. On a two-day trip, strong hikers can pitch their tent at Kicking Horse by early afternoon, walk to Nicomen Ridge and back carrying only fanny packs, then hike out the next day.

Don't be tempted to exit via the Grainger Creek trail from Nicomen Lake. Even if you could arrange a shuttle between trailheads, you'd be in forest the entire last day and you'd miss repeating one of the most amazing meadowland walks in the North Cascades.

FACT

By Car

Drive B.C. Highway 3 to Manning Park. At 5.8 miles (9.3 km) southeast of Allison Pass, across the highway from the Manning Park Lodge, turn north onto the road signed CASCADE LOOKOUT. Drive 9.3 miles (15.0 km) to Blackwall Peak's farthest north parking lot, at 6400 feet (1950 meters).

On Foot

The trail leaves the northeast side of the Blackwall Peak parking lot and immediately passes the outhouses. Follow the signed Viewpoint Loop north. In ten minutes, where the loop turns sharply left back to the parking lot, continue straight (northeast) to descend off Lone Man Ridge. In places, the trail is quite wide. It's on an old fire-access road for 3.1 miles (5 km), dropping 400 feet (125 meters) to Buckhorn Camp. There's a creeklet just south.

The tent sites at Buckhorn are within view of the trail, but nicely separated from each other. Here and at Kicking Horse Camp (farther northwest) are wood tent platforms, which help preserve the groundcover, keep your tent from getting muddy, and even provide comfortable seating. If you have trouble anchoring your tent to the platform, try moving the screw-in hooks.

From Buckhorn, ascend northwest through an old burn. Starting at 4.0 miles (6.4 km), wind through gently rolling subalpine meadows. Frosty Mountain and other peaks are now visible to the southwest. Typical North Cascades wildflowers, such as lupine and paintbrush, are profuse here. Look in seeps for the less common white bog orchid and elephant's head. The bog orchid resembles the flying nun's hat. It has 10 to 30 tiny flowers on a green stem up to 25 inches tall. The stem and flowers of the elephant's head are pink to reddish. The head and trunk of the elephant are only fingernail size. There are about 6 to 12 rows of heads around the terminal end of the 8- to 15-inch stem.

At 5.0 miles (8.0 km), pass the Bonnevier trail forking right (southeast). Continue straight (northwest) and walk under 7029-foot (2143-meter) Big Buck Mountain. You can soon see 7452-foot (2272-meter) First Brother Mountain peeking over the ridge to the north. (The 1990 Ministry of Environment map labels it Three Brothers Mtn, but the 1993 B.C. Park map identifies it accurately as First Brother Mtn.) You get a clear view of First Brother's talused summit ridge from a saddle below its southwestern arm, where the trail skims the edge of a dropoff. East you can see the low forested mountains of the southern Interior Plateau.

After a brief ascent, at 6.2 miles (10.0 km) reach the side trail (not shown on the topo map) leading 0.6 mile (1.0 km) to the summit of First Brother. Even without going to the summit, you get a good view south to Frosty Mountain and southwest to Hozomeen Mountain. The main trail, continuing northwest, then skirts the slopes of Second and Third Brother mountains—both slightly lower than their more popular sibling. In the basin just north of Second Brother, about 1 mile past the side trail up First Brother, is a creek.

From the saddle below Third Brother, the trail descends 490 feet (150 meters) into a basin. Kicking Horse Camp is at 8.4 miles (13.5 km). It has 8 tent platforms well off the trail to the left. Some sites have views of Third Brother. A creeklet crosses the main trail 0.3 mile east of camp.

At 9.0 miles (14.5 km), the trail begins the ascent out of the Kicking Horse basin through rolling subalpine meadows. At 11.2 miles (18.0 km), drop 246 feet (75 meters) into a forested bowl only to regain that elevation climbing up the other side. At 11.7 miles (18.8 km) pass two tarns. The trail levels out here, becoming faint and narrow. Continuing in subalpine forest, pass a third and fourth tarn. Water is probably available here all summer. Slightly off trail to the right is a view east across the Copper Creek drainage toward Cathedral Park. Top out on Nicomen Ridge at 13.0 miles (21.0 km).

The scenery beyond Nicomen Ridge sends a clear message: you've hit the end of the North Cascades. Low, rolling, forested mountains spread north and east. If you're turning around here, first follow the trail far enough down the north end of the ridge to get a peek at Nicomen Lake, to the northwest. The lake and campground are 1.3 miles (2.1 km) and a drop of 655 feet (200 meters) below the ridge.

It's possible to make this a one-way trip by descending the Grainger Creek trail 7.0 miles (11.5 km) west from Nicomen Lake to the junction at 3198 feet (975 meters) with the Hope Pass trail. Then go left (southwest) to parallel the Skaist River 5.0 miles (8.0 km) to Cayuse Flats on Highway 3. This makes a total shuttle trip of 26.3 miles (42.3 km). From there, it's difficult to hitchhike the 15.5 miles (25.0 km) to the Manning Park Lodge. And it takes a magic thumb to catch a ride all the way back up the Cascade Lookout road to the Blackwall Peak parking lot. A pre-arranged shuttle makes the one-way more feasible.

Tent platform at Kicking Horse Camp

Trip 87

Horseshoe Basin /
Boundary Trail

Location	Pasayten Wilderness / Okanogan National Forest.
Distance	12.4-mile round trip to Horseshoe Pass; 26.4-mile round trip to Teapot Dome.
Elevation gain	1200' to Horseshoe Pass; 1400' to Teapot Dome.
Maps	Green Trails No. 21–Horseshoe Basin, No. 20–Coleman Peak; US Forest Service–Pasayten Wilderness.

OPINION

Horseshoe Basin is unique. The attraction of most mountain terrain is rugged, vertical topography. Here it's a vast, ethereal expanse of rolling meadowlands. Alpine destinations are often distant, but this one's just 4.5 gently-ascending miles from road's end. And while high-country trails are usually snow-covered until late July, consistently sunny skies and open, sparsely forested terrain make this one hikeable in late June, when the dazzling flower display begins.

Don't even think about dayhiking. Hoist your backpack and spend at least one night. Reaching this remarkable landscape only to leave immediately would be a wasted effort, because the approach is not scenic. It's only after the basin comes into view that this hike earns its Premier rating. You might want to sit and stare. You might want to explore. Probably both. So allow enough time.

The rounded summits will seduce you into roaming higher. Though the views on top are not spectacular, wandering at will in such openness is wonderful. Trekking farther west along the Boundary Trail is another temptation. From Horseshoe Basin it's 94 miles to Harts Pass. Teapot Dome is a satisfying destination for a 3- to 4-day trip. You'll have adequately sampled the area by

Joyous meadow-walking in Horseshoe Basin

then, but more is sometimes better. If you push on, the trail clings to the 7000-foot level as far as Cathedral Peak—a good turn-around point for a 5- or 6-day trip. Staying so high for so long is a rare delight in any mountain range. Upper Cathedral Lake, at the base of Amphitheater Mountain's granite cliffs, is an out-standing destination. Beyond Cathedral Peak the trail skulks in the forest for long periods.

You don't have to steel yourself for a staggering elevation gain or loss. In the 20 miles from the basin to Cathedral Peak, you lose only a few hundred feet in a couple places and gain only 1000 feet over Apex Pass. So you can relax and and enjoy the journey. Just go as far as you feel compelled, then camp wherever you want (with minimal impact, of course). Permits, reservations and rigid itineraries are not required here in Pasayten Wilderness, as they are in the National Park.

The initial four miles through scrawny lodgepole pines can be discouraging. Just press on. You'll soon burst into tundra mead-ows more like the Scottish Highlands than the craggy Cascades. Fields of luscious, lavender lupine and bright-yellow subalpine buttercup blanket the slopes. A closer look will reveal velvety, pink-plumed avens, and magenta shootingstars. Of course, you'll also see the ubiquitous, red Indian paintbrush.

Too bad the mosquitoes are so horrendous. Otherwise you could lollygag in the meadows for days. Given enough time in such a halcyon atmosphere, you might learn aromatherapy from the flowers or maybe even levitation from the cottonball clouds. But the reality is, without a steady, stiff breeze to keep the bloodsuckers down, it can be difficult to sit for long outside your tent. Take consolation in the fact that at least it doesn't rain much here, which might allow you to leave your tent fly off.

On the north side of Rock Mountain, a mile past Horseshoe Pass, you exit the meadows and enter dry, sparse, airy forest offering occasional open views. Dusty trail gives way to crushed gravel—very pleasant. Your eye is drawn to twisted, silver deadfall, instead of sweeping tundra. Granite slabs and outcroppings give the land sharper edges. From here on it's not a particular feature of the scenery that pulls you on, but rather your emotions, evoked by this expansive environment. You might sense a lightness, a peacefulness—very different from the solemnity you might experience in a deep valley, or the exhilaration you probably feel on a mountaintop.

Mountain bikes are not permitted in this fragile area. Riding all the way to Cathedral Peak in a day would be a blast, but you can get an adrenalin rush lots of other places. Horseshoe Basin deserves to be appreciated more fully.

FACT

By Car

From British Columbia's Highway 3, enter the U.S. at the Chopaka-Nighthawk border crossing. Continue south to Loomis. From within Washington, travel north on Highway 97 to Ellisforde, then drive 12.0 miles northwest to Loomis.

In Loomis, drive 0.3 mile through the hamlet to a green sign at the T-intersection. Go right 1.9 miles to Toats Coulee Road 39 and turn left onto it near the valley bottom, before the highway turns sharply right. On Road 39, 1.3 miles from the highway, ignore the ascending dirt road; continue straight on pavement. At 7.9 miles go left at the signed junction, toward Iron Gate trailhead. North Fork Campground is on the right at 8.2 miles. At 13.7 miles (milepost 36) reach a junction; turn right (northwest) onto Road (3900) 500. It's another 6, rough miles to the trailhead at Iron Gate campground, which is really just a parking lot and is not on a creek, 5800 feet. After July, water becomes scarce in this arid region. Bring enough in your vehicle so you can start the trip with full water bottles. Once on the trail, refill at every opportunity.

On Foot

A sign at the trailhead announces CLOSED TO BICYCLES AND HANG GLIDERS. The trail is initially an abandoned mining road. In 0.5 mile (marked 1.0 mile on the Green Trails 1979 map) stay straight at a junction. Right leads 2 miles to Deer Park, 5 miles to Fourteen Mile Camp. Twenty yards beyond the first junction is another. From here, the Clutch Creek trail leads southwest to a trail going northwest over Windy Peak. That longer route (not recommended) reaches Sunny Pass in 10.0 miles. So again, continue straight (northwest) toward Horseshoe Basin.

At 3.0 miles enter an open area of grass and flowers, then re-enter trees. After a steep stretch, the trail leaves lodgepole pine at 4.5 miles and enters Sunny Basin. You'll cross a creeklet just before arriving in the basin. There's a campground at 6900 feet, east of the trail, in trees, beside a small creek.

From Sunny Basin, grass and flowers are continuous to Horseshoe Basin and most of the 6.0 miles to Haig Mountain. At 5.0 miles you reach 7200-foot Sunny Pass. Here, and at many points along the Boundary Trail, you can look southwest to the jagged peak of 8685-foot Remmel Mountain. The multi-track trail on the left (the old mining road) completes the loop from Windy Peak to the southwest. Sunny Pass overlooks your immediate goal— Horseshoe Basin—and allows you to survey the tame, grassy peaks above it. Rock Mountain is in the northwest; Arnold Peak in the northeast. North 0.1 mile from Sunny Pass ignore the narrow, overgrown Albert Camp trail on the right.

Horseshoe Pass is at 6.2 miles, 7000 feet. In early season, there's a lovely creek here. There's also water at Smith Lake (reached by a trail leading 1.0 mile east from the pass). To continue on the Boundary Trail, go left (northwest) from Horseshoe Pass. In 1.0 mile you'll reach Louden Lake. Both lakes can dry up in late summer. You'll find comfortable campsites above the southwest shore of Louden Lake.

At 7.4 miles, at the northeast edge of Rock Mountain, there's a side trail leading north to pretty campsites in meadows beneath larch and whitebark pine trees. The main trail continues west

though open forest and low shrubs. Boulders and flowers decorate the hillsides.

A pond sits south of the trail at 9.8 miles. An otherwise inviting
campsite, it can be infested with mosquitoes. You might escape
them somewhat 2.2 miles farther, on the breezier, open slopes
south of Haig Mountain. A small creek (through early summer)
crosses the trail here, and there's a view southeast to Windy Peak.
The drawback is that flat spots for a tent are harder to find.

You gain and lose 100 feet a couple times between Horseshoe
Basin and the south side of Haig Mountain. The elevation varies
from 6900 to 7200 feet. The trail then drops 320 feet in 2.5 miles to
Teapot Dome, which is 7.0 miles southwest from Horseshoe Pass,
13.2 miles from the trailhead. There's a creeklet here in early
summer and flat campsites beneath the dome's southeast wall.
Granite outcroppings, boulders, and the silver skeletons of fallen
trees comprise the setting.

The terrain after Teapot Dome is similar to what you will
already have traversed between Rock and Haig mountains. The
easy-to-follow Boundary Trail has only one junction, 6.6 miles
after Teapot Dome, where trail 534 heads southeast along Tung-
sten Creek. Continue straight (northwest) toward Cathedral Pass,
gaining 1000 feet to Apex Pass en route. The trail crosses creeks
occasionally, but some are unreliable in late summer. Fill your
water bottles whenever you can. Reach 7600-foot Cathedral Pass
at 25.8 miles. Its vicinity is more sheerly vertical than any place
along the Boundary Trail this far. 8601-foot Cathedral Peak towers above to the north. Upper Cathedral Lake is 0.8 mile below
and southwest of the pass, at the base of Amphitheater Mountain's granite cliffs.

Trip 88   🦶🦶🦶🦶
Copper Ridge /
Chilliwack River / Whatcom Pass

Location	Mt. Baker Wilderness / North Cascades National Park.
Distance	34.5-mile loop.
Elevation gain	10160′.
Maps	Green Trails No. 14–Mt. Shuksan, No. 15–Mt. Challenger; Trails Illustrated No. 223–North Cascades National Park Complex.

OPINION

On Copper Ridge you'll witness exploding horizons. At Whatcom Pass you'll stand in awe of cloud-bursting Whatcom Peak and the heart-stopping Challenger Glacier. For those whose place of worship is the mountains, hiking this grand loop feels like a pilgrimage. Spiritual journeys, however, always pose tribulations. Here you must tramp many miles through viewless forest between the sacred sites.

Your trek begins in the Ruth Creek valley. Cliffs, waterfalls, avalanche greenery and snowfields will stoke your enthusiasm on the easy walk to Hannegan Pass. You then plunge past the colorful soils of ancient volcanoes into the headwaters of the Chilliwack River. From there, a burst of energy will vault you onto Copper Ridge, where you can see the trail scratching the ridge's back.

Fanatics pressed for time can dayhike the 20.4-mile round trip to the Copper Ridge Lookout, but backpacking is better. Beyond the lookout, the trail rides the sky, offering a string of supreme vistas that rival any in the range. The intricacies of the ridge itself are fascinating too. Copper Lake sits in a classic alpine cirque. The trail wiggles through fields of rectangular boulders, some resembling beds and chaise lounges, that entice you to drop your pack and sprawl. Eventually the ridge affords the closest view of mighty Mount Redoubt that non-climbers can enjoy. Then the good times are over, temporarily, as you descend into the Chilliwack River valley. Your knees take the brunt of this brutal, 3.8-mile, 3440-foot drop. Your legs will struggle to keep your ready-to-roll body upright.

After wading across the braided Chilliwack River, you face 8.7 miles—most of it forested, much of it level, little of it exciting—to Whatcom Pass, where the scenery will blow away your memory of the boring approach. Wander the slopes north of the pass for superior views of the peaks and glaciers and choice camping at the Tapto Lakes cross-country area. It's one mile and 600 feet above the trail, so allow at least an extra hour of daylight to get there.

If you must choose between the two scenic climaxes, go to Copper Ridge. Whatcom Peak and Challenger Glacier are visible from there, plus you'll see infinitely more. Also, by hiking out and back on the ridge instead of looping down along the Chilliwack River, you can avoid spending time in forest. Whether you go directly to Whatcom Pass or include it on the grand loop, you'll be in trees for the better part of two days. Still, the ideal plan is to hike it all, from Hannegan to Copper to Whatcom, then out.

Steep, rugged stretches of Copper Ridge typically hold snow until August. Don't go earlier unless you're properly equipped or certain the snow is gone. September is when you're most likely to get good weather for the four or five days you'll need to complete the loop. The Ruth Creek and Chilliwack River valleys are known for particularly thick swarms of black flies. That's another good reason to delay this hike until fall when they're gone. September is also when the trail is busiest, which means more competition for the limited campsites. From Boundary Camp on, you're in the National Park and need a permit to camp. Fires are not allowed on Copper Ridge.

Try to reach a National Park office in person the day before you start hiking, to make backcountry camping reservations. If you wait until just before you hit the trail, you're less likely to secure the sites you want. (For details, read the introductory section *Backcountry Permits*.) Here's the schedule most people prefer: first night at Silesia Camp/Egg Lake (8.2 miles) or Copper Lake (11.4 miles), second night at Indian Creek (19.7 miles), third night at Whatcom Camp (27.6 miles) or Tapto cross-country (about 28.5 miles), fourth night at U.S. Cabin Camp (34.8 miles), and out the fifth day. Rangers are strict about enforcing the permit system. To preserve the campgrounds, as well as the camping experience, they limit the number of tents at each campground to the number of designated sites—usually no more than two or three. If you can't keep to your pre-determined schedule (which is almost to be expected, since the unknown looms large in any wilderness) and you happen to encounter a ranger, explain your situation. You might meet one at the Copper Ridge Lookout. Ask about campsite availability. If necessary, the ranger will radio the park office for you and check the status of the campgrounds on the loop. You should also ask hikers you meet where they're planning to spend the night. You might find they too are off schedule and will be leaving a tent site empty where you want to camp. Most hikers pitch their tents by 5 P.M. If you arrive at a campground later than that, any vacant site will probably go unclaimed. Wait until dusk. If nobody shows, you're home free.

FACT

By Car

From the Glacier Public Service Center on Highway 542, drive 13.1 miles east. Just before the Nooksack River bridge, turn left (east) toward Hannegan Pass on Road 32. At the junction in 1.3 miles, stay left on Ruth Creek Road 32. At 5.4 miles reach Hannegan Campground and the trailhead at road's end, 3100 feet. On weekends, expect to see dozens of vehicles in the parking lot.

On Foot

Read Trip 23—Hannegan Pass for details about the first 4.1 miles. To proceed to Copper Ridge, descend the northeast side of the 5066-foot pass. The trail loses 500 feet in 0.7 mile, then crosses a rockslide and a creek. The white talus and grayish clay slope on the right (south) is an arm of Ruth Mountain. The slopes to the left (north) display colorful, striated soil. This is the headwaters valley of the Chilliwack River.

At 5.0 miles, 4480 feet, the trail forks at the boundary of North Cascades National Park. Left ascends through forest to Copper Ridge. Straight ahead dives deeper into the Chilliwack River valley—your return route on the grand loop. Below the fork, 40 yards to your right, is Boundary Camp. It's in subalpine trees, next to a corn-lily meadow, above the Chilliwack River, which at this early stage is merely a creek. It's also just inside the National Park, so you need a permit to camp.

At 6.1 miles, on the way to Copper Ridge, there's a view southwest back to Hannegan Pass and south to the enormous wall of Icy Peak. At 6.5 miles, traverse the upper reaches of Hells Gorge. At 6.7 miles, after gaining 1000 feet from Boundary Camp, attain the southwest end of Copper Ridge, cloaked in heather and berry meadows. The Silesia Creek valley is far below to the north. Beyond it are the Border Peaks.

The trail undulates generally east along the knobby ridge to Silesia Camp at 8.2 miles, 5689 feet. There are only two tent sites here: one is somewhat sheltered beneath a tree, the other is an exposed patch of cement-hard dirt. The views southeast to Mineral Mountain and Easy Ridge are exceptional. Below Silesia, a side trail drops 300 feet northwest to Egg Lake and three more tent sites. The lake is the only water source in the area.

Continuing northeast along the ridge, the trail drops 280 feet, then ascends 1100 feet on tight switchbacks to the Copper Ridge Lookout at 10.2 miles, 6260 feet. In summer and early fall a ranger often occupies the lookout. To the southwest, Ruth Mountain, Icy Peak, Mt. Shuksan and Mt. Baker are visible. Mt. Blum is directly south. Southeast across the Chilliwack valley is the Picket Range massif, including Whatcom Peak and Mt. Challenger.

From the small summit where the lookout is perched, the trail descends 250 feet. The views continue, with Bear Mountain and Mt. Redoubt visible to the northeast. After contouring 0.5 mile, the trail makes a steep, rugged descent to a three-site camp and vivid-blue Copper Lake at 11.4 miles, 5200 feet. At 11.8 miles rockhop across a tumbling creek. At 12.2 miles pass through a boulder garden, followed by the last ascent on the ridge. After gaining 400 feet via steep switchbacks, the trail regains the ridge-crest and offers a view straight south up Brush Creek—the way to Whatcom Pass. Farther north on Copper Ridge, the eastern horizon is dominated by Mount Redoubt. You can also survey the Indian Creek valley on the south side of Bear Mountain. During this final ridge run, the trail contours 1.4 miles through heather meadows.

Before the trail plunges off the north end of Copper Ridge, Chilliwack Lake makes a surprise appearance far below in the distance. At 14.5 miles the trail drops steeply below a cliff and a lingering snowfield, then darts 20 yards upward to get above a rockslide. Descending again, the trail takes you farther north than seems necessary. Be patient and observant. The trail is rooty and at times is a narrow trench—awkward to stay in without tripping. Rocks on the path might be hidden by tall grass. (The Copper Mountain trail is supposed to be improved in 1998.) The trail then traverses the top of another rockslide before fully committing to the eastward plunge to the Chilliwack River.

On the long, forested descent, cross a reliable spring and a stream at 15.4 miles. Nearing the valley bottom at 18.3 miles, the trail is faint. At one point, you have to jump onto a toppled cedar that appears to block the trail. Walk along it, watching for cairns. Near the end of the log, jump off the right side. Walk around the rest of the log and go left through boulders. The trail resumes in 20 yards where there's a ribbon blaze on a tree branch, and soon reaches the Chilliwack River.

By September, the river's main branch should be only about 15 inches deep and 25 feet wide. You also have to wade across a smaller, middle branch, then a third one (actually a tributary—Indian Creek) about the same size as the main branch. On the far side, go right. It's another 0.25 mile to the junction with the Chilliwack trail at 18.9 miles, 2300 feet. Turn right (south) at the junction and reach Indian Creek camp at 19.7 miles. It has three official sites and room for two more tents beneath giant cedars. Continuing south, cross bridged Indian Creek just after the camp. The trail gains only 300 feet in the next 2.7 miles to the junction with the Hannegan-Whatcom trail at 22.4 miles, 2600 feet.

Left (south) leads to Whatcom Pass. Following Brush Creek upstream, it's 2.2 miles to several campsites at Graybeal Camp, 3200 feet. A separate camp at Graybeal is designated for horse packers. After Graybeal, the trail ascends steeply, gaining 2000 feet in 3.0 miles. Whatcom Pass is at 5.2 miles, 5206 feet. There are two constantly-in-demand, no-fire campsites at Whatcom Camp, just west of the pass. 7574-Whatcom Peak is directly south of the pass, and 8236-foot Mt. Challenger rises southeast, above the Challenger Glacier.

A boot-beaten route leads to the Tapto Lakes cross-country camping area, a bit west of Whatcom Pass and 0.5 mile to 1.0 mile north of the trail. Your tent must be at least 200 feet from any water source. Fires are prohibited. After the initially steep ascent, the route reaches leveler ground in meadows. The lakes are at 5760 feet. You can also find suitable cross-country camping near the Middle Lakes, north and east of the pass, on the east side of the ridge separating them from the Tapto Lakes.

To see more of Mt. Challenger than is visible from Whatcom Pass, ascend 0.2 mile and several hundred feet along the ridge directly south of the pass. You can also see more of the Challenger Glacier by following the main trail through the pass and dropping a couple hundred feet down the east side.

Back at the 22.4-mile junction with the Hannegan-Whatcom trail, the Chilliwack trail crosses Brush Creek on a solid, plank bridge. The trail forks at 23.2 miles. Go left to reach the cablecar. Right leads to the horse ford. At 23.9 miles use the cablecar to propel yourself across the Chilliwack River. The trail resumes above the north bank, heading southwest. At 24.4 miles reach U.S. Cabin Camp in forest, near the river. The next 2.0 miles are virtually level. The trail then ascends gently to Copper Creek Camp at 27.0 miles. From there the ascent steepens, gaining 1200 feet in 2.5 miles to rejoin the Copper Mountain trail at Boundary Camp. The loop mileage at this point (excluding the side trip to Whatcom Pass) is 29.5. Right (northeast) is the trail you took to Copper Ridge. Stay left (west) and ascend the trail you originally descended from Hannegan Pass. Beyond the pass, the final stretch northwest back to the trailhead provides nearly constant views of Nooksack Ridge and Mt. Sefrit. Reach Hannegan Campground and the end of the loop at 34.5 miles.

Cable car across the Chilliwack River

Trip 89
Lake Byrne

Location	Glacier Peak Wilderness.
Distance	15.4-mile round trip.
Elevation gain	3300'.
Maps	Green Trails No. 111–Sloan Peak, No. 112–Glacier Peak; US Forest Service–Glacier Peak Wilderness.

OPINION

Lake Byrne is the cover girl of North Cascades lakes. The setting is sublime: deep turquoise water cupped beneath whitish rock escarpments, at the end of a high ridge, directly across a valley from Glacier Peak. You'll admire the lake, look at the peak, then continue glancing back and forth, risking whiplash.

This perspective of the icy volcano's western slope reveals a crater more jagged than Mt. Baker's. You can also see the Kennedy and Scimitar glaciers clawing at the peak from sky to forest. It's a view that might inspire you to hike from Kennedy Hot Springs northeast to Kennedy Ridge and on to Fire Creek Pass.

The approach to Kennedy Hot Springs is a breeze, but from there it's a wickedly steep 2300 feet in 2.5 miles up the end of Lost Creek Ridge. Soon after piercing the forest crown you arrive at the lake. Ascend an additional 250 feet for a better vantage.

FACT

By Car

From Darrington on Highway 530, drive the Mountain Loop Highway southeast 9.5 miles. Shortly after you cross the Sauk River bridge, the second road on the left is signed WHITE CHUCK TRAIL, MEADOW MOUNTAIN TRAIL. Turn left (northeast) here, onto White Chuck River Road 23, and drive 10.4 miles east to the trailhead and Owl Creek Campground at road's end, 2300 feet.

On Foot

Read Trip 63 for directions to Kennedy Hot Springs at 5.2 miles, 3300 feet. From the Kennedy Hot Springs guard station, cross the bridge to the west bank of the White Chuck River. The springs are to the left. Go right 0.1 mile to a sign LOST CREEK RIDGE TRAIL NO. 646, LAKE BYRNE. Take the trail angling southwest, immediately ascending short, steep switchbacks. Two thirds of the way up, the grade relaxes in a small heather meadow amid mountain hemlocks. At 7.4 miles Glacier Peak is visible. The ridge of Meadow Mountain is northwest, across the valley.

Reach Lake Byrne at 7.7 miles, 5600 feet. Black Mountain rises south of Byrne. Experienced scramblers can circle the lake on the ridges surrounding it. The optimal viewpoint is on a knoll 500 feet above the south end of the lake.

Rangers are trying to rehabilitate the tiny, fragile meadows beside Lake Byrne. They urge you to camp elsewhere. There's almost no flat spot big enough to pitch a tent here anyway, so most people push on. After grazing the north end of the lake, the trail climbs 250 feet to a superior view of the cirque. Ascend a bit more, then drop west to Camp Lake at 8.5 miles, 5700 feet, where you'll find a couple good tent sites. The Green Trails map shows the distance from Kennedy Hot Springs to Camp Lake as 4.0 miles. It's closer to 3.3.

Lake Byrne atop Lost Creek Ridge

Trip 90
Red Pass / White Chuck River / Lost Creek Ridge Loop

Location	Glacier Peak Wilderness.
Distance	33.1-mile loop if you walk or hitchhike 3.7 miles between trailheads.
Elevation gain	8000'.
Maps	Green Trails No. 111–Sloan Peak, No. 112–Glacier Peak, No. 143–Monte Cristo, No. 144–Benchmark Mtn; US Forest Service Glacier Peak Wilderness.

OPINION

St. Peter's is not Rome. Disneyworld is not Florida. Glacier Peak is not Glacier Peak Wilderness. Landmarks often deceive. Overshadowed by a dominating mountain, the scenery in this immense wilderness is more marvelously varied than you might think. That's why this is a premier backpack trip. Your enjoyment won't depend on seeing Glacier Peak. It's only one of many powerful sights.

And this loop is only one of several you can choose from in the area. Our favorite covers 46 miles in four to seven days, linking Pilot Ridge, Blue Lake, Dishpan Gap, Indian Pass, White Pass, Red Pass, White Chuck River, Kennedy Hot Springs, Lake Byrne, and Lost Creek Ridge. For a shorter, three- to five-day version, start by hiking up the North Fork Sauk River, then continue the loop from Red Pass north. That's the trip described here. If you're hiking the longer loop, also read Trip 91.

As you set out, you'll be greeted by nobility: giant cedars and gargantuan Douglas firs. The trees are so tall it's hard to look up at them while carrying a big pack. For a shoulder-season dayhike, keep in mind this section along the North Fork, between the trailhead and McKinaw Shelter. It passes through an exceptionally grand ancient forest.

Above, on the Pacific Crest Trail, is a 3.5-mile stretch between

Lower White Pass and Red Pass that's one of the supreme, sustained-high-elevation hikes in the North Cascades. The other is on Miners Ridge, east of Image Lake (Trip 94).

Then there's the view from Red Pass. Wow! Make sure you hit it in good weather, or you'll miss one of the most impactful scenes in the United States: the alpine vastness of the White Chuck River's headwaters valley, with the White Chuck Glacier beyond. After surveying this ethereal valley, you get to walk through it. The tussocky meadows, rock gardens, lyrical, omnipresent meltwater streams, and particularly the elegant, swooping walls are more typical of the Canadian Rockies than the gnarly North Cascades.

Once you're below the upper basin, you could happily walk to Kennedy Hot Springs during a rainstorm—an occurrence so common here you should expect it. The trail descends through prelapsarian forest, beside the raging White Chuck River whose lusty roar resounds. Try to include a side trip up to the White Chuck Glacier for a rock-and-ice extravaganza.

Kennedy Hot Springs is the Grand Central Station of Glacier Peak Wilderness. The trails radiating from it lead to wilder, lonelier environs: Red Pass, Kennedy Ridge, Fire Creek Pass, and Lost Creek Ridge. In the vicinity of the springs and on the slopes above, you'll find berries galore.

If possible, allow a full day for the 8.6-mile side trip from Kennedy Hot Springs to Kennedy Ridge, where you'll see the Kennedy and Scimitar glaciers. But if all you have time for is the first 2.0 miles, even that's worthwhile. The ancient forest decorated with sphagnum moss is enchanting. Half a mile before joining the PCT, the trail surprises you by suddenly dancing along a knife-edge ridge.

Fire Creek Pass is another excellent side trip from Kennedy Hot Springs. Fit, determined hikers can make the 19.0-mile round trip in a day—if you're here when the days are long, and you start close to sunrise. But it's worth allowing two extra days. Less ambitious hikers can camp at Glacier Creek, 4.3 miles up, then dayhike a 10.4-mile round trip to the pass. Or hike all the way to the pass on day one, camp on the other side at Mica Lake, then hike back over and down on day two. You might also consider arranging a shuttle, so you can hike over Fire Creek Pass, drop down past Mica Lake, and exit via the Milk Creek trail. But don't do that if it means missing Lake Byrne and Lost Creek Ridge.

Lake Byrne, atop the eastern end of Lost Creek Ridge, is as pretty as any place in the North Cascades. Ideally, you should backpack the whole ridge, but only if you're strong and experienced. The route is sketchy in spots, rough in others, and always works you hard. It straps you in and thrashes you around like a bucking bronco. But the challenge can be enjoyable, the continuous views exhilarating, the relative isolation rejuvenating.

Want to see part of this loop, but don't have time to backpack? It's possible to dayhike up the North Fork Sauk River to Red Pass (20.0 miles round trip) or up the White Chuck River to Lake Byrne (15.4 miles round trip, Trip 89), but these are marathons that will severely test your mettle. If you have only one day and are bursting with energy and desire, go for it. You'll see the scenery. You might even attain a greater sense of physical accomplishment. What you'll miss is ephemeral: a sense of intimacy with the land, the feeling of having lived there. Visitors rarely get to know a place as well as residents. Dayhikers are visitors. Backpackers are temporary residents.

We recommend starting the loop by hiking up the North Fork, as described here, because you can ease into it this way, rather than immediately grinding straight up to Round Lake and flinging yourself at the mercy of Lost Creek Ridge.

FACT

By Car

From Granite Falls, drive the Mountain Loop Highway southeast to Barlow Pass. Continue 7.2 miles beyond the pass. Or, from Darrington on Highway 530, drive the Mountain Loop Highway southeast 16.5 miles. From either approach, turn east onto North Fork Sauk River Road 49. Drive 3.1 miles (road sign states 4 miles) up Road 49 to the Lost Creek Ridge trailhead. It's on the left, at 1900 feet. If you're hiking the loop as suggested, this is where the trail ends. If you have a shuttle vehicle, leave one here. Otherwise, to complete the loop, you'll have to walk the road from here to the North Fork trailhead—where we recommend starting. To get there, continue up Road 49. At 6.7 miles turn left at the sign N. FK SAUK TRAIL ¼. The North Fork trailhead is at 6.8 miles, 2100 feet. Twenty yards beyond the trailhead, the road ends at Sloan Creek Campground.

On Foot

The trailhead sign states BLUE LAKE TRAIL 1.75. It's actually 2.0. You'll bypass it on this loop. The sign also states MCKINAW SHELTER 5. It's actually 5.5. That's along the North Fork Sauk River— the way you'll be going.

Heading southeast, the trail begins in ancient forest. In a few minutes, the Red Mountain trail branches left (north). Proceed straight. At 1.4 miles the trail is close to the river. At 2.0 miles, 2400 feet, come to a junction. There are two fine campsites here, beside the river. The right fork climbs south to Pilot Ridge. Continue straight (east) on the North Fork trail.

At 5.5 miles, 3000 feet, reach McKinaw Shelter, near the river. At 5.8 miles the trail goes vertical, switchbacking northeast through deep forest. At 6.4 miles you get a 0.4-mile reprieve before it steepens again. At 7.3 miles reach subalpine slopes. The trail then veers southeast. It gains 500 feet in the last 0.5 mile to the junction with the Pacific Crest Trail, at 8.3 miles, 6000 feet. Go left (northwest) to Red Pass. Or, for an even more commanding view of the White Chuck Glacier and the headwaters valley of the White Chuck River, first detour right (southeast) 0.7 mile to White Pass. Look up to your left (north) at 7030-foot White Mountain. A 0.6-mile, cross-country ascent will grant you the summit.

Continuing northwest on the PCT, from the junction with the North Fork trail, traverse pink-heather slopes. Arrive at 6500-foot Red Pass at 10.0 miles total. Below to the west is a scenic campsite with a few trees for shelter and a snowpatch for water. From the pass you can see Monte Cristo and Kyes peaks to the southwest and, a bit closer, all of Pilot Ridge to Johnson Mountain. In the near southeast are Indian Head and Kodak peaks. The pass itself is a narrow defile bounded on the north by Portal Peak and on the southeast by the ridgeline of White Mountain. Looking west from the pass, the White Chuck Glacier gleams in the distance, and below you spreads the headwaters valley of the White Chuck River.

The trail drops east from the pass through 1.0 mile of rock gardens and creeklets. Official campsites are 1.2 miles down, where you enter forest. The best site is on the left, alone in hemlocks, 10 yards after you pass a creek. Switchback down a bit and come to more campsites and berry patches. Cross another creek on logs. Then drop into a gully lined by hemlocks where you're next to a narrow, rushing creek. More switchbacks steeply

White Chuck Glacier and south arm of Glacier Peak, from Red Pass

descend north to the high, stable bridge over the milky, mighty White Chuck River at 14.8 miles, 4050 feet. On the far (northeast) side of the bridge there's a big, plank bench—convenient for a rest break.

Proceed north, descending gradually, almost imperceptibly, through forest. Near 15.8 miles the trail hits Baekos Creek. There are campsites on the south bank. Follow a path 25 yards upstream to a log crossing. At 17.0 miles reach Chetwot Creek—a series of channels crossed with the help of footbridges. This is an area of stunted evergreens, deciduous trees, sandy soil, and profuse berries. At 18.0 miles, 3900 feet, cross Sitkum Creek on two barely usable footlogs. On the north side are three campsites and the junction with the Sitkum Creek trail.

You now have a choice. To reach Fire Creek Pass, 9.5 miles north via the PCT, go right. You'll eliminate a 600-foot descent and 900-foot ascent by not dropping to Kennedy Hot Springs. To continue the loop described here, turn left onto heavily used, often muddy, White Chuck trail 643A, and walk 1.8 miles northwest to Kennedy Hot Springs. You'll be in giant trees the whole way. The last 0.75 mile descends steeply, losing 600 feet, but by then the tread is solid, the switchbacks comfortable. You get views over the White Chuck River canyon.

The Kennedy Hot Springs Guard Station (only occasionally occupied by a ranger) is at 3300 feet, between the White Chuck River and Kennedy Creek. Your total distance here is 19.8 miles. A map posted on the log cabin indicates the many permitted tent sites in the area. The hot springs are on the far (west) bank of the White Chuck River, across the solid footbridge and 75 yards upstream. The steep ascent to Lake Byrne also departs from that side.

Bears have been sighted at Kennedy Hot Springs. So they don't become a problem at this popular destination, hang your food properly. The small, roughly four-feet-square, hot springs pool is just warm enough to defrost you on a frigid day. To soothe trail-sore feet, it's better to plunk them in a stream. Cold alleviates inflammation.

For the side trip to Kennedy Ridge and Fire Creek Pass, cross the Kennedy Creek bridge just north of the guard station. Turn left, walk 0.3 mile, then turn right on trail 639. It's immediately steep, gaining 900 feet in 1.7 miles to the junction with the PCT. Turn left there, climbing past rock outcroppings and into heather. At 2.7 miles attain a view east into Kennedy Creek chasm, and at 3.5 miles a view northeast to Kennedy Peak. Reach the campsites beside Glacier Creek at 4.0 miles. You can see Lost Creek Ridge to the west. For Kennedy Ridge, leave the trail at Glacier Creek and ascend east cross-country as far as you feel compelled—0.5 mile through open subalpine forest on an old moraine, then on the boulders of an obviously much younger moraine. For Fire Creek Pass, continue north on the PCT at Glacier Creek. The Pumice Creek campsites are at 5.3 miles, 5900 feet. From there the trail heads west, loses 700 feet, then gains 1000 feet in the last 1.6 miles north to 6300-foot Fire Creek Pass, 9.5 miles from Kennedy Hot Springs.

If you choose to leave Kennedy Hot Springs via White Chuck River trail 643, it's 5.2 miles northwest to that trailhead. Of course, without a pre-arranged shuttle, you'll have to hitchhike—not impossible in this frequently visited area.

To leave Kennedy Hot Springs via the Lost Creek Ridge trail, cross the bridge to the west side of the White Chuck River, then go right. Angle up southwest 0.1 mile past a couple campsites. Soon the trail is even steeper than the Pilot Ridge ascent. Reach a meadow basin at 1.8 miles. Seventy-five yards beyond, a view east to Glacier Peak reveals a crater more jagged than Mt. Baker's.

THE NORTH CASCADES

You can also see Kennedy and Scimitar glaciers slightly northeast. The ridge of Meadow Mountain is northwest, across the valley. You'll ascend 2300 feet in 2.5 miles from Kennedy Hot Springs west to Lake Byrne, at 5600 feet. After grazing the north end of the lake, the trail climbs 250 feet to a superior view of the lake cirque. Ascend a bit more, then drop west to Camp Lake at 5700 feet, where you'll find a couple good tent sites. Camp Lake is about 3.3 miles from Kennedy Hot Springs—less than the 4.0 miles on the Green Trails map. Your total distance on the loop, which started at the North Fork Sauk River trailhead, is now 23.1 miles. Fill your water bottles at Camp Lake; hiking the ridge you'll find only a few convenient water sources.

The Lost Creek Ridge trail heads generally west. It winds 1.25 miles from Camp Lake, ascending briefly, then dropping 200 feet as it curves to Hardtack Lake. It's then a series of ups and downs, mostly through heather and rock, sometimes in trees, all the way to Round Lake. There are a couple campsites along the trail, west of Camp Lake. The first is in heather and grass, 1.0 mile past Hardtack Lake, west of the long ridge jutting beyond the lake.

Views diminish after Camp Lake. Mostly you're looking north at unremarkable Meadow Mountain and the blight of a logging road leading to it. From a gap west of Hardtack Lake, you do attain open views southeast to the glaciers on Black Mountain and east to Glacier Peak.

Soon after Hardtack Lake, the trail stays closer to the ridgecrest but becomes narrower and less defined. Sometimes it's no wider than the length of a boot, though it is always distinguishable. In places it's on very precipitous slopes, so avoid hiking here in times of limited visibility.

A mile and a half west of Hardtack Lake, the trail crosses the ridgecrest to the south side. This allows an unobstructed view of Black and Red mountains (southeast and south), Sloan Peak (southwest), and the North Fork Sauk River canyon (southwest) far below you. After miles of heather, re-enter trees. At 28.5 miles (8.7 miles from Kennedy) reach a junction at 5500 feet.

The right fork immediately crests a ridge, then drops north 500 feet in 0.7 mile to Round Lake and campsites. To avoid having to descend to Round Lake for water, fill up just east of this junction, where streams trickle through a rocky basin. Here, in addition to water, you might find the waxy, deep-purple king gentian flower, rare in the North Cascades. Look for it in moist, grassy areas.

At the junction, stay left on the main trail to complete the loop. The tread is now in better condition than on the ridge, but still rough and narrow. Follow it west off the ridge to Bingley Gap (not noticeable as such) then south to the Lost Creek Ridge trailhead on Road 49. Always in trees, constantly switchbacking, you'll lose 3600 feet in the 4.6-mile descent from the Round Lake junction. Your total distance when you reach the road is 33.1 miles. The North Fork Sauk River trailhead where you began the loop, however, is 3.7 miles left (southeast) on Road 49. Try hitchhiking if you didn't pre-arrange a shuttle.

Sloan Peak from Lost Creek Ridge near Round Lake junction

Trip 91

Pilot Ridge / White Pass / North Fork Sauk River Loop

Location	Glacier Peak Wilderness.
Distance	29.3-mile loop.
Elevation gain	5800'.
Maps	Green Trails No. 111–Sloan Peak, No. 112–Glacier Peak, No. 143–Monte Cristo, No. 144–Benchmark Mtn; US Forest Service Glacier Peak Wilderness.

OPINION

Once in a great while, you see an image that instantly earns a permanent place in your mental gallery, where you can return to it again and again for emotional and physical renewal, perhaps even spiritual sustenance. Glacier Peak Wilderness is replete with such sights. You'll experience many on this premier backpack trip.

And this is only one of several loops you can choose from in the area. Our favorite covers 46 miles in four to seven days, linking Pilot Ridge, Blue Lake, Dishpan Gap, Indian Pass, White Pass, Red Pass, White Chuck River, Kennedy Hot Springs, Lake Byrne, and Lost Creek Ridge. For a shorter, three- to five-day version, start the long loop but exit earlier: drop from White Pass down the North Fork Sauk River. That's the trip described here. If you're hiking the longer loop, also read Trip 90.

After a memorable beginning through exceptionally grand ancient forest, the excitement continues. Topping out on Pilot Ridge you can see a massif so awesome you might not recognize it as Monte Cristo. No other vantage reveals Monte's full stature like this one. Of course, Glacier Peak soon leaps into view and does so repeatedly throughout the trip. You can also see the ridge, southwest, where the Bald Eagle trail bumps along in trees. If you'd ever thought about hiking it, you won't anymore. The views here on Pilot Ridge are superior.

Pilot is, like most ridges, decidedly unlevel. Walking it you feel like a tiny ship in rough seas, cresting waves then plunging into troughs. But the meadows you cross later are so long and languorous they more than compensate.

Hiking north on the Pacific Crest Trail, approaching White Pass, you can see the White River valley yawning to the east. In case you're tempted to explore it, a warning: it's more impressive for its size than its beauty. Except for the first 1.5 alpine miles, a few avalanche swaths, and a 2.0-mile stretch of meadow, the valley trail is forested the remaining 11.5 miles out to White River Road 6400.

Before descending White Pass to hike out along the North Fork, be sure to make the short off-trail hike up White Mountain for the supreme view of the White Chuck Glacier and the sweeping headwaters valley of the White Chuck River.

Between Pilot Ridge and the North Fork valley bottom, the trail affords little protection from sun or inclement weather. There are few trees for shade or shelter. If it's wet, you'll get very wet; if it's hot, you'll be very hot. Clear skies are almost a necessity for enjoying high-elevation trails like this, but when the temperature soars you'll want a wide-brimmed hat and maybe a bandana you can moisten and wrap around your neck. Also bring plenty of water and fill up at every opportunity. Except near the North Fork, the trail can be dry for long stretches.

Expect company at Blue Lake, Dishpan Gap and Meander Meadow. Dishpan is the confluence of several popular loop trails, and it's a short hike here from the Little Wenatchee River trailhead just south.

Which way should you hike the loop? It's a coin toss. Both directions have pros and cons. We describe it starting with the ascent of Pilot Ridge. That way, if it's hot, your steepest ascent will be through forest, probably in the cool of the morning; rather than on a sun-blistered slope in the afternoon.

Because there's no desirable campsite and little water on Pilot Ridge, start early and hike all the way to Blue Lake the first day. It's a rigorous 11.8 miles, but doable if you're strong.

FACT

By Car

From Granite Falls, drive the Mountain Loop Highway southeast to Barlow Pass. Continue 7.2 miles beyond the pass. Or, from Darrington on Highway 530, drive the Mountain Loop Highway southeast 16.5 miles. From either approach, turn east onto North Fork Sauk River Road 49. Drive 3.1 miles (road sign states 4 miles) up Road 49 to the Lost Creek Ridge trailhead. It's on the left, at 1900 feet. If you're hiking the loop as suggested, this is where it ends, so you might want to leave a shuttle vehicle here. Otherwise drive farther on the North Fork road to the North Fork trailhead, where you'll start hiking the loop. At 6.7 miles go left at the sign N. FK SAUK TRAIL ¼. Arrive at the North Fork trailhead at 6.8 miles, 2100 feet. Twenty yards beyond the trailhead, the road ends at the Sloan Creek Campground.

On Foot

The trailhead sign states BLUE LAKE TRAIL 1.75 MILES. It's actually 2.0. That's the way we recommend starting—over Pilot Ridge. The sign also states MCKINAW SHELTER 5 MILES. (It's actually 5.5.) That's along the North Fork Sauk River—the way we recommend returning.

Heading southeast, the trail begins in ancient forest. A few minutes in, pass the Red Mountain trail branching left (north). At 1.4 miles, the trail is close to the river. At 2.0 miles, 2400 feet, come to a junction. There are two fine campsites here, beside the river. The North Fork trail continues straight, reaching the Pacific Crest Trail near White Pass. To ascend Pilot Ridge, turn right (south) toward the riverside camp and ford the river.

By early August, fording the river where the trail drops to it should be easy. But if you want to keep your boots on, try a short detour. Follow the path branching left at the water's edge. Go upstream 70 yards to a giant fallen cedar bridging the main channel. Cross it. Then walk downstream over logs and brush to the end of the island. Rockhop the smaller second channel. Then pick up the path leading back downstream 20 yards to the main trail.

On the south side of the river, the trail climbs a long serious of steep, tight switchbacks south through forest. The last dependable water on the entire ridge is 1.9 miles up, where the trail crosses a creeklet. After gaining 1600 feet in that distance, the grade eases slightly. The first possible campsite—a small flat spot beside the trail—is 4.3 miles from the trailhead.

At 4.6 miles a rockslide splits the forest, which is mostly big,

Looking north from lower White Pass

healthy hemlocks. At 5.1 miles, cross an unreliable creeklet. Glacier Peak (northeast) now makes its first appearance. Just before you pop onto the narrow, western end of the ridge at 5.4 miles, you see Red Mountain on the left and Glacier Peak again. The ascent continues steeply and the view improves. You can see (left to right in the northeast) Black Mountain, Portal Peak above Red Pass, and White Mountain across the North Fork valley and above White Pass. At 5.5 miles you can see Mt. Baker and Pugh Mountain to the northwest, the massive glacier on Sloan Peak nearby to the west, and the Monte Cristo massif to the southwest. You can also see Alpine Lakes Wilderness to the southeast, and the Icicle Group farther east above Leavenworth. Mt. Rainier is visible too, on the southern horizon. Below you in the foreground (southwest) are the Sloan and Cadet creek valleys, at the base of Monte Cristo Peak.

Enter heather and berry bushes atop the ridge. Heading southeast, the trail is in the open for 0.3 mile, then in forest again. It's level for only 0.5 mile before it plunges. There's a flat but otherwise poor campsite in a depression at 6.5 miles. The trail loses 240 feet, then levels in forest. At 6.9 miles the trail crosses a flat spot where you could, if necessary, pitch a tent. Finally, the ridgewalk is mostly level for 1.0 mile. At 8.5 miles, there's an adequate tent site on the right, in trees, just below the trail.

The walking becomes easier as you contour southeast across subalpine slopes. At 10.5 miles, 6080 feet, go right (west) at the directional sign JOHNSON MOUNTAIN ⇐, BLUE LAKES ⇒. If you crane over the slope, you can see Little Blue Lake, far below to the south. At 11.5 miles, 5500 feet, reach a junction and sign BLUE LAKE HIGH ROUTE NO. 652A. Follow the sign left (southeast), taking the smaller trail 0.3 mile up the slope. As you come over the lip of a narrow, slippery, rooty stretch, there's a good campsite to the left, above upper Blue Lake. The lake is at 5625 feet, in a steep-sided grassy bowl. As its name suggests, the water is a deep blue. Campsites are limited; the few obvious ones are likely to be occupied at this popular destination.

Back at the 11.5-mile junction, a longer, gentler trail to the PCT goes right (south) toward Little Blue Lake and June Mountain. At a junction in 1.5 miles, it heads northeast to join trail 652A at 5800 feet, 3.2 miles from upper Blue Lake. Most hikers opt for the high route—a precarious, somewhat exposed short cut from upper Blue Lake. It ascends steeply above the narrow south end of the lake and in 0.8 mile reaches a gap between two knolls. There's just enough room for a small tent here. The view is extensive: south to Mts. Daniels, Hinman, The Cradle in Alpine Lakes Wilderness, even Mt. Rainier; and northeast to Indian Head Peak. The trail then heads east, abruptly descending a steep, rocky buttress to a junction at 12.6 miles with the longer trail from Little Blue Lake and June Mountain.

It's now a fairly level 0.8 mile through meadows, southeast then south, to a four-way junction at Dishpan Gap. The gap is a broad, flat meadow, dotted with tarns, rimmed by hemlocks. There are campsites here, but don't expect solitude; it's a busy crossroads. Right descends east to the Skykomish River. Straight south, the PCT leads to Lake Sally Ann (Trip 99) and eventually Stevens Pass. Turn left (north) onto the PCT, heading toward Indian and White passes.

Meadows and subalpine trees continue 1.6 miles. At 14.1 and 14.3 miles stay straight, passing the trails dropping southeast into Meander Meadow—unless you want to camp in the basin. At 15.0 miles pass the Wenatchee Ridge trail forking east. Here the PCT turns sharply north, offering an unobstructed view of 7442-foot Indian Head Peak to the northeast, its smooth green slopes reminding of U.S. Glacier National Park. You've now rounded the base of Kodak Peak. Kodak earned its name by being a good vantage point for photographers, not because it's prominent or photogenic itself. If you need water, you'll probably find seeps beside the trail near 15.5 miles, on Kodak's northeast side. Bees and flies can be rife on these alpine slopes.

Drop 700 feet north to 5000-foot Indian Pass, at 16.0 miles. The pass is forested and has sheltered campsites. Small meadows and brackish tarns are surrounded by hemlocks. Pass the trail descending right (east) to Indian Creek. Proceed north on the PCT, following the sign directing you toward the White River trail.

At 18.0 miles reach lower White Pass and the White River trail dropping right (east) off the PCT into the White River valley. There are campsites at the pass; also 0.3 mile beyond, in the trees beside Reflection Pond.

Having gained 900 feet since leaving Indian Pass, reach White Pass at 20.3 miles, 5904 feet. Above you, straight ahead (north), is 7030-foot White Mountain. A 0.6-mile, cross-country ascent will grant you the summit, with a commanding view of the White Chuck Glacier and Glacier Peak. Camping is not allowed at White Pass, only in the basin immediately below, reached via the spur trail left (west). At a fork 30 yards beyond, pass the side trail leading right (east) to Foam Basin. Proceed straight (north) on the PCT, toward Red Pass. Reach a water source (several rivulets pouring off White Mountain) 0.4 mile from White Pass. Beyond White Pass 0.7 mile, reach a junction at 6000 feet. The total distance here is 21.0 miles. The PCT continues straight (north), crossing Red Pass and dropping into the White Chuck River valley. For the shorter loop, turn left (west), leaving the PCT, descending trail 649, and reaching the North Fork Sauk River in 2.8 miles and the trailhead in 8.3 miles.

Trail 649 descends 450 feet in 0.5 mile, then descends gently for 0.8 mile. After that it switchbacks steeply 1.5 miles, reaching the North Fork Sauk River at 3000 feet. You can camp here near the river at McKinaw Shelter. From there, it's 3.5 mostly level miles through deep, cool, virgin forest to the junction with the trail to Pilot Ridge, which you ascended days ago. Continue straight 2.0 miles to the trailhead, where your total distance is 29.3 miles.

Trip 92

Railroad Creek / Lyman Lakes

Location	Glacier Peak Wilderness / Wenatchee National Forest.
Distance	18.6-mile round trip.
Elevation gain	2400'.
Maps	Green Trails No. 113–Holden; US Forest Service–Glacier Peak Wilderness.

OPINION

A boat trip up Lake Chelan and a bus ride to Holden village propel you into sublime hiking country, starting with the resplendent Railroad Creek valley. Here, centerfold mountains reveal their beauty within a couple miles.

In the North Cascades, attaining scenery of this magnitude can require a full day's slog. But at Holden, you're already 12 miles up a mountain canyon. Your gratification is then instantaneous as you begin to follow Railroad Creek upstream. Soon, Hart Lake appears. The slopes northeast of it are look-alikes of those in Waterton National Park, in Alberta, Canada. To the south is Dumbell Mountain. With its red-orange soil and streaks of alpine-greenery, it could be a stand-in for similar leviathans in the San Juan Wilderness of Colorado.

Along the way, you'll notice the forest understory is home to a fetching variety of vegetation. You'll hear streams all around you. In early summer, cascades grace the valley walls. And the trail is so smooth and well-maintained that often you can stare at the captivating peaks and continue to hike without tripping.

The Lyman Lakes basin is the *pièce de résistance* of the hike. It's a world apart from the green hues of Railroad Creek below. Walk past turquoise Lyman Lake, into the desolate, Tibetan-like, upper lake basin, where Lyman Glacier chews away at Chiwawa Mountain. The mosquitoes and black flies will be chewing on you in this bug-infested glacial pocket, so don't camp there. Pitch your tent higher, near Cloudy Pass.

Just getting to Holden is a journey, so allow at least three days for exploring the wilderness at its back door. The boat ride up Lake Chelan and the hike to Lyman Lake are well worth your time and effort, even if that's all you do in the area. But an additional day or two will grant you the supreme experience of extending the adventure to Cloudy Pass and Image Lake (Trip 94). The alpine saddle of Cloudy Pass sits between Cloudy Peak (northeast) and a looming arm of Chiwawa Mountain (southwest). You can see commanding 7759-foot Sitting Bull Mountain to the northwest. Walk half a mile west and below Cloudy Pass for a clear view down the valley of South Fork Agnes Creek. The trail west to Suiattle Pass and across 3 meadowy miles on Miners Ridge to Image Lake should be on every Northwest hiker's I've-Gotta-Do-It list. And while you're in Holden, also visit Holden

Lyman Lakes Basin

Lake (Trip 15), a sweet, easy dayhike that ends in a glorious cirque.

Holden was originally a mining settlement. Copper ore was discovered here in 1896. After production began in 1937, track was laid in Railroad Creek valley with the intention of hauling ore from Holden down to Lucerne. But the railroad was never completed. Instead, the ore was trucked to the barges waiting on Lake Chelan. After the trip down-lake to the town of Chelan, the ore was transported to Tacoma, then shipped to points beyond. Be thankful the rugged geography around Cloudy and Suiattle passes discouraged surveyors from pushing a road west through the mountains. Otherwise, this exciting, wild valley would be just another mundane victim of man's avarice and myopia.

FACT

By Car

See the Chelan Lakeshore description (Trip 108) for directions to the Lake Chelan boat landing.

By Boat & Bus

See the Holden Lake description (Trip 15) for details about the boat to Lucerne and the bus to Holden, at 3209 feet.

On Foot

Follow the dirt road west from Holden village. Pass the ranger station, some mining junk, the trailhead sign GOAT TRAIL, a bridge over Railroad Creek, and the cement foundations of the long-gone miners' village. In 1.0 mile come to the village baseball field, which also serves as the Holden Campground. You can pitch your tent here for free. A trailhead sign is posted on the northeast corner. The trail to Holden Lake and Lyman Lakes continues from the northwest corner of the field, where you enter Glacier Peak Wilderness.

The trail gently gains 300 feet in 0.9 mile, through cottonwood, mixed conifer and giant willow, to a signed junction at 1.9 miles from Holden village. Right leads to Holden Lake. Continue straight as the almost-level trail contours northwest. Open forest allows views southwest across the valley to 8421-foot Dumbell Mountain. At 2.7 miles cross the bridged stream issuing from Holden Lake. The trail steepens at 3.5 miles.

Reach the northeast end of Hart Lake at 4.75 miles. Campsites are in cottonwoods above the lake. Above the north side of the lake the trail crosses a stream, which can be difficult to ford until August. After a level mile, at 6.0 miles the trail tilts upward from 4000 feet, switchbacking steeply near 7 miles, to climb the Railroad Creek headwall, from which Crown Point Falls plunges.

At 9.1 miles, 5500 feet, reach a junction with the 3.0-mile trail that climbs south over a low ridge to the upper Lyman Lakes basin at 6000 feet. There are subalpine fir and a scattering of larch in the upper basin. The notch above and left (southeast) of Lyman Glacier is 7100-foot Spider Gap. Only competent mountaineers with ice axes should attempt the snowfield ascent to the gap. Hikers can scramble to the gap from its south side, via Spider Meadow (Trip 14).

The major Lyman Lake at 5600 feet is reached 0.2 mile southwest of the 9.1-mile junction. A trail skirts the west shore of this 0.6-mile-long lake. 6438-foot Cloudy Pass is 1.0 mile northwest of Lyman Lake and 840 feet above it. 5983-foot Suiattle Pass is 1.2 miles southwest of Cloudy Pass. From there it's 4.2 miles west via Miners Ridge trail 785 to Image Lake.

Trip 93

Thunder Creek / Park Creek Pass / Cascade Pass

Location	Ross Lake National Recreation Area / North Cascades National Park.
Distance	19.4 miles one way to Park Creek Pass, 8.0 miles to Stehekin Road, 9.1 miles out via Cascade Pass, 36.5 miles total for the shuttle trip.
Elevation gain	5700' up Thunder Creek to Park Creek Pass, 2600' from Stehekin Road to Cascade Pass, 8300' total for the shuttle trip.
Maps	Green Trails No. 4–Diablo Dam, No. 49 –Mt. Logan, No. 80–Cascade Pass, No. 81–McGregor Mtn; Trails Illustrated No. 223–North Cascades National Park Complex.

OPINION

Park Creek Pass is a scenic treasure, but you'll have to earn it. Whichever way you approach, you'll hike several miles before a gold coin—a glimpse of the glacier-clad peaks above—is tossed your way. Endure. You'll be richly compensated for your effort.

The best route for this four- to-five-day backpack trip starts at Colonial Creek Campground. Hike southeast over Park Creek Pass and down to Stehekin Road. Catch the shuttle bus northwest to Cottonwood Camp, then hike northwest over Cascade Pass. If you're with friends, it's easy to leave one car at the Cascade Pass trailhead. But enough people dayhike to Cascade Pass that you can probably hitch a ride to Marblemount on Highway 20 and another ride from there back to Colonial Creek Campground.

The next best option is to ride the shuttle bus from Stehekin, on Lake Chelan, to Park Creek Camp. From there, the trail north climbs 3800 feet in 7.2 miles to Park Creek Pass. Robo hikers can make it a round-trip dayhike. Others can crash overnight below the pass.

A third option is to backpack from Colonial Creek Campground on Highway 20 to Park Creek Pass, then about-face and return the same way, with the possible variant of exiting over Easy Pass. We don't recommend either—too much time in deep forest.

And the fourth option—after backpacking from Colonial Creek over Park Creek Pass and down to Stehekin Road—is to walk Stehekin Road to Bridge Creek (Trip 103), then hike the Pacific Crest Trail northeast to Highway 20 near Rainy Pass. Forget it! This section of the PCT is monotonous, a scenic zero. The side trail up the North Fork Bridge Creek is wild and offers views of Goode Mountain, but it's not enough to justify the rest of the slog.

Even our recommended approach from Colonial Creek Campground will test your patience—granting you only an occasional skyward view. It's like a swimming-pool bully who keeps dunking your head under water. Try to simply enjoy the lush rain forest en route. The pass is sublime, but it's a long way off, deeply embedded in the South Unit of North Cascades National Park. And you can expect the 3 B's to make the trip seem even longer: bears, bugs and brush. We saw loads of bear scat between the Skagit Queen and Thunder Basin camps. They probably won't bother you, but their obvious presence might keep you on edge. The Cascades' notorious biting flies *will* bother you in mid-summer—only at the pass will you escape them. As for brush, expect nettles the last couple of miles before Thunder Basin, thick alder on the descent south from the pass, and a veritable jungle on parts of the PCT (if you hike out Bridge Creek).

The trail begins at the feet of giants: fir, cedar, and hemlock. It leads you upstream along Thunder Creek, by most people's standards a river. Creeks are generally small enough, after spring runoff has subsided, to rockhop across—but not in the North Cascades. Here, nature is big. Big trees. Big fungi. Big creeks. And big mountains, often requiring a big journey like this to fully appreciate them.

If you make it to Park Creek Pass, you'll be transformed into a fountain of appreciation, gushing with superlatives. Pull up a rock, toast your accomplishment, and marvel at the scenery above and below. The pass itself is 0.2 mile long, the boulder-strewn north and meadow-laced south sides separated by a narrow gap. Allow plenty of time to roam over all of it, and maybe scramble high onto the slopes of Buckner Mountain. Since camping is prohibited at the pass, we recommend pitching your tent below the north side, in Thunder Creek basin; devoting most of the next day to the pass; then hiking down the south side to spend the night at scenic Buckner Camp.

Continuing south from the pass, once you drop below treeline, hiking through the Park Creek drainage is anticlimactic. You've been booted out of heaven, back to earth. The forest is drier and less impressive here than in the Thunder Creek valley. But the pass is worth it. And if you plan to exit via Cascade Pass, you have a lot to look forward to.

FACT

By Car

On Highway 20, drive 4.3 miles southeast from the Diablo-townsite turnoff to Colonial Creek Campground on Diablo Lake. Turn southeast into the big parking lot, but keep going through the campground to the smaller parking area at the trailhead, 1200 feet.

On Foot

The trail contours the west side of Diablo Lake's Thunder Arm for 0.8 mile. In 1.4 miles cross a bridge to the east side of Thunder Creek and continue upstream. Pass the spur trail to Thunder Creek Camp at 1.8 miles. At 2.1 miles reach a junction. Fourth of July Pass is to the left (southeast). Go straight (south). Neve Camp at 2.5 miles is in big timber. At 6.4 miles a spur trail crosses Thunder Creek and heads north to isolated creekside campsites at McAllister Camp. The trail as far as McAllister gains little elevation, so it's usually snow-free in early and late season. At 6.8 miles you enter the National Park.

Still in trees, cross Fisher Creek at 7.7 miles and arrive at Tricouni Camp. To avoid the largest swampland in the Cascades, the trail then veers left and in 0.5 mile begins a 1000-foot ascent to Junction Camps at 9.9 miles, 3100 feet. A few campsites are on the south side of the trail; a spur trail on the north side leads to more sites. On the trail south to Park Creek Pass, this is the only campground with views. You can see the upper reaches of Thunder Creek, as well as west across the canyon to Tricouni and Primus peaks. From Junction Camps, the Fisher Creek trail climbs east over Easy Pass to reach Highway 20 in 14.9 miles. Continue south on Thunder Creek trail, dropping 800 feet, passing views of Boston Glacier, then ascending to the turnoff to Skagit Queen Camp at 13.7 miles, 3100 feet. A spur trail drops right 0.2 mile to the campsites. In the early 1900s, miners penetrated the North Cascades, and you'll see evidence of that near Skagit Queen Creek.

Beyond Skagit Queen, the trail climbs 900 feet southeast in 1.2 miles, passing huge moss-covered boulders beneath Mt. Logan and entering a hanging valley. Just after gaining your first view of Park Creek Pass, you must cross the creek to your left. If you reach a brushy deadend, go back a short way to find an easier passage on rocks. Reach Thunder Basin Horse Camp at 16.6 miles, 4300 feet. Above you to the southeast is Park Creek Pass. It looks close but is still two hours away. At the first switchback that jogs north away from Thunder Creek, near 17.6 miles, 4900 feet, is a newer camp for hikers only. It will be called Steamboat, after a miner's faithful pack mule, or Upper Thunder Basin. Reach Park Creek Pass at 19.4 miles, 6100 feet. Descending the south side of the pass, you can see the glaciers of 9112-foot Buckner Mountain directly west and the cliffs of 8280-foot Booker Mountain looming close to the southwest. 8515-foot Storm King and 9197-foot Goode mountains are southeast. Walk a mile through heather and meadowland before switchbacking down into the Park Creek valley. At 22.4 miles (a little farther from Park Creek Pass than the Green Trails map shows) reach Buckner Camp and, about 0.4 mile beyond, Fivemile Horse Camp. The trail continues descending in forest now, with limited views except for glimpses of Park Creek Ridge (southwest) and Goode Ridge (northeast). At 25.4 miles reach tiny Twomile Camp. From there, you leave the hanging valley of Park Creek and drop 1060 feet, switchbacking down to Park Creek Camp and Stehekin Road at 27.4 miles, 2300 feet.

Before planning to exit along Bridge Creek, read Trip 103—a Don't Do. If you go that way, hike 3.0 miles east on Stehekin Road to the Bridge Creek trail, then 12.8 miles and 2300 feet to the Bridge Creek trailhead parking lot on Highway 20. The one-way shuttle trip totals 43.2 miles.

If you're continuing to Cascade Pass, either catch the shuttle bus or walk the road 4.5 miles northwest to Cottonwood Camp at road's end, 2800 feet. Call or write a National Park Service information center for the current bus schedule.

From Cottonwood, it's 9.1 miles northwest, including a 2600-foot ascent and an 1800-foot descent, to the trailhead at the end of the Cascade River road on the west side of Cascade Pass. First, the trail traverses the green valley bottom, with open views to forested slopes. Reach Basin Creek Camp at 1.5 miles, 3160 feet. At 2.4 miles, the 1.5-mile side trail to Horseshoe Basin branches off northeast. It ascends 1200 feet to a cirque with tumbling waterfalls beneath glaciers on Sahale Mountain and Boston Peak.

Continuing west to Cascade Pass, ascend a talus slope and at 3.1 miles, 4000 feet, ford Doubtful Creek. At 4.6 miles, 4800 feet, reach Pelton Basin and the most attractive campsites on this hike west of Park Creek. Here, wood tent platforms enable you to pitch your tent in open meadows without damaging them. If you're strong and make the bus connection, it's possible to start at Buckner Camp and hike the 10.4 miles to Pelton Basin in a day. Both of those camps offer great scenery.

After gaining 600 feet from Pelton Basin Camp, reach Cascade Pass (Trip 8) at 5.4 miles, 5400 feet. From there, descend 1800 feet in 3.7 miles northwest to the trailhead at the end of the Cascade River road, at 3600 feet.

Booker Mountain from south side of Park Creek Pass

Trip 94

Image Lake / Miners Ridge / Cloudy Pass

Location	Glacier Peak Wilderness / Mt. Baker-Snoqualmie National Forest.
Distance	32.6-mile round trip to Image Lake; 44.0-mile round trip to Cloudy Pass.
Elevation gain	4440' to Image Lake, including ups and downs; 5900' to Cloudy Pass, including ups and downs.
Maps	Green Trails No. 112–Glacier Peak, No. 113–Holden; US Forest Service–Glacier Peak Wilderness.

OPINION

Smell something burning? Don't worry, it's just your thighs, on this arduous but worth-every-step journey. It's a classic among Northwest backpack trips, so start building up for it now. Because the glories you'll be coming to witness are widely known, avoid camping at the most famous of all, Image Lake, on a weekend. Arriving midweek will increase your chance of a private bonding with this tiny, natural beauty and perhaps grant you the solitude to fully appreciate the image it captures of colossal Glacier Peak beyond.

Road Runner wannabes can smoke the round trip to Cloudy Pass in three nights, four days. Most people should plan at least four nights, five days. Longer is better. We urge you to be patient on your trek. Flow into it. Let the enchanted forests enthrall you with their complex tapestry. Let the steep ascent to Miners Ridge become a time to view your own inner landscape. Then, when you finally emerge above, you might feel you've become part of the mountains. The sense of having grown into the rapturous scenery you behold is delicious, and readily attained here by those who pace their bodies and open their minds.

The trip begins with a meditative forest walk along the Suiattle

River. Tread is soft underfoot. The powerful, rushing water is often within view for about 3 miles. Good shade makes this a pleasant stretch even on a hot day. If it's not raining, all the mosses and ferns will remind you how lucky you are.

When you're ready for a change, the trail offers a radical one: a 4.7-mile, 3200-foot climb to Miners Ridge. It's a doozy, switch-backing at least two dozen times in just the lower 2.5-mile section. It's not an enjoyable ascent after 10 A.M. on a sunny day; you'll cook. And there's no water after the first creek 0.75 mile up, so the first night it's smart to camp below at 10.8 miles, then start by 7 A.M. to reach Miners Ridge before noon. Yes, it could very well take four or five hours. Glimpses of the white volcano provide encouragement. But for refreshment, you'll have to rely on your water bottle until reaching the creek beside the Image Lake camp-ground.

The thousands of strides, the streams of sweat, however, are necessary to fully appreciate Glacier Peak. Seen from afar, it's merely a jumbo snowcone. Here, up close, it takes on an all-con-suming personal significance. Atop the ridge, in clear weather, it's as if you'd been granted a private audience with The Volcano God. The physical price you paid for the experience will seem utterly trivial. Were it not for Glacier Peak, the northern horizon, crowded with lesser but still very impressive mountains, would be captivating and need nothing else to seem a worthy reward for the effort.

From your Image Lake campsite, definitely walk northeast up the heathery slope to the crest of Miners Ridge and wander toward Plummer Mountain. It's only a few hundred feet up to where you can see a parade of jagged spires and look back down

Image Lake and Glacier Peak

on the entire bowl surrounding the lake.

Also walk up the 6758-foot knoll just north of the lake. From there you can peer north at Canyon Lake. If you've allowed yourself a week for this trip, you might enjoy dayhiking the rough, unmaintained trail to that lonely gem. If your time is limited, skip Canyon Lake. After romping up the knoll and ridge above Image Lake, hoist your pack and make for Cloudy Pass, enjoying one of the all-time-great meadow walks farther east on the Miners Ridge trail. Pay particular attention one mile east of Image Lake, where Kennecott Copper has in the past threatened to desecrate the scene by digging an open-pit copper mine! Such exquisite natural beauty should be sacrosanct. The existing hiking path is enough of a scar. Anything else is unconscionable.

Don't think of Suiattle Pass as a destination. It's just a narrow, tree-choked notch. Push on to Cloudy Pass for supreme views. Pray you're here when it's not cloudy, so you can see the sky-raking mountains that surround you. From the pass, you can also survey the Lyman Lakes below to the southeast. Walking down to the lakes and the small glacier is not a significant event, and will likely be a miserable one, due to the plentiful, voracious mosquitoes. Do wander at least part way northeast up the slope of Cloudy Peak.

Turning around at Cloudy Pass, you have a choice when you get back to Suiattle Pass: return the same way via Miners Ridge, or take the Pacific Crest Trail. If you had clear weather and therefore views coming in, stay on the PCT now for a different route back to the Suiattle River trail. Total distances are the same. Dropping from Suiattle Pass, your legs will struggle to hold back your ready-to-roll body. The roar of Miners Creek fills the valley here. This portion of the PCT soon eases into a gradual descent through magnificent, ancient trees. We didn't see any furry Ewoks, but we're sure they live here.

Upon reaching the Suiattle River, you quickly rejoin the trail you entered on. You then retrace your initial 10.8 miles. But by looping back on the PCT, you'll add another dimension to the journey. Also keep in mind, the forested PCT provides more protection from heat or foul weather than the exposed Miners Ridge trail.

Some people hike one-way from the Suiattle River trailhead, over Suiattle Pass, then 19.8 miles north on the PCT through South Fork Agnes Creek valley (Trip 107), to the Stehekin River.

To complete that circuit, you must pay for the shuttle bus to Stehekin and the boat trip down Lake Chelan, then have a shuttle vehicle waiting for the 10-hour drive around the mountains back to the Suiattle trailhead. It's a navigating nightmare. Also, after 4.0 miles through subalpine gardens, the South Fork is a monotonous walk through forest that we think you can easily skip and not be sorry.

FACT

By Car

From the junction of Highways 20 and 530 at Rockport, drive south 11.3 miles on 530. Or, from Darrington on Highway 530, drive north 7.2 miles on 530. On the east side of the Sauk River bridge, turn east onto Suiattle River Road 26 and drive 23.0 miles southeast to Sulphur Creek Campground. Road's end and the trailhead are just beyond, at 1600 feet.

On Foot

Begin by walking 0.8 mile to a fork where Milk Creek trail 790 crosses the Suiattle River and goes southeast. Staying on the northeast side of the river, continue straight (southeast) on Suiattle River trail 784, which is mostly level for 10.0 miles through forest, gaining only 1000 feet. At 6.5 miles, 2350 feet, cross Canyon Creek. There's a campground to the right of the trail on the west side of the creek. At 10.8 miles, near a small creek, just west of the junction with Miners Ridge trail 785, there are small campsites at 2800 feet. At the junction, go left (northeast). There's a creek 0.75 mile up where you can refill water bottles. After steeply ascending 2.5 miles to 4800 feet and another junction, go left (north) and ascend 2.2 miles and 1200 feet to reach Miners Ridge at 6000 feet. Your total distance to this point is 15.5 miles. Drop your pack and walk 0.2 mile northwest along the ridge to the old fire lookout. Dome Peak and Dome Glacier are the preeminent sights north. Glacier Peak dominates the southern horizon.

Image Lake is 0.8 mile farther northeast (right), at 6050 feet. On the way, you'll come to a fork where a trail circles the lake. Stay right, hugging the southern edge of the lake, for the quickest route to the campground 0.5 mile farther. It's in the basin southeast of the lake. Though you don't see the lake from the campground, many sites have views of Glacier Peak. There's a creek trickling past the campground. Be sure to hang your food at night and whenever you leave your site. The bold, rampaging marmots won't hesitate to maraud your tent if they smell something appealing. They'll frolic right beside you; even pose for pictures.

For the daytrip to Canyon Lake, start 0.2 mile off the southeast end of the trail around Image Lake. Hikers with off-trail knowhow can drop from the ridge north of Image Lake down to the Canyon Lake trail. This shortcut will probably be snow-covered until mid-August. The trail descends north, heads east on the northern side of Miners Ridge, then traverses north above the upper end of the Canyon Creek drainage beneath Sitting Bull Mountain, and arrives at 5700-foot-high Canyon Lake in 7.0 miles.

Continuing east from Image Lake, pick up Miners Ridge trail above the campground. It immediately ascends several hundred feet, then is fairly level through flower-filled alpine meadows before descending 500 feet to a junction at 5500' with trail 795. Go left, continuing east 1.6 level miles on Miners Ridge trail to a junction with the PCT. Just before reaching the PCT, you'll pass campsites near a tributary of Miners Creek plummeting down from Plummer Mountain. Now going straight (east) on the PCT, ascend 0.8 mile to 5983-foot Suiattle Pass. A right turn south on the PCT descends to Miners Creek (take that trail on your return from Cloudy Pass). Just west of Suiattle Pass and below the trail is a campsite in a tiny meadow. Total distance from the Image Lake campground to Suiattle Pass is 4.0 miles.

Suiattle is not a classic alpine pass. Trees and other vegetation obstruct views. On your way through, take the path angling right instead of following the PCT north down into the South Fork Agnes Creek drainage. The 483-foot descent on the PCT going left might not be necessary if you're going to Cloudy Pass. The boot-beaten path stays high and traverses a headwall, allowing you to maintain your elevation on a more direct line to the pass, and providing a view several miles down the South Fork valley. If you're here after late July in an average snowfall year, the rocky chute you scramble through should have little snow and therefore be less precarious. It's a 1.2-mile, 538-foot ascent from Suiattle Pass to Cloudy Pass this way, and a total distance of 22.0 miles from the Suiattle River trailhead. If the headwall traverse is snow-covered, however, go back and take the longer, safer route on the PCT that drops to 5500 feet.

Opting for the PCT, you'll descend 0.5 mile to a junction. Take the right fork east and in 0.3 mile, at 5500 feet, come to where the old PCT, now labeled trail 1239, branches north. Continue straight (east), ascending 0.4 mile to where the headwall traverse comes in from the right; then ascend 0.5 mile more to 6438-foot Cloudy Pass—1.7 miles via this longer route from Suiattle Pass. The mountains surrounding you are: Sitting Bull in the northwest, Cloudy above you northeast, Fortress south, and Chiwawa southeast.

If you're hiking the PCT south through the South Fork Agnes Creek valley on your way to Cloudy Pass, avoid Suiattle Pass by turning left at the junction described at the beginning of the previous paragraph. That way is easier and faster.

From Cloudy Pass, it's a 1.0-mile, 840-foot descent to Lyman Lake. You can camp in the basin north of the lake, but it's usually mosquito- and fly-infested, so you might prefer a high camp somewhere off the pass, where the bugs will be less bothersome. If you've arranged to hike all the way through to Holden and boat down Lake Chelan, it's 9.3 miles from the north end of Lyman Lake, paralleling above Railroad Creek (Trip 92), to Holden village and the shuttle bus that'll take you down to the *Lady of the Lake II* on Lake Chelan. But then you have the problem of getting back to your vehicle on the Suiattle River road.

If you're returning from Cloudy Pass to the Suiattle River trailhead, hike back to the junction 0.8 mile west of Suiattle Pass. From here, the PCT descends to a footlog crossing of Miners Creek and arrives in 2.8 miles at a 4600-foot junction with trail 789 heading south over Buck Creek Pass. Go right on the PCT on a long, gradual descent west through ancient forest. In 4.8 miles, after losing 1800 feet, you'll reach the Suiattle River and another junction at 2798 feet. The PCT crosses the river to ascend the northern slopes of Glacier Peak. Stay on the east bank, heading northwest on trail 784. There's a campground here, in tall trees between the river and Miners Creek. Cross the creek on a footlog and go slightly uphill 1.25 miles to a junction with the Miners Ridge trail. Just before that, a landslide path grants you a view southwest to grassy Gamma Ridge. At the junction, bear left and walk 10.8 miles back to the Suiattle River trailhead. If you take this PCT route on your return, your total round trip to Cloudy Pass is 43.8 miles.

Trip 95
Buck Creek Pass / High Pass

Location	Glacier Peak Wilderness / Wenatchee National Forest.
Distance	19.2-mile round trip to Buck Creek Pass.
Elevation gain	3100′.
Maps	Green Trails No. 113–Holden; US Forest Service–Glacier Peak Wilderness.

OPINION

Idyllic meadows undulate from pass to pass. Imposing Glacier Peak crowds out the sky. Ice-laden Clark Mountain vies for attention with the great volcano. The deep, green Suiattle River valley adds dimension to the scene. Memorize those four sentences and repeat them aloud, mantra-like, on this disheartening trail. It will help you endure the badgering bugs, disenchanted forest, deadfall difficulties, enervating heat, and virtual viewlessness. The only external inspiration will be a glimpse of massive, angular Buck Mountain. Though impressive, it alone might not buck you up sufficiently to persevere. And you should; you'll be well rewarded. Exhilaration will kick in about a mile before the pass.

The Buck Creek Pass environs offer a choice of compelling explorations. From the subalpine basin a mile east of Buck Creek Pass, you can traverse spectacular alpine country beneath Helmet Butte and find superb campsites. At Buck Creek Pass you can continue south along the slope of Liberty Cap toward High Pass—the scenic climax of the trip. The pastoral summit of nearby Flower Dome is also a worthwhile excursion, but less so than the others.

Black flies can be nightmarish until you escape up the headwall of Buck Creek valley. On this hike, you really should bring a bevy of friends. Together you'll stay sane by keeping the mood light and distracting each other from your misery. Be prepared to eschew rest stops for the first 8 miles. Slurping water and chuffing down snacks on the go is more comfortable than stopping, because of the swarming flies. Stand still and you'll immediately have 60 of the little blighters crawling all over you. However, they usually don't show up for work until it gets warm, around 10 A.M., so it helps a lot to start hiking before 7 A.M. And because they usually go to bed as soon as it cools off, around 5 P.M., you should begin your return hike from Buck Creek Pass after 3 P.M. Either hike all the way out that evening, or camp part-way and finish the next morning.

Speedsters can smoke the trail to Buck Creek Pass on a Saturday, then visit High Pass and hike all the way back out on Sunday. But most people should allow at least three days, with the second day devoted to high-elevation exploring.

FACT

By Car

Drive Highway 2 to Coles Corner, 19.5 miles east of Stevens Pass, or 16.0 miles northwest of Leavenworth. Turn north onto Highway 207 and head toward Lake Wenatchee. Pass the state park and the road to Plain. At 4.3 miles, go right (east) toward the Chiwawa Loop Road. At 5.7 miles turn left onto Meadow Creek Road, which takes you north to Fish Lake and the Chiwawa River valley. Pavement ends at 16.8 miles. At 20.2 miles pass the entrance to Riverbend Campground, the first of several excellent free campgrounds in the valley. At 28.1 miles reach a fork and a sign PHELPS CR T.H. 2 ⇒, PHELPS CR CAMPGROUND ⇑. Take the left fork. Pass Phelps Creek Campground on the left at 28.4 miles. Arrive at the trailhead parking lot at 28.7 miles, 2800 feet.

On Foot

Begin by crossing Phelps Creek on a bridge. The trail initially meanders around the Trinity mining operation. Stay left at 0.4 mile where a sign directs you toward the Buck Creek trail. You're now on an old road. At the next fork (not on maps), go right. Enter Glacier Peak Wilderness at 0.7 mile. The road soon dwindles to trail. Go left (northwest) at the junction in 1.4 miles, 3100 feet. The Red Mountain trail is right. The forest is more verdant after 1.7 miles.

Cross the Chiwawa River on a bridge at 3.0 miles. There are campsites above the west bank. To this point, elevation gain is hardly noticeable. Beyond, the trail ascends moderately through drier forest. Near 4 miles, just before a meadow, 8573-foot Buck Mountain appears to the left (southwest), rising 5000 feet above you.

Here the ascent northwest begins in earnest, but long switchbacks allow a comfortable pace. There's a stream and a flat campsite at 5.7 miles. Proceed through dense, tall timber. Pass a larger campsite at 6.0 miles. The valley narrows and you can see both walls, the one to the southwest distinguished by rocky escarpments and green avalanche slopes.

At 7.0 miles a new route has been forged through a huge swath of downfall flattened by an avalanche. You can see where the avalanche shredded the opposite wall of the valley, then careened up the northeast wall where you are. After following the trail among the downed trees, you'll reach the edge of standing forest. Don't cross the boggy drainage ahead of you; the trail stays left, heading up-canyon into more deadfall. Go to the edge of the deadfall. There's a campsite 50 yards beyond where standing forest resumes. The long switchback darting southeast on the Green Trails map is well after the deadfall.

Via this switchback at 7.5 miles the trail goes sharply right, away from Buck Creek, then begins ascending steeply northwest—600 feet in the next 0.8 mile. Then the grade eases on a high traverse. Near 8.3 miles the forest opens, revealing the headwaters of Buck Creek, the forested pass, and the meadowy slopes under Helmet Butte. Water is available at 8.8 miles, in the basin below Pass No Pass. This is where a narrow spur trail ascends north beneath Helmet Butte.

At 9.6 miles, 5900 feet, reach a slope 100 feet above Buck Creek Pass. Trail 789 continues northwest through the pass to Middle Ridge. There's a creeklet at the south end of the pass and campsites scattered in trees below the southeast side.

To reach High Pass, take the trail dropping into Buck Creek Pass. Follow it south through trees and meadows 0.25 mile and pick up signed trail 1562.2. It jogs northwest, around the ridge. Once on the ridge, it turns south. There's no reliable water source en route to High Pass, so carry plenty.

Ascending the west side of Liberty Cap, the trail is in grass and heather. Miners Ridge and Plummer Mountain are visible north, across the Suiattle River valley. Dome Peak is beyond. At 1.5 miles, on the grassy slope of Liberty Cap, 8876-foot Clark Mountain leaps into view south. At 1.75 miles reach an open saddle. Here you can look east and see the trail that led you up the Buck Creek valley toward Helmet Butte and Fortress Mountain. To the west, Glacier Peak looms large.

Continuing south to High Pass, the trail is a narrow, rough, sometimes exposed path above a sheer drop into the valley. If you're confident and capable, you can easily follow the path as it contours along the ridgecrest. Hikers' tread ends 3.0 miles from Buck Creek Pass, at a 6900-foot saddle above Triad Lake, which is cupped in a cirque to the southwest.

Wandering near Liberty Cap

Trip 96

Pyramid Mountain

Location	Chelan Mountains / Wenatchee National Forest.
Distance	18.4-mile round trip.
Elevation gain	2800' in, 1100' out.
Maps	Green Trails No. 114–Lucerne, No. 113–Holden (to identify Entiat Peaks in the northwest), No. 115–Prince Creek (to identify peaks across Lake Chelan).

OPINION

If you're willing to pay with sweat, rather than cash, you can enjoy an airplane-view of Lake Chelan, from the summit of Pyramid Mountain. Walking is better anyway. It gives you a fuller experience. Any climax, scenic or otherwise, is more impactful in context. And this is a view to absorb, not just see. The lake is 7145 feet directly below. Mountains ring the horizon. Virtually nothing of human construction is in sight. It's enough to bring you to your knees in gratitude for the gifts of creation.

Chelan is the deepest gorge in North America. From the lake's highest surface level at 1098 feet, mountains rise above 8000 feet. Its deepest point, 386 feet below sea level, is due east of Pyramid Mountain, near Big Goat Creek. Unlike broad Hell's Canyon on the Oregon-Idaho border or Copper Canyon in Mexico, which often claim the appellation "deepest gorge," Chelan actually looks like a gorge; its walls average less than 2 miles apart. Atop Pyramid you can also see much of the lake's east bank, where the incomparable Chelan Lakeshore trail clings to the water's edge.

Being a former fire-lookout site, Pyramid has a view of more than just water. You can see the monster peaks of Glacier Peak Wilderness northwest and those of Lake Chelan-Sawtooth Wilderness across the lake. Though no particular mountain or ridge is startling, the enormity of the scene is enrapturing.

Henry David Thoreau would love it here. Solitude is your constant companion on the high, dry trail to Pyramid. Very few people from Puget Sound drive out of their way to hike in the east Cascades, and very few locals hike up here. The Entiat is popular with motorcyclists, but the obnoxious machines are prohibited on this trail.

With so few people around, you'll notice something else special: the silence. It's joyous. There aren't even any water sounds. Perhaps just a zephyr whispering through the trees. There's an expansiveness to these wide open mountainsides that tends to amplify silence. The generally cooler temperatures at this high altitude might also heighten your sensitivity to the lack of sound. The sun feels gentler, the air lighter, the silence larger. Be aware of this when you're here. Maybe you'll agree.

The Pyramid Mountain environs resemble the dry Pasayten Wilderness. The trails are dusty, sometimes gravelly. Grass grows in tussocks instead of carpet-like meadows. Forests are open and unimpressive. The sky is frequently brilliant blue. And the billowing, white cumulus clouds usually dissipate before turning mean. Pack plenty of water and fill up at every opportunity.

Looking at a map, you'll see it's possible to make Pyramid a loop trip. Don't try it. Return the same way, on the high route, and savor the views again. If you hike the other trails—Pugh Ridge or South Pyramid Creek—you'll plod through boring forest the whole way.

Dayhiking Pyramid via the route described here takes about ten hours, but can be enjoyable if you're up to the challenge. Afterward you can camp at the trailhead or the Shady Pass Road junction. At either place you'll still probably be alone.

FACT

By Car

Drive Highway 97 ALT to the town of Entiat, between Chelan and Wenatchee. If you're driving east on Highway 2/97, when you reach the northwest side of Wenatchee take the Spokane exit, then the second exit onto 97 ALT.

In Entiat, turn west at the sign ENTIAT RIVER RECREATION AREA— GLACIER PEAK WILDERNESS. After passing Lake Creek Campground at 27.8 miles, slow down and look for your turn. At 29.0 miles go right at the sign COTTONWOOD CPGRD 8 ⇑, HALFWAY SPRINGS 4 ⇒, SHADY PASS 8 ⇒, LAKE CHELAN 31 ⇒. You'll then be on Road 5900. The drive to the Big Hill trailhead is on a decent, fairly smooth road. It's passable in a low-clearance, two-wheel-drive vehicle. Just go slow enough to spot the few dips, washboards, and deep-sand patches.

At 4.1 miles from the Entiat River road, continue past Halfway Springs. The campsites are pullouts in trees beside the road. At 8.5 miles, reach Shady Pass in an old burn. The only facility for the campsite is one fire grate. From the pass, take narrow Road 112 left. Don't start down the hill going east. At 9.3 miles, look right to see Lake Chelan far below. At the fork at 10.4 miles, go straight on Road 113. The signpost might be down in the dirt. Don't go right. That way cuts back sharply to ascend Big Hill. Arrive at the large, open trailhead parking area at 10.8 miles, 6500 feet.

On Foot

Start walking on the old fire-break and in 30 yards cut left onto the trail, marked by cairns. It switchbacks 0.3 mile up to rejoin the fire-break. The trail is a bit longer than the firebreak, but it's smoother, easier to walk.

Leave the burn area of a 1970s fire at 0.9 mile, where the trail turns north. The view west is over the Entiat River valley, to the Entiat Mountains. Your goal is visible to the north: Pyramid is the bald, rounded mountain on the right. There's a feasible campsite just past the 1.0-mile sign. You can see east into the Chelan gorge, but you can't see the lake yet. The trees here are tamaracks, or golden larches.

At 1.4 miles, 7000 feet, start contouring the west side of Crow Hill, through grass and lupine. Begin a 600-foot descent at 1.8 miles. At 2.7 miles reach a junction. Butte Creek trail 1440 goes left (west) to South Pyramid Creek. Stay right, descending deeper into forest. At 3.2 miles come to the head of Butte Creek. On both sides are pleasant campsites. The shallow creeklet makes it hard to use a water filter, but it's possible. There's a scattering of wildflowers: pearly everlasting, paintbrush, lupine. You'll also find yarrow, which has numerous tiny white flowers in a clump at the top of a stalk with parsley-like leaves.

After this forested basin, the trail ascends 600 feet in 0.7 mile via steep switchbacks up the rocky western slope of Graham Mountain. Then the grade is more gentle. At 4.5 miles the trail starts a 300-foot descent. At 5.3 miles, from a saddle on the northwest slope of Graham Mountain, you can look east and glimpse Lake Chelan below the Graham Harbor Creek drainage. This is a good rest spot. Then, 0.2 mile beyond the saddle, there's a trickle of water through a meadow.

The optimal campsite is at 5.8 miles, in trees beside a flat meadow. The scenery is comparable to that at Butte Creek. Proceed through more forest. The trail disappears for 40 yards through the next meadow, but keep going the same direction (west) and you'll see it resume on the rocky ascent ahead. The junction at 6.3 miles, 6800 feet, has a sign 6 MILES—BIG HILL ROAD. The trail to Pyramid Creek, Pugh Ridge, and Emerald Park drops left. Stay right to ascend north on Pyramid Viewpoint trail 1441.

Pyramid Mountain looms closer, directly north. Near its base, there's a small meadow and an unreliable dribble of water. Look in seeps here for the pinkish-red elephant's head. At 7.4 miles you start contouring the south side of Pyramid Mountain. The trail then begins the climactic 1245-foot ascent in the final 1.7 miles.

As you climb, Pugh Ridge is below you to the west. The tread is now solid dirt and granite. You pass through scattered rocks, clumps of grass and whitebark pine, all the way to the top. You don't ascend the steep side of Pyramid that was visible the first 7 miles. Instead, the trail traverses around to ascend the mellow west side. Moderately graded switchbacks allow you to maintain momentum. Yellow stonecrop and faint-pink spreading phlox add color to the final rocky slope.

Reach the 8245-foot summit of Pyramid Mountain at 9.2 miles. Directly northwest is the ridge of Cardinal Peak. Pinnacle Mountain is just beyond it. Seven Fingered Jack and Mt. Maude are way northwest. Across the Lake Chelan gorge are mountains of the Lake Chelan-Sawtooth Wilderness.

On Pyramid Mountain—7000 feet above Lake Chelan

Trip 97
Cathedral Provincial Park Core Area

Location	Cathedral Provincial Park.
Distance	17.4-mile (28.0-km) round trip to Quiniscoe Lake via the jeep road; 19.8-mile (32.0-km) round trip via the Lakeview trail.
Elevation gain	3936' (1200 m).
Maps	the free B.C. Parks brochure–Cathedral Provincial Park; National Topographic Series for Canada: Ashnola River 92 H/1.

OPINION

Above sweeping forested slopes, hidden from the valleys below, is this kingdom of piercing peaks and lovely lakes crowning a high plateau. Once you're up there, the dayhike possibilities to open ridges, granite outcroppings, and azure waters beneath serrated mountains—all connected by a generous trail network—make it an alpine playground. But playgrounds get crowded and noisy, and this one's no exception. There's a private resort on the shore of the park's central lake, Quiniscoe, and guests are shuttled in on a jeep road. So if you've always yearned to penetrate the realm of the persistent hiker, but would rather pay for it with money instead of muscle, here's your chance.

Cathedral's location between the Cascade rain forests and the arid Okanagan Highland makes it unique. So does its trail system, which offers vantages at varying altitudes, giving you a more complete picture of the geography. And Cathedral's Rim trail is uniquely rewarding, because it provides a sustained alpine experience: you don't plunge back into forest immediately after climbing above treeline, as so often happens in the Cascades.

There are several ways to storm this bastille: Lakeview Creek, Ewart Creek, Wall Creek. Since all the approaches are in trees, we recommend the shortest—either the Lakeview trail or the jeep road that parallels Lakeview Creek—so you can enjoy more time up top. Officially, hikers aren't allowed on the road, but as long as you politely yield the right-of-way to the resort's shuttle vehicles, they don't mind. The road and the trail are both featureless endurance tests. The trail grants you a few more glimpses of the distant horizon, but you'll see it all while dayhiking above. The road is more direct and therefore quicker than the trail, and the one or two vehicles you'll encounter aren't enough to be annoying. Both approaches are aggressive, rocketing onto the plateau. The level lapses are few and short, with liftoff resuming immediately.

Once you've powered your way up to Quiniscoe Lake at 6888 feet (2100 meters), you can establish your launchpad there, at nearby Lake of the Woods, or even at Pyramid Lake. All are gorgeous, but the latter two feel wilder and are only a 10-or 15-minute walk from Quiniscoe. Quiniscoe offers cages to keep your food safe from marauding squirrels. Pyramid has the most dramatic view, with the cliffs of Pyramid Mountain in your face. We prefer Lake of the Woods, where the sites are sprinkled around the lake.

Grinding up to Quiniscoe Lake is hardly worthwhile until the trails above it are snow-free. That's usually mid-July, possibly late June in years of light snowfall. Keep in mind, although Cathedral is conducive to a basecamp-and-dayhike setup, it isn't necessarily the ideal first backpack trip of the season. You'll find the wickedly steep approach less challenging later in the summer, after you've developed your mountain muscles; however, that's when the area gets busy.

Although you might enjoy a week-long Cathedral trip, consider four days the minimum: one in, two for dayhiking, and one out. Devote the second day to the Rim trail, the third day to Lakeview Mountain via Goat Lakes.

Now a few suggestions on dayhiking. If the sky is clear, burst out of your tent and race onto the Rim trail for a spectacular, high-elevation tour. If you see serious weather moving in, get down quickly. At 8573 feet (2614 meters) on the south end and 8367 feet (2551 meters) on the north, you'd be a red flag for a bullish lightning bolt. Low clouds can pose a danger here, by obscuring the route and making it impossible to follow the cairns. The loop is more rugged than the park map indicates, especially when gaining the lip of the rim, so don't expect the trip to go quickly. Allow a full day.

If the weather is threatening, and you don't want to venture onto the rim, you can still enjoy descending into the upper reaches of Lakeview Creek and visiting Goat Lakes. If you're lucky, a break in the clouds will grant you a view of Denture Ridge taking a bite out of the sky. They should have named it Monster Mouth.

On a clear day, think of the Goat Lakes cirque not as a destination but rather a point of interest en route to Lakeview Mountain. Ascending its rounded slopes is easy and will afford you a tremendous view southwest to Denture Ridge, Matriarch Mountain, Macabre Tower and Grimface Mountain. Even if you only scurry above the trees, it's worthwhile.

Once you attain the broad, open saddle between Lakeview Mountain and the Boxcar, you can ascend either or both. Go south to the Boxcar for a fix of rock and rubble. If you're a capable scrambler, you'll grok the way. Starting from a campsite at the core lakes near Quiniscoe Lake, experienced, fit hikers can bag the Boxcar and Lakeview Mountain in a single day—if the pleasant roaming at the saddle, amidst talus and alpine forget-me-nots, doesn't weaken your resolve to push on.

If possible, turn the ascent of Lakeview Mountain into a loop excursion. Enjoy the creek-and-meadow walk southeast to Goat Lakes. Ascend Lakeview Mountain from there. Then, if the weather holds, you have the option of traversing the mountain and picking up the Centennial trail, descending to Lakeview Creek, and looping back to the core lakes.

Finally, be sure to take in Glacier Lake before you leave the park. Surrounded by mountains on three sides, it seems wilder—higher and more remote—than the other lakes. Also, from the ridge separating Quiniscoe and Glacier lakes, you can see Lakeview Mountain southeast and the Similkameen Valley northeast. If bad weather is keeping you off the rim, it's worth checking out the views from lower ridges like this one.

FACT

Because Cathedral is in Canada, if you're from the U.S., you might be wondering, "is this grizzly country?" Cougar, wolverine, deer, and black bear inhabit the park, but not grizzlies—they were all shot long ago by ranchers. And the black bear stay down in the valleys, because it's such paltry dining for them at higher elevations.

Before leaving home, get the B.C. Parks brochure and map of Cathedral Provincial Park by contacting the Okanagan District Manager. Mountain bikes are not allowed on any trails in the park. Dogs are prohibited in the core area surrounding Quiniscoe Lake because they've harassed wildlife and people in the past.

By Car

Driving Highway 3, near the western edge of Keremeos, you'll see a B.C. Parks sign 24 KM CATHEDRAL LAKES PROVINCIAL PARK. Turn south onto the Ashnola River Road. If you're going to pay for the shuttle up to Quiniscoe Lake, drive 13.8 miles (22.2 km) southwest to the Cathedral Lakes Resort Base parking lot. Pick-up times are 10 A.M., 2 P.M., and 4 P.M. The round trip costs $50 CDN per person and will continue to get more expensive. Call (604) 499-5848 for reservations. If you're going to hike up, drive 1.0 mile (1.6 km) farther to the Lakeview Creek trailhead and campground, 2952 feet (900 meters). There are walk-in tent sites here along the Ashnola River, 30 yards/meters from the parking area.

On Foot

From the Lakeview Creek trailhead, you can hike to Quiniscoe Lake 8.7 miles (14.0 km) on the jeep road or 9.9 miles (16.0 km) on the trail. Start by crossing the Ashnola River on a footbridge, then ascending a trail southeast to the jeep road.

For the shortest route, stay on the road. You'll initially ascend the east side of Lakeview Creek (locally referred to as Noisy Creek) then, at approximately 1 mile (1.6 km), cross a bridge to the west side for the rest of the way. You'll see the mileage posted on trees along the road. Camping is not allowed anywhere along the road. The steepest sections are at 5.0 miles (8.0 km) and 7.5 miles (12.1 km). The only view from the road is at 8.0 miles (12.9 km), where you can see the barren summit of 8620-foot (2628-meter) Lakeview Mountain (southeast), the highest point in the park. Arrive in 8.7 miles (14.0 km) at Quiniscoe Lake, 6888 feet (2100 meters).

If you opt to hike the trail to Quiniscoe, after ascending 0.6 mile (1.0 km) on trail, rejoin the road just before crossing Lakeview Creek. At 2.2 miles (3.5 km) up, you'll see a sign where trail

Goat Lake and Denture Ridge, Cathedral Park

resumes off the road to the right (northwest). Halfway up there's a campground on the north side of Lindsey Creek. Farther southwest the trail breaks out of the trees and you reach a junction at 7.7 miles (12.4 km). Stay straight, continuing southwest on the Lakeview trail to arrive at Quiniscoe Lake in 9.9 miles (16.0 km).

If you take the side excursion from the 7.7-mile junction, the Diamond trail goes right (northwest), circling around Scout Mountain. Stay left at junctions with the Centennial and Rim trails to rejoin the Lakeview trail 0.5 mile (0.8 km) before Quiniscoe. This route adds 2.0 miles (3.2 km) to the total trip. Check in at the ranger cabin at Quiniscoe Lake and get the park map showing all the trails. There's a $2-a-night fee to camp at Quiniscoe.

Radiating from the core lakes, all the Cathedral trails are well maintained, clearly signed, and marked on the park map. The Rim and Lakeview Mountain trails, however, are actually routes, not trails, and are marked by cairns, not signs. Beginning at Quiniscoe Lake, these are the approximate distances and elevation gains for the possible dayhikes:

Lake of the Woods—0.8 mile (1.3 km) one way, level; Glacier Lake—0.9 mile (1.5 km) one way, 410 feet (125 m); Ladyslipper Lake—1.9 miles (3.0 km) one way, 490 feet (150 m); Goat Lakes—3.1 miles (5.0 km) one way, 490 feet (150 m); Lakeview Moun-

tain—8.0-mile (13.0-km) loop, 1970 feet (600 m); Rim trail, south
end—7.0-mile (11.3-km) loop, 1770 feet (540 m); Rim trail, north
end—6.0-mile (9.7-km) loop, 1570 (480 m).

To reach Goat Lakes, head southeast from the east end of
Quiniscoe, toward Pyramid Lake. Just past Pyramid, come to a
junction. Go left (east), descending about 15 minutes to another
junction. Then turn right (south), staying west of Goat Creek. (If
the weather allows a traverse of Lakeview Mountain, this junction is where you'll loop back on the Centennial trail.) There are
no more junctions south to Goat Lake.

The routes up Lakeview Mountain and the Boxcar begin near
the rocky, tussocky Goat Lakes outlet. Look for a sign and cairns
indicating where to hop across the stream. Then go east, following orange blazes on trees. At the trailer-size boulders, turn left
onto a narrow route. It's steep and lacks switchbacks, but it's
short—only about 15 minutes to the saddle. From there, turn
right (south) to scramble up the Boxcar, left (north) to reach the
summit of Lakeview Mountain. The route down the north side of
Lakeview Mountain joins the Centennial trail to loop back to the
core lakes.

The Rim trail offers three choices. You can hike it end-to-end:
from Stone City in the south, to Red Mountain in the north. Or
you can start by ascending above Glacier Lake, then hiking just
the south or north end of the rim.

To hike the rim end-to-end, first walk from Quiniscoe Lake
southeast to Pyramid Lake. Just past it, stay right at the junction
and ascend south to Ladyslipper Lake. Before the final drop into
the Ladyslipper basin, there's a view south of Goat Lakes and
Denture Ridge, and southeast to the saddle between Lakeview
Mountain and the Boxcar. From Ladyslipper's southeast side,
cross the outlet stream and follow the trail climbing steeply
southwest through rock piles. When the ascent eases and you
attain the rim, keep following the cairns. To see the rock formations called Smokey the Bear and the Giant Cleft, detour left
(southeast) before continuing north along the rim.

To hike either end of the rim, first walk along the south side of
Quiniscoe Lake. Go through the campground and ascend southwest on the ridge separating Quiniscoe Lake from Glacier Lake.
This trail will meet the trail coming up from Glacier Lake. Continue climbing the talus slope above Glacier Lake to the south end
of a saddle.

To hike the south end of the rim, when you reach the saddle above Glacier Lake turn left (southeast). You'll swing around Pyramid Mountain, skirting the unusual geologic features called Devil's Woodpile and Stone City. Just after Stone City, you'll see a trail descending left to Ladyslipper Lake. To visit Smokey the Bear and the Giant Cleft, detour straight (southeast), then return to the junction, drop to Ladyslipper and follow the well-defined trail back to Quiniscoe.

To hike the north end of the rim, when you reach the saddle above Glacier Lake, turn right (north). Following cairns, pick your way through scree, boulders, and meadows. This King-of-the-Mountain route will lead you over 8367-foot (2551-meter) Quiniscoe and 8098-foot (2469-meter) Red mountains. From a northeast arm of Red Mountain, the Rim trail descends southeast to a junction with the Centennial trail. Descend right to the Lakeview trail, then go right again to head south to Quiniscoe Lake.

Trip 98
Snowy Lakes

Location	North Cascades Scenic Highway Corridor / Okanogan National Forest.
Distance	19.6-mile round trip.
Elevation gain	2580' in, 600' out.
Maps	Green Trails No. 50–Washington Pass; Trails Illustrated No. 223–North Cascades National Park Complex.

OPINION

On this stretch of the Pacific Crest Trail, you feel you're actually trekking along the crest. After an easy ascent to Cutthroat Pass, the trail stays high for 6 miles. The highlight is the 2.3-mile, level traverse above the sweeping expanse of Swamp Creek valley. You can see it from above Granite Pass—an airy vantage where, on a sunny day, you might experience a lightness of being, which is how we imagine the wing-footed messenger god Hermes must have felt.

Here on the east side of the North Cascades, the peaks aren't jaw-droppers that inspire emotional verbosity. And they're certainly not verdant, like the ranges farther west. They're simply stark. But the arid scenery does have a calming, cleansing affect, much like the desert. It reminds us of Nevada's Great Basin. Even the heat can be similar. On a hot summer day, be sure to haul plenty of water. Better yet, make this a cool weather, late-season hike, when you can count on the steeply descending switchbacks to Granite Pass being safely snow-free.

Above Granite Pass, at the switchbacks, pause to survey Swamp Creek far below and, north across the upper valley, the jags of 8444-foot Tower Mountain and 8366-foot Golden Horn. At this point, you might question the need to descend, since the trail all the way to Methow Pass is now visible. Ah, go on. Don't let logic hold you back. Careen downhill to the pass, like a gleeful kid in a red wagon. The pleasure of walking the narrow traverse to the Snowy Lakes side trail more than compensates for the brief struggle up from Granite on the return.

Herculean hikers can make this trip a real challenge, bounding all the way to the Snowy Lakes and back to Rainy Pass in one day. Allow nine or ten hours, including breaks for resting, refueling and spectating. From the Snowy Lakes side trail branching off the PCT, it's possible to attain the upper lake in 20 minutes. Here, the orange granite of the Golden Horn is a commanding sight. So is the huge wall and piercing spires of Mount Hardy, to the southwest.

From the ridge west of the upper lake, you can see into the West Fork Methow River valley. That should convince you not to proceed. After Methow Pass, it's 12 forested miles before the PCT climbs back onto a scenic ridge, above Glacier Pass. Skip that section. Instead, after hiking out to the Snowy Lakes and back, drive farther east and hike the PCT to Grasshopper Pass (Trip 29).

The fragile, abused meadows around the Snowy Lakes need your help. You'll have far less impact if you camp down near the PCT. But if you insist on lying next to the lakes all night while your eyes are closed, pitch your tent on gravel, not on grass. There are flat rocks to sprawl and cook on, so there's no excuse for destroying the vegetation.

FACT

By Car

On Highway 20, drive 37.2 miles southeast of Newhalem, or 20.8 miles southwest of the Early Winters Information Center, to the Rainy Pass trailhead parking lot. It's on the east side of the road, at 4880 feet. Don't turn into the Rainy Pass Picnic Area parking lot on the west side.

On Foot

Initially follow the directions to Cutthroat Pass (Trip 40). Reach Cutthroat Pass at 5.0 miles, 6800 feet. Beyond, the PCT contours northeast 1.4 miles over barren slopes above Cutthroat Creek canyon to a knoll directly above Granite Pass. Here you can look northwest over Swamp Creek valley and see the long traverse ahead. From the knoll, switchbacks plunge 600 feet in 0.5 mile to 6200-foot Granite Pass.

It's 2.3 level miles northwest from Granite Pass to a stream trickling down from the Snowy Lakes. Still on the PCT, you're now 9.3 miles from Rainy Pass. You can camp here in a worn meadow of heather and grass. The side trail to the lakes leaves the PCT near the hitching post and climbs to the prominent gap you see up to your right (north). Gain 500 feet in 0.5 mile to Lower Snowy Lake, at 6735 feet. It's 0.2 mile farther to the upper lake, at 6840 feet.

From the worn meadow and hitching post, it's 1.2 miles southwest on the PCT to 6600-foot Methow Pass. The PCT then drops to 4400 feet in 4.9 miles. At a junction in 18.4 miles, it goes left (northwest) up Brush Creek to reach Grasshopper Pass, approximately 23.4 miles from Rainy Pass.

Trail above Swamp Creek to Snowy Lakes

Trip 99
Skykomish Loops

Location	Henry M. Jackson Wilderness / Wenatchee National Forest.
Distance	18.3 miles for short loop; 24.8 miles for long loop.
Elevation gain	2800' for short loop; 4200' for long loop.
Maps	Green Trails No. 144–Benchmark Mtn; No. 143–Monte Cristo for long loop.

OPINION

Loopsters rejoice. Off the North Fork Skykomish River Road are two backpack trips, the longer of which doesn't require you to retrace a single step. Too bad neither requires you to bring extra film.

The short one reaches Dishpan Gap, rounds Skykomish Peak, crosses Cady Pass, then exits via Pass Creek. The long one is an extension, skipping Pass Creek, rounding Benchmark Mountain and exiting via West Cady Ridge. The short loop is fairly easy, mostly pleasant, through pretty forest and a couple miles of meadow. The environs of Dishpan Gap are a meadowland mecca. The grass and flowers continue south along the east slope of Skykomish Peak. It *is* a peak, but it's nothing special. On the long loop you'll attain far-reaching vistas from atop Benchmark Mountain and enjoy four more miles of meadow.

These and other trails on the Green Trails Map 144 wallow in forest. When they rise above, the scenery is mellow, less distinct than farther north in the range. There are no electrifying sights here. The Skykomish Peak loops are worthwhile partly because of the quick access they provide to Dishpan Gap and the outstanding excursions you can make from there. A half-day hike from Dishpan to Blue Lake or Kodak Peak might set your fireworks off. The panorama from Benchmark Mountain includes Mt. Rainier, Mt. Baker and Glacier Peak, but they're too distant to cause heart palpitations.

For a more exciting, scenic and solitudinous adventure, hike to

Blue Lake and Dishpan Gap via the North Fork Sauk River trail and Pilot Ridge (Trip 91). That approach, however, is longer and tougher.

Lake Sally Ann is merely a pond. It's popular only because it's one of the few reliable water sources in the area, and because it's conveniently close to the busy junction at Dishpan Gap. Many people camp at Sally Ann, then dayhike to Blue Lake—a lovely jewel set in a steep-sided bowl. It's worth shouldering a full pack all the way to Blue, if you can snag one of the few tentsites there.

Can you muster a little extra time and effort? Hike the longer Skykomish Peak loop and ascend Benchmark Mountain. From there you can see the Monte Cristo peaks and Sloan Peak to the northwest, in addition to the three big volcanoes already mentioned. Then comes a glorious meadow tour of West Cady Ridge. Fit hikers can complete the long loop in two days. But if you have to choose between the long loop and side trips to Blue Lake or Kodak Peak, opt for the latter.

As in most North Cascades valleys, you'll be plagued by mosquitoes and flies here from late July to early September. They abate somewhat on the ridges. Brush can be another nuisance here. Ask at the Wenatchee Ranger Station if the North Fork Skykomish and Pass Creek trails have been brushed. If not, hiking them can be an invective-inducing tribulation.

FACT

By Car

From Highway 2, take the Index turnoff. Don't cross the bridge into the town. Drive northwest on the paved North Fork Skykomish River Road 63 to a junction at 14.5 miles. There are several free campsites along the way. Bear left at the junction, staying on Road 63, which is now gravel. Pass the Blanca Lake trailhead at 16.7 miles. The West Cady Ridge trailhead is on the right (south) at 18.8 miles. If you hike the longer loop, this is where you'll come out to the road. To start either of the loops, drive farther to the North Fork trailhead and road's end at 20.2 miles, 3000 feet.

On Foot

Heading generally northwest, the trail penetrates the North Fork Skykomish River valley but is almost never beside the river. You'll ascend 320 feet above the drainage, then stay about 0.5 mile away until the Pass Creek trail junction at 1.5 miles. This first stretch, which you'll repeat on the short loop, is marshy.

Where the Pass Creek trail goes right (east), continue straight (northwest) through open forest and several large meadows. At 4.2 miles cross the North Fork on a footlog. There's a campsite here. After 5.0 miles the trail is level for 1.0 mile through huckleberry bushes and meadows. At 5.8 miles, 4600 feet, switchbacks climb 1000 feet in 1.5 miles to reach 5600-foot Dishpan Gap at 7.3 miles. This is a 4-way junction. Left (north) leads 0.8 mile to the Bald Eagle Mountain trail and 1.6 miles to Blue Lake. Straight ahead (northeast), the Pacific Crest Trail skirts Meander Meadow in 1.0 mile then offers a view north as it contours the east shoulder of Kodak Peak. Turn right (south) onto the PCT to continue the loop.

South of Dishpan Gap, ascend 200 feet through meadow to 5680-foot Wards Pass. Reach a junction at 8.7 miles, 5300 feet (incorrectly labeled 5800 on the Green Trails 1986 map). Left (southeast) follows Cady Ridge 6.5 miles to Little Wenatchee River Road 6500. Bear right on the PCT, reaching campsites at meadow-rimmed Lake Sally Ann at 9.1 miles.

On the PCT from Dishpan Gap to Kodak Peak

The PCT then traverses the open east slope of 6368-foot Sky-komish Peak. From the 5560-foot high point on the south end of the ridge, descend 1.8 miles in trees to forested 4300-foot Cady Pass at 13.0 miles. The Cady Creek trail goes left (east). Bear right (southwest) on the PCT to continue the loop. At 13.3 mile turn right (north) onto Pass Creek trail 1053 if you're doing the short loop. There are campsites here, on the east side of Pass Creek.

The Pass Creek trail descends through thick forest, crossing the creek at 14.5 and 15.8 miles. At 16.4 miles reach a footlog over the North Fork Skykomish River. Rejoin the North Fork Skykomish River trail at 16.8 miles. Turn left (southwest) and retrace the initial 1.5 marshy miles to the trailhead, completing the 18.3-mile loop.

If you're doing the long loop, stay straight on the PCT at the 13.3-mile junction with the Pass Creek trail. Climb sweeping switchbacks 700 feet in 1.6 miles to another junction. The PCT goes left (south). You go right, ascending yet another 700 feet in 1.5 miles to a fork at 5600 feet. Here, a spur trail climbs 0.3 mile north to the 5816-foot summit of Benchmark Mountain. The main trail proceeds southwest, dropping then rising again, touring the open meadows of West Cady Ridge for 4.0 miles. Near 20.4 miles, begin a 3.0-mile, 2000-foot descent through forest to the North Fork Skykomish River Road. Unless you pre-arranged a shuttle, turn right (northeast) and walk an additional 1.4 miles up the road to where you started, at the North Fork trailhead. This completes a 24.8-mile loop.

Trip 100

Cascade Loop /
Monuments 78 and 83

Location	Manning Provincial Park / Pasayten Wilderness / Okanogan National Forest.
Distance	33.8-mile (54.4-km) loop.
Elevation gain	4200' (1280 meters).
Maps	the free B.C. Parks brochure–Manning Provincial Park; Manning Park and Skagit Valley Recreation Area topo by the B.C. Ministry of Environment; Trails Illustrated No. 223–North Cascades National Park Complex; Green Trails No. 17–Jack Mountain, No. 18–Pasayten Peak.

OPINION

What's fun about most loop trips is enjoying new scenery the entire way. But that's presuming the scenery changes, and on this loop it hardly does. There's not enough variety to keep you awake on your feet. It's a long trudge through trees, with only a few fleeting exceptions: small meadows here and there, a view of Ptarmigan and Cathedral peaks from Monument 83, and a view of Joker and Castle peaks from Frosty Pass.

Not only is the scenery somnolent, much of the "trail"—13.5 dreary miles—is actually an old fire-lookout access road. And don't let the international aspect of this hike tempt you. If not for the two unexciting border monuments and the border swath-cut, you'd never know which country you were in.

You shouldn't set foot here. The North Cascades, even in Manning Park, have so much more to offer, like the thrilling panorama atop Frosty Mountain, or the Heather trail's marathon meadows.

Anyone completing the Pacific Crest Trail north of Harts Pass has to hike from Castle Creek to B.C. Highway 3, but at least they only have to endure the scenery once. If you're a PCT through-hiker coming up from the U.S., and you've never experienced the mountains of Canada, please don't assume this stretch through Manning Park is representative. Plan a trip to the stupendous Canadian Rockies. Pick up a copy of *Don't Waste Your Time in the Canadian Rockies, An Opinionated Hiking Guide to Help You Get the Most from this Magnificent Wilderness*.

Trip 101
Beaver Loop

Location	North Cascades National Park / Ross Lake Recreation Area.
Distance	27.0-mile shuttle trip using a water taxi.
Elevation gain	3500'.
Maps	Green Trails No. 15–Mt. Challenger, No. 16–Ross Lake, No. 48–Diablo Dam; Trails Illustrated No. 223–North Cascades National Park Complex.

OPINION

In a mountain range infamous for brushy trails, this could be the worst. Tunneling your way through the towering vegetation can make you feel like a character in "Honey I Shrunk the Kids." When you're not flailing at the stinging, clinging plants, you'll be swatting mosquitoes, flies and bees, as thick here as anywhere in the range. Don't go. It's a jungle odyssey suited only for those seeking a crash course in misery. Marching 26 mostly frustrating miles with only occasional up-periscope views of peaks isn't worth it. The ancient trees, including many giant cedars, are magnificent. But you can hike to equally impressive groves elsewhere—more easily and enjoyably. Try the North Fork Sauk River (Trip 90), or the White Chuck Bench (Trip 83).

If you're tempted by what appears on a map to be a creekside route nearly the whole way, bear in mind that Little and Big Beaver creeks are rarely visible or even audible. You might think Beaver Pass would be a wonderfully scenic climax. It's not—too many trees. Maybe you're drawn to the deep-forest campsites. They are beautiful, especially Stillwell Camp. But you'll find the beauty hard to enjoy with the incessant bugs. And if you're assuming such a low-elevation route would make an ideal early-season backpack trip, you could again be disappointed. Deep snow lingers surprisingly long in Beaver Pass, which angles north/south. Before mid-June, the trail is clear only to within a couple miles on either side of the pass.

If you insist on seeing this area, do it after mid-September, when the bugs are gone and (keep your fingers crossed) a trail crew might have brushed the trail. Better yet, take the water taxi (supplied by Ross Lake Resort) only as far as Big Beaver Landing, or hike there 7.3 miles from Ross Dam trailhead. Camp there, near the cascades of the wild river mouth, amid the fiord-like scenery, then either dayhike up the Big Beaver or do an over-nighter to Beaver Pass and back. If there are only two of you, it's not worth paying $50 (the 1995 price) for a water taxi to do the entire loop.

Certainly don't hike either of the Beavers if your goal is What-com Pass. The access is easier, the ascent less steep, and the hiking more pleasant on the Chilliwack River trail (Trip 88).

Obstacles on the Beaver Loop

Trip 102

McMillan Park / Devils Park / Jackita Ridge / Devils Dome

Location	Pasayten Wilderness / Mt. Baker-Snoqualmie National Forest.
Distance	15.2-mile round trip to Devils Park; 41.9-mile loop; 26.4-mile shuttle trip from Canyon Creek to Ross Lake using a water-taxi.
Elevation gain	4900' to Devils Park; 8350' gain / 8500' loss for loop starting at Canyon Creek; 7200' gain / 7500' loss from Canyon Creek to Ross Lake.
Maps	Green Trails No. 16–Ross Lake, No. 17 Jack Mountain, No. 48–Diablo Dam, No. 49–Mt. Logan; Trails Illustrated No. 223–North Cascades National Park Complex; US Forest Service–Pasayten Wilderness.

OPINION

Beware the monster of monotony. Surmounting 3400 feet in 4 miles, you expect to respond "Wow!" to what you see. But arriving at McMillan Park, you'll look around and mutter "Oh." The scenery is just as insipid as what you plodded through to get there. Punishing ascents like up Sourdough Mountain (Trip 27) are worth it, because ultimately the experience is superlative. This one is all agony and no ecstasy. It's a waste of time, energy, and knee cartilage.

Adding distaste to misery is the trail itself—pulverized to dust by the hooves of many horses. Remember the Peanuts cartoon character Pigpen? That's you hiking here. Mountain air should cleanse your lungs, not clog them. It should smell fresh, too, not reek of horse manure.

Typical of arid landscapes, convenient water sources are uncomfortably far apart on this trail. Yet the bug population rivals that of a Louisiana swamp. Only in late September do the flies and mosquitoes abate. Deer hunting season, however, starts mid-September, and you don't want to be here after the shoot-out begins.

So, you need a Walkman for entertainment, a surgical mask for the dust, a nose plug for the horse manure, a beekeeper's suit for the bugs, and a fluorescent orange hat and vest for the hunters. What's the benefit of all this? Not much.

Devils Park does offer a broad view, but the mountains east are nondescript and Jack Mountain looks just as good from the highway. Traversing the slopes of Jackita Ridge is frustrating. You feel like a mule, repeatedly hauling your load up and down huge, seemingly pointless changes in elevation.

Roaming ridgeline meadows northeast of Devils Dome, with amazing views of Jack Mountain's northern glaciers, can be heavenly. But getting there—a 18.6-mile, 7200-foot trek—is hell. If it were fun, they would have called it Bacchus' Dome. Place names are often meaningful. Even if you take the shorter approach via water-taxi to Devils Junction Camp, it's still a purgatorial 5400-foot, 7.8-mile climb to the Dome.

Shallow Crater Lake is unappealing. The vertical cirque walls are impressive, but overall the setting is not beautiful. Beyond the lake, scaling the easternmost summit of Crater Mountain might be worthwhile, but it presents a more difficult challenge and offers a less exciting panorama than Sourdough Mountain. Crater doesn't afford a complete view of Diablo and Ross lakes.

The solitude you're likely to find in this area might compensate somewhat for the lack of high-voltage scenery. But don't be lured by the prospect of a big loop. You'd have to hike the Ross Lake East Bank trail, and that's a monster of monotony too.

Trip 103
Bridge Creek / North Fork Bridge Creek

Location	North Cascades National Park / Wenatchee National Forest.
Distance	12.8 miles from Stehekin Road to Bridge Creek trailhead on Highway 20.
Elevation gain	2320'.
Maps	Green Trails No. 50–Washington Pass, No. 81–McGregor Mountain, No. 82–Stehekin; Trails Illustrated No. 223–North Cascades National Park Complex.

OPINION

Avoid this stretch of the Pacific Crest Trail. It's no fun. The peaks you see from the highway at Rainy Pass are far more rugged and interesting than anything you'll spy here. Does it provide a sufficient wilderness experience to excuse the lack of scenery? We think it offers only misery. And a surprising number of hikers ply this route, so you can't even be miserable in peace. During mid-summer, what you'll probably encounter is heat and horseflies, on a long, dusty trail, mostly in trees or head-high brush. Trying to enjoy this trail could rank up there among the major challenges of your hiking career.

So there are only two reasons to walk it: (1) you've traversed Park Creek Pass and don't want to exit via Cottonwood Camp and Cascade Pass, because you've already been there; or (2) you're a through-hiker on the PCT, committed to walking every step of the way.

If you insist on persisting, hike early or late in the day, and try to spend a night at the soothing North Fork campground. It's on a peninsula, with Bridge Creek and the North Fork Bridge Creek raging past you on either side.

A side trip up the North Fork of Bridge Creek can add interest to this journey—if a trail crew has brushed the trail. If not, the tall, dense growth will be too discouraging for most hikers. Exploring the North Fork is best left until September, when the flies abate, or you'll be flapping your arms like a puppet gone mad. Hike at least as far as Walker Park, where the view of Goode Mountain will overwhelm you. Trekking to trail's end, 7 miles deep into this isolated valley, will probably reward you with solitude, as well as tantalizing views of Mt. Logan, waterfalls, and hanging glaciers.

Cooling off in Bridge Creek

Trip 104
Meadow Mountain

Location	Mt. Baker-Snoqualmie National Forest / Glacier Peak Wilderness.
Distance	18.9-mile shuttle trip.
Elevation gain	3500'.
Maps	Green Trails No. 111–Sloan Peak, No. 112–Glacier Peak; US Forest Service–Glacier Peak Wilderness.

OPINION

Yes, you can walk through miles of meadow on the slopes east of Meadow Mountain. Yes, you'll enjoy grand views of Glacier Peak, the White Chuck valley, and Lost Creek Ridge. But it would take more than that to justify the approach here: a dusty, dreary, punishing slog on an abandoned logging road. With almost no shade, the miserable road can be a heat-stroke danger zone on a sunny day. And it's 5 miles long! So what if you get views of Mt. Pugh and glimpses of Glacier Peak along the road? This masochistic trudge is followed by 5 miles on trail, mostly through forest, before reaching the promised meadowlands. Then, after a mere 3 miles along an alpine ridge, the trail slinks back into forest beneath Fire Mountain. Why pay such an exorbitant price for so little pleasure? Other, equally pretty meadows are much easier to reach. Check out Skyline Divide (Trip 1), Green Mountain (Trip 12), or Spider Meadow (Trip 14).

Trip 105

Meander Meadow / Cady Ridge

Location	Henry M. Jackson Wilderness.
Distance	15.8-mile loop.
Elevation gain	2900'.
Maps	Green Trails No. 144–Benchmark Mtn, No. 145–Wenatchee Lake (shows Road 65); US Forest Service–Glacier Peak Wilderness.

OPINION

Brush, bugs, and ball bearings will torment you on this loop.

Though gorgeous, Meander Meadow isn't worth all the vegetation you'll battle to get there. The trail up the Little Wenatchee River valley is beneath beautiful, big trees that you'll hardly notice if the trail hasn't been brushed. Grass and brush in the frequent glades grow 5 feet high. The path is choked for 4.5 miles, until the final ascent to the meadow. If a Forest Service trail crew gets here to clear the path, it's usually not until August. Nevertheless, if you must come, do so by mid-July. The trail is usually snow-free then, except for patches on the upper meadow. Later it gets wickedly hot here and the black flies and mosquitoes are, in the words of a ranger, worse than the plague of Egypt.

As for Cady Ridge, it's forested and cottonmouth dry. The limited views are of trifling mountains. The trail itself is slippery steep, composed of gravel ball bearings that almost ensure a butt-sliding descent.

Consider this circuit only as part of a longer trip that takes in Blue Lake and the views north of Kodak Peak. And if those are your goal, reaching them via the Pilot Ridge / White Pass loop (Trip 91) is a thrill you shouldn't miss.

If you insist on hiking in this area, your first choice should be Poe Mountain (Trip 49). It starts at the same trailhead and quickly ascends to an enjoyable panorama, including an overview of the Little Wenatchee River valley, which should squelch your curiosity about hiking there.

Trip 106
Ice Lakes / Entiat Meadows

Location	Wenatchee National Forest / Glacier Peak Wilderness.
Distance	26.8-mile round trip to the lower Ice Lake; 25.0-mile round trip to Entiat Meadows.
Elevation gain	3700' to the lower Ice Lake; 1900' to Entiat Meadows.
Maps	Green Trails No. 113–Holden, No. 114–Lucerne; US Forest Service–Glacier Peak Wilderness.

OPINION

Add the following important statistics to those above. Number of times you'll be glad you're here: 1, at Ice Lakes. Number of times you'll wish you were someplace else: 562, throughout the rest of the hike. Locals will tell you the Ice Lakes are the jewels of the Entiat. It's true. But they're at the end of an unbearably tedious trail. Leave these jewels embedded in the rough. Hike elsewhere.

The Entiat River valley is disappointing overall. Severe fire damage has left unsightly scars visible from the road. Trailhead access is rough and rocky. Free camping is limited and undesirable. Trails are unscenic for long distances. Motorcyclists, mountainbikers and horseback riders are nearly as prevalent as hikers. Flies are as much a nuisance here as anywhere in the range; wasps can be worse.

What's most memorable about hiking to Ice Lakes is the trail surface. Empty your vacuum cleaner bag, kick up the contents, and take a deep breath. There, now you know what it's like. Imagine enduring it for miles. The land is already so dry that when you spit, it raises a poof of dust. Soil like this doesn't resist speeding tires and pounding hooves; the dust just gets deeper. And that's only one of the travesties of "multiple use." Multiple abuse is more like it.

As for the disenchanted forest, there's nothing pretty about the scraggly trees this trail drags you through. And rarely is the trail close to the river, so you can't take solace in the sight and sound of running water. Visiting the beautiful Entiat Meadows is possible, but seeing them doesn't compensate for the journey, most of which is on the same blah trail as the one to Ice Lakes.

Hiking to Ice Lakes would be particularly discouraging to beginning backpackers; they might never hike again. A surprising number of locals return here repeatedly, yet many seem not to have heard of Pyramid Mountain (Trip 96), which is also in the Entiat, or Spider Meadow (Trip 14), which is just one valley over. Both are vastly more rewarding than Ice Lakes. Pyramid would be an excellent introductory, multi-day adventure for beginners. It's the only destination that warrants a trip up the Entiat. Locals who haven't revelled in the glory of Spider Meadow should be ashamed of themselves. It's one of the jewels of the North Cascades, and hiking there is a joy.

Trip 107
South Fork Agnes Creek

Location	Glacier Peak Wilderness / Wenatchee National Forest.
Distance	19.8 miles one way to Suiattle Pass.
Elevation gain	4800'.
Maps	Green Trails No. 81–McGregor Mountain, No. 113–Holden; Trails Illustrated No. 223–North Cascades National Park Complex; US Forest Service–Glacier Peak Wilderness.

OPINION

Leaping into a boat bound for Stehekin, then forging into the mountains to trek the Pacific Crest Trail sounds like a grand, romantic endeavor. But it's a fool's journey. This is the longest mind-numbing section of the PCT in the North Cascades.

From High Bridge, you can glimpse peaks only at the 5- and 10-mile points, until you reach open subalpine heights at 14 miles. Of course, heroic hikers can vanquish that distance in a single day. And forest is all you should expect to see in any deep North Cascades valley. But only Monet could make this forest look appealing. Besides, the trail makes a point of keeping you away from the creek. And the tread is less maintained than you'd expect of the PCT. For a memorable tour through truly resplendent ancient forest, wander up the White Chuck River to Kennedy Ridge or Red Pass (Trip 90), or along the PCT from the Suiattle River to Suiattle Pass (Trip 94). If you're curious about the South Fork Agnes Creek, you can see a big chunk of it from just east of Suiattle Pass (refer to Trips 94 and 92), without having to actually walk the South Fork.

Trip 108 Shoulder Season

Chelan Lakeshore Trail

Location	Wenatchee National Forest / Lake Chelan National Recreation Area.
Distance	17.0 miles from Prince Creek to Stehekin.
Elevation gain	roughly 2200'.
Maps	Green Trails No. 115–Prince Creek (the first mile of trail), No. 114–Lucerne, No. 82–Stehekin; US Forest Service– Glacier Peak Wilderness.

OPINION

A unique mix of Norway and Greece, this extraordinary trail ranks among the world's greatest. The journey begins with a 20-mile boat ride up a fantastic inland fiord to the trailhead at Prince Creek on the east bank of Lake Chelan. Continuing north, the trail dances along the rocky, rugged, Mediterranean-like shore. You're often within view of the deliciously clear, deep water and the gargantuan mountains that hold it in place.

The most stirring stretch is between Moore Point and Flick Creek. The lake-to-sky spectacle from high on Hunts Bluff is galvanizing. Several possible campsites on the north end of Hunts Bluff offer head-spinning views north to Stehekin and south as far as Domke Mountain, but you'll have to haul drinking water up there.

You'll be about 200 feet above the lake most of the way. At several points you'll be within 50 feet of the lapping water. For about 5 miles (a little less than a third of the total mileage), the trail winds away from the lake into ponderosa-pine forest and lush, creek grottos—cool, moist respites from the generally hot, dry lakeshore. In damp spots, look for tiger lilies flying on high stems like miniature orange space capsules.

Unless you're a desert rat accustomed to heat, don't hike here between June and September. If you must hike in June, wait for a cool spell, or go right after a rainy period. The mercury can rise to 105°F by mid May, and the steep shoreline makes it difficult to cool off in the water as often as you might like. The lake's popularity with boaters is another reason to hike here in early spring. The later you come, the more boaters you'll have to share the campgrounds with. This is rattlesnake country too, so be alert. Also check yourself thoroughly for ticks at rest stops and at the end of the day.

You'll disembark at Prince Creek around 11 A.M. That enables strong hikers to cruise the 11 miles to Moore Point for the first night's camp. The Meadow Creek campsites at 7 miles are unappealing. If you reach Moore Point the first day, you can finish the hike the next day in time to catch the boat departing from Stehekin at about 2 P.M. for its down-lake journey. If you only want to dayhike, disembark at Moore Point and walk the 6.8 miles north to Stehekin. You can arrange to leave gear on the boat and have it dropped at Stehekin Landing. In Stehekin, you can camp at Purple Point or stay in one of the lodges.

To fully appreciate the deepest gorge in the U.S., hike the Chelan Lakeshore in spring, then come back after July and hike to the top of Pyramid Mountain (Trip 96). From there you can look straight down at the lake, more than 7000 feet below, and see just how colossal the surrounding mountains really are.

FACT

By Car

Drive north of Wenatchee to the town of Entiat. If you're driving east on Highway 2/97, when you reach the northwest side of Wenatchee take the Spokane exit, then the second exit onto 97 ALT to Entiat. From Entiat, continue 9.0 miles north. Turn left onto Highway 971, the Navarre-Coulee Road. It climbs over the hillside. At the junction in 9.1 miles, you've reached Lake Chelan. Turn left and continue up-lake on the highway.

From Chelan, drive Highway 971 west 10.0 miles along the lakeshore. At the junction with the Navarre-Coulee Road, stay right and continue up-lake.

From either approach, you'll soon see Chelan State Park on the right. On your way back, keep this park in mind: you can get a shower here even if you don't pay to camp. At 7.5 miles north of the Navarre-Coulee / Highway 971 junction, turn right into the Wenatchee National Forest and Lake Chelan National Recreation

Area parking lot. This is Fields Point landing. By embarking here rather than in Chelan, you cut 45 minutes off the boat ride without missing any remarkable scenery. There's a $4 per night charge for parking here, as there is in Chelan.

By Boat

At the boat landing office or on the boat, pick up the informative "Discover Lake Chelan" brochure. Hikers on their way to the lakeshore trail have to take the slower boat, the *Lady of the Lake II*, in order to disembark at Prince Creek. If you want to hike the lakeshore as well as trails out of Holden, the logical plan is to hike the lakeshore first. Then, on the down-lake boat trip, disembark at Lucerne to catch the bus up to Holden. Be sure to tell the purser or the captain where you want off. From Fields Point the boat ride is about an hour and a half to Prince Creek, two hours to Lucerne, two and a half hours to Stehekin.

The *Lady of the Lake II* offers daily service May 1 through October 31. So if you want to hike the lakeshore earlier, you have to go directly to Stehekin on the *Lady Express.* It runs throughout the year and makes daily trips March 15 through April 30, and June 1 through September 30. The *Lady Express* doesn't stop at Prince Creek or Moore Point, so you'd have to hike the lakeshore trail south, then back north to Stehekin.

In the past *The Lady of the Lake II* has left Fields Point at 9:45 A.M. The round-trip price to Stehekin has been $21 per person. November through April a round trip on the *Lady Express* has been $21, increasing to $39 May through October.

Check with the Lake Chelan Boat Company for current fares and schedules. Call (509) 682-4584 for a live person, or (509) 682-2224 for a recorded message. You can write them at P.O. Box 186, Chelan, WA 98816.

During the long boat ride, contemplate this: you're in the deepest gorge in the United States. The Grand Canyon is a mile deep. Kings Canyon in California is 7800 feet deep. Hells Canyon on the Idaho/Oregon border is 8200 feet deep. Lake Chelan gorge is deeper still, measuring 8631 feet. It was gouged by glaciers 14,000 to 17,000 years ago. Some say Hells Canyon is the deepest, but they're measuring from a high point 8 miles away from the low point along the Snake River. The Lake Chelan gorge is measured from the 8245-foot summit of Pyramid Mountain—about three-quarters of the way up the lake, on the west side. That high point is only 3 horizontal miles west from the low point at the bottom of Lake Chelan—386 feet below sea level. So Lake Chelan gorge is 431 feet deeper than Hells Canyon. After Crater Lake in Oregon, Lake Chelan is the second deepest lake in North America.

By Bus

From Stehekin Landing, near the north end of Lake Chelan, there are two shuttle-bus operations: the National Park Service (NPS) and the Stehekin Adventure Company. From mid-May to June 8, they usually go 11 miles northwest to High Bridge. From June 10 to June 30, they go 16 miles to Bridge Creek. And from July 1 to September 30, they go 22.8 miles to road's end at Cottonwood Camp, 2800 feet. You can bring your bike at no extra charge.

The NPS shuttle bus costs $5 one way per person, per zone. Stehekin to High Bridge is one zone; from there to Cottonwood is another. It leaves from Stehekin Landing at 8 A.M. and 2 P.M. and takes one hour to High Bridge. Reservations are required. You can reserve your seat (two days ahead in person, longer by phone) at any National Park ranger station in the North Cascades. No reservations are necessary with the Adventure Company. They charge $4 per zone, leave the landing at 8:15 A.M., 11:15 A.M., 2:15 P.M., and 5:15 P.M., and reach High Bridge in 45 minutes. The NPS leaves High Bridge for the return trip to Stehekin at 10:30 A.M. and 5:40 P.M.; the Adventure Company at 9 A.M., 12 noon, 3 P.M., and 6 P.M. Check with both operations for current fares and schedules.

For bus reservations, trail information, or other details about the national recreation area, contact the Golden West visitor center. Call (360) 856-5703, extension 14. Address letters to the National Park Service, P.O. Box 7, Stehekin, WA 98852. They're open from 8 A.M. to 4:30 P.M. daily beginning May 15. Weekdays year-round you can call the Chelan Ranger District at (509) 682-2576. Address letters to P.O. Box 189, Chelan, WA 98816.

On Foot

The boat drops hikers either south or north of Prince Creek, at 1100 feet elevation. The following distances start from the south side of Prince Creek, where there's a campground with tables. Just north of the campground, the trail crosses the alluvial fan of the Prince Creek drainage. The creek is bridged. Another camp-

On the Chelan Lakeshore Trail

ground is in meadows and ponderosa pines 0.1 mile north of the creek. It has no tables but is often less crowded, and the creek is more audible here. At 0.3 mile pass the Prince Creek trail heading upstream to Cub Lake. Soon after, the lakeshore trail gains 200 feet. You'll be heading generally northwest.

The trail is often level, but has some short, steep climbs. At 3.0 miles (where you can see Domke Falls west across the lake) there's a very steep ascent. The trail then descends to an easy ford of Rex Creek at 3.5 miles. The next ford, Pioneer Creek, can be difficult after a hard rain. Beyond it is a 0.25-mile flat area where you could pitch a tent in the trees. Notice that some of the giant ponderosas and Douglas fir have survived severe fires. Domke Mountain dominates the western horizon across the lake for a long stretch. Cross Cascade Creek near 6.25 miles.

At 7.7 miles reach the lush environs of Meadow Creek. There are a couple tent sites with firepits in scruffy pines below the Meadow Creek shelter. Private property here makes it difficult to access the lake or find an attractive campsite. To do that, proceed 0.7 mile past the shelter, then cut left off the trail and walk cross-country toward the lakeshore. Descend 150 feet in 0.2 mile. Look for a flat spot in ponderosa pines on a bench above the lake. It's hard to find at dusk.

After a long, gradual ascent, partly on an old road, the main trail reaches its 1700-foot high point 1.0 mile south of the Moore Point junction. A view to the north opens up, then switchbacks drop steeply toward Moore Point. Pass a broad meadow. Continue north until the trail almost runs into the creek. At 10.7 miles, on the south side of the Fish Creek bridge, turn left and go downstream to reach Moore Point Camp. Shortly, there's a bridge over a roaring stream and directional signs for Moore Pt. Dock. It's a 300-foot, 0.5-mile descent from the Fish Creek bridge to the lake at 1100 feet. In 1889 the upper lake's first hotel was built here on an alluvial fan. During a catastrophic regionwide-flood in 1948, Fish Creek raged across the fan, dragging pieces of the hotel with it. That was the end of business. The rest of the building burned in 1957. Stone walls around a pasture are all that remain. Moore Point is now a large Forest Service campground offering a rough shelter, tables, toilets, fire pits, space for 10 tents, and a secluded tent site in trees near the toilets. Boaters often claim the lakeshore sites before hikers arrive. Fish Creek is audible even from the most distant campsites at the south end.

Continuing north from the Moore Point junction, cross the bridge over Fish Creek. Ascend 200 feet in 0.4 mile to the junction with the Fish Creek trail. Just after the junction, there's a confusing network of old, abandoned roads. At a seeming fork near a creek, stay right and go toward the creek. Don't follow the wide road heading down. Look for the sign pointing north to Stehekin and south to Prince Creek.

After ascending a rocky traverse (not precarious), reach the high point of Hunts Bluff at 12.2 miles, 1600 feet. Views are expansive south down the lake to Pinnacle Mountain.

Gradually descend, crossing Hunts Creek, then an unnamed stream. Just after private property ends, enter the National Recreation Area at 13.3 miles. For the next 0.4 mile, the trail is within 20 vertical feet of the lake. Flick Creek campground, on the lakeshore, is at 13.7 miles. It's small, with room for only two comfortably spaced tents; three otherwise. It also has a shelter, a table, and a toilet.

Beyond Flick Creek the trail is beneath cliffs, about 100 feet above the water. It darts in and out of forest. Cross Flick Creek at 14.5 miles, then bridged Fourmile Creek at 15.2 miles. Just past Fourmile is a campsite in trees overlooking the lake. It could be handy if Flick is full. The trail makes a couple ascents around rock outcroppings. Lake views are frequent the remaining distance to Stehekin. Pass private summer homes just before Hazard Creek and a waterfall at 16.7 miles. Arrive in Stehekin 17.0 miles from Prince Creek (park sign states 17.2 MILES). You'll first see the North Cascades Lodge and a sign for overflow camping. It has 10 tent sites, two toilets, and a water faucet up the slope behind the ranger station.

To reach Purple Point Campground in Stehekin, continue 0.4 mile north. It can be difficult to find the trail that contours the hillside, so just walk the lakeshore road through Stehekin. Pass the ranger station, the visitor center, and the visitor services at the boat landing. The campground is just north of Purple Creek. It has tables, fire pits, toilets, and seven campsites well-separated in the woods. The sites are above the infrequently used road and across from buildings; views of the lake and mountains are obscured. A shower and laundry, just south of the campground, are open 9 A.M. to 6 P.M. To camp at Purple Point or any other campground in the National Recreation Area or National Park, get a free permit from the Golden West visitor center in Stehekin.

Trip 109 Shoulder Season

Canyon Creek / Chancellor

Location	Mt. Baker National Forest / Pasayten Wilderness.
Distance	18.0-mile round trip.
Elevation gain	1140′ in, 640′ out.
Maps	Green Trails No. 49–Mt. Logan, No. 17 –Jack Mountain; Trails Illustrated No. 223–North Cascades National Park Complex; US Forest Service–Pasayten Wilderness.

OPINION

Most early-season hikes are too short to be an adventure for experienced hikers. Canyon Creek is an exception. Usually open in May, it's a strenuous 18.0-mile, full-day trek, or a less ambitious but still challenging overnighter. For such a low-elevation route, it penetrates surprisingly deep into the mountains. It even offers a fascinating and unusual destination: the ghost town of Chancellor, 9.0 miles from the trailhead.

The scenery isn't a shutter-clicker, but it will keep you entertained. You'll be high on a canyon wall most of the way, enjoying glimpses of the creek below and occasional views of peaks. Within the first few miles, you'll see snowmelt waterfalls catapult off the southern buttress of Crater Mountain. The trail continually meanders in and out of gulleys, ravines and side canyons, adding surprise and variety to the journey. And the final stretch is alongside furious Canyon Creek, a liquid locomotive careening downhill out of control.

Overcast skies or even rain won't ruin this hike, because the experience doesn't hinge on seeing what's above you. But if you're lucky enough to be here on a hot day in May or early June, you'll be glad the sun remains just below the high southern wall of the canyon, keeping long stretches of the trail shaded.

Two nemeses of the early-season hiker—brush and dangerous, unbridged stream crossings—are absent on this high trail. Only during the final 1.6 miles to Chancellor will you wade through grasping vegetation. There are numerous creek crossings, including one of Canyon Creek itself at 8.5 miles, but all the major ones are spanned by reliable bridges. The smaller ones pose no danger, although they might require an impressive pirouette to avoid wading. One potential obstacle is a badly eroding section of trail shortly after Mill Creek, which could become impassable after a long spate of rain. Acrophobes might hesitate to cross it at any time. Others will find the between-your-knees view of Canyon Creek, 500 feet below, exhilarating.

Traces of the old narrow-gauge truck road used by miners are evident on the last stretch into Chancellor. Reaching the ghost town will give you a sense of completion. Several log cabins and placer-mine timbers remain from the 1880s. Because the road access over Harts Pass is blocked by snow well into summer, if you hike here in early spring you're likely to be alone, which will make it easier to imagine the town when it was booming.

FACT

By Car

On Highway 20, drive 16.7 miles northwest of Rainy Pass, or 11.1 miles east of Colonial Creek Campground on Diablo Lake, to the signed Canyon Creek trailhead. It's 0.25 mile east of milepost 141. Turn north into the parking area at 1900 feet.

The other end of the trail is at the ghost town of Chancellor, which is accessible by road usually by early August. That gives you the option of making this a one-way hike, if you can set up a shuttle or arrange to have someone pick you up or drop you off at one end. To drive to Chancellor, start at Mazama. On Harts Pass Road 5400, go 19.0 miles northwest to 6200-foot Harts Pass and road junctions. Take Chancellor Road 700. Descend, paralleling Slate Creek, to road's end at Chancellor.

On Foot

Signs for Jackita Ridge trail 738 and Chancellor trail 754 are at the far end of the trailhead parking area. The trails begin at the same point: where Canyon and Granite creeks meet and become Ruby Creek. Walk a few minutes upstream beside Granite Creek, turn left and cross the creek on a bridge. On the other side, ignore the unmarked trail veering right. Go left and in another few minutes come to a signed fork. Turn right on trail 754, climbing northeast above the south bank of Canyon Creek, toward Chancellor. Left quickly leads to historic Beebe's Cabin, crosses Canyon Creek on a bridge and continues to Jackita Ridge.

Trail 754 briefly switchbacks upward after the fork, then follows the canyon upstream. At 0.75 mile, a long, loud waterfall is visible north across the canyon in early season. At 1.5 miles you can look up at McMillan Park and Crater Mountain, both to the north. The first 1.75 miles are a steady, gradual ascent.

At 2.0 miles, watch for the trail left to Rowley's Chasm. It's a couple-minute side trip. The deep abyss is only 4 feet wide at the top. You can peer all the way down at Canyon Creek. Walk cautiously: the ground is crumbling into the chasm, and the bridge might still be missing.

Continuing generally northeast on the main trail, rockhop across Pete Miller Creek at 2.3 miles, and across Old Discovery Creek at 2.6 miles. Looking north over the canyon here, you can see Nickol Falls, fed by streams tumbling down Crater Mountain. At 3.0 miles, you might have to get your feet wet crossing Holmes Creek during spring runoff, but it's not difficult.

Reach the sturdy footlog over Boulder Creek at 3.5 miles, 2400 feet. There's a single campsite next to the creek, just before the crossing and a little downstream. At 0.75 mile beyond Boulder Creek, there's a larger campsite with a fireplace-like firepit. It's left of the trail, across from a rockslide and a tiny pond.

From here, the trail ascends 400 feet. At 5.0 miles, 2800 feet, don't take the unmarked side trail angling south up the hillside. That's trail 729, which ascends the Boulder Creek drainage and is difficult to follow. There's a tree branch across it, to keep hikers from going that way by mistake. Before switchbacking down to Mill Creek, you can look southeast up Mill Creek Canyon and see a trail zigzagging over Cady Pass.

At 5.5 miles, 2650 feet, Mill Creek is spanned by a plank-bridge. On the other side, the trail ascends 240 feet in 0.5 mile beside an old burn. At 6.5 miles, the trail hangs on the edge of a severely eroded slope. In wet weather, this short section could wash out and become dangerous. At 7.4 miles, reach the hefty plank-bridge over Canyon Creek. Before crossing, look for the metal plaque announcing the Lucky Seven Mining Syndicate claim. It's on a tree, left of the bridge.

At 8.0 miles you can see a large waterfall south across the creek. Chancellor is at 9.0 miles, 2800 feet. Chancellor is not marked on the Green Trails map. It's where Road 700 from Harts Pass meets the confluence of Canyon and Slate creeks. A steel-and-wood bridge enables you to cross Canyon Creek to the road's end, parking area, and townsite on the east bank.

You could camp in a grassy area under trees on the far side of the dirt parking area. For a 10-minute tour of the townsite, take the path heading up the slope beside the grassy area. It leads to an old cabin in the woods. The narrow path to the left of the cabin will lead you past mining junk and circle back to the parking area.

Canyon Creek Canyon

Trip 110 Shoulder Season

Ross Lake East Bank

Location	Ross Lake National Recreation Area.
Distance	16.1 miles one way.
Elevation gain	1300'.
Maps	Green Trails No. 16–Ross Lake, No. 48–Diablo Dam, No. 49–Mt Logan; Trails Illustrated No. 223–North Cascades National Park Complex.

OPINION

Suffering from cabin fever? Of all the North Cascade trails accessible early, this is probably the longest. And it offers scenic, lakeshore campsites. It's not, however, as glorious as you might imagine by looking at a map. Consider it only if you're desperate to get out and stay out, and then only in spring, when more scenic trails are still snow-covered.

The East Bank trail grazes the water's edge for one scant stretch. Mostly it's well back from shore, the lake often obscured by trees. Unfortunately, the forest is mostly unimpressive second-growth lodgepole pine. Although early season is the time to hike here, that's also when plummeting water levels expose broad, unsightly, stump-studded mud flats around the lake perimeter. Later, a full lake is more visually pleasing, but by then you might find the afternoons uncomfortably hot at such a low elevation on this sun beaten, west-facing slope. Besides, that's when you should be hiking over nearby Fourth of July Pass (Trip 61) instead.

In early spring, we like the nearby Canyon Creek trail (Trip 109) to Chancellor better than the East Bank trail. On the East Bank you're usually so far from shore that you don't feel you're exploring a lake. In Canyon Creek you're definitely exploring a canyon. Without using a water taxi, the East Bank also requires a long march to get over Hidden Hand Pass before you're near the lake.

If you do hike the East Bank trail, a one-way hike from Lightning Creek to Panther Creek makes the most sense. It does, however, require a pricey water-taxi ride from Ross Lake Resort to the mouth of Lightning Creek. To further complicate matters, you'll need a shuttle vehicle waiting for you at Panther, unless you're willing to hitchhike back to the parking area above the resort. An out-and-back hike from Panther is a mistake; the scenery is too monotonous to endure twice. If you're fit and eager, you can dayhike the 16.1 miles between Lightning and Panther. The added challenge might help compensate for the dull scenery. But an overnight backpack trip lets you take advantage of this trail's best feature: several beautiful campgrounds that are right on the lake and often deserted in early season.

If you're already paying for a water taxi to Lightning Creek, consider allowing an extra day for the grueling, 4400-foot trudge up Desolation Peak. This monster trail starts 2.1 miles north of Lightning Creek. From up top you can survey the length of Ross Lake. You can also see north to Hozomeen Mountain, east over Pasayten Wilderness, and west into the heart of the North Cascades. Desolation Peak is usually snow-free by mid-June. By itself, it's not worth the expense and hassle of riding the water taxi to and from Desolation Landing. Sourdough Mountain (Trip 27) is a better hike, offering a more convenient trailhead and a superior summit panorama. But tagging Desolation onto your East Bank hike will likely be the highlight of an otherwise unremarkable outing.

FACT

By Car

To make this a one-way trip, as recommended, you'll have to ride the water taxi from Ross Lake Resort to where you'll begin hiking at Lightning Creek. If you're including Desolation Peak on your agenda, take the water taxi farther north to Desolation Landing, so you won't have to hike the stretch north of Lightning Creek twice.

The Ross Dam trailhead is a large parking lot on the north side of Highway 20. It's near milepost 134, which is 3.9 miles northeast of Colonial Creek Campground on Diablo Lake, or 23.9 miles northwest of Rainy Pass.

Unless you plan to hitchhike back to your starting point, leave

Lightning Creek Bridge on Ross Lake East Bank Trail

a shuttle car where the hike ends, at the East Bank trailhead. This is a pullout on the north side of Highway 20. It's 4.3 miles southeast of the Ross Dam trailhead parking area. You probably can't drive to the East Bank trailhead until the end of April. Before then, the highway is closed just east of the Ross Dam trailhead.

On Foot

The East Bank trail is in the Ross Lake National Recreation Area. Motor vehicles are prohibited; horses allowed. All the lakeside campgrounds have fire rings, picnic tables and pit toilets. To camp, you need a backcountry permit, available at any nearby ranger station.

Call the Ross Lake Resort (206-386-4437) for water-taxi information and reservations. In 1995 the water taxi cost $40 to Lightning Creek, $45 to Desolation Landing. It's the same price for one person or a full boatload of six. Ask if anyone else is scheduled close to when you want to go; maybe you can ride together. The taxi generally runs June 1 through October 31.

To catch the Ross Lake Resort water taxi, walk the initial, switchbacking descent 0.8 mile from the Ross Dam trailhead parking area toward the lake. When you reach a dirt road, turn right, go over a wooden bridge and follow the road down 40 yards—not all the way to the lake. Cut left on the side road here and switchback down past the sign NO CAMPING. Just beyond the shed and across from an outhouse, you'll see a small, grey, metal box on a telephone pole. Inside the box is a phone you can use to call the resort. The phone number is posted on the phone. After calling, walk back up to the road, turn left and follow it 0.2 mile down to the lakeshore. The boat will pick you up here, on the small, floating dock.

At Desolation Landing, walk from the lake 0.1 mile uphill to a fork. Left ascends 4300 feet in 4.7 miles to the summit of Desolation Peak. Right (south) parallels the lakeshore and reaches Lightning Creek in 2.1 miles.

At Lightning Creek, the water taxi will probably drop you north of the mouth. Scramble up the rocks to the trail. Lightning Creek Camp is off a spur trail to the left. Switchbacking up the north side of the creek, the Lightning Creek trail heads east to join the Three Fools trail. For the East Bank trail turn right (south) and proceed over the bridge. You'll pass a horse camp immediately on the right. From here south, conveniently spaced campgrounds allow you to hike long days or short.

A side trail 1.3 miles south of Lightning Creek forks right to Ponderosa and Dry Creek camps on the lake. Stay high on the main trail to continue south. At 2.1 miles cross bridged Dry Creek. At 3.6 miles reach a junction: Devils Dome trail left, spur trail to the lake and Devils Junction Camps right, East Bank trail straight ahead (south).

Five miles south of Lightning Creek, the trail finally breaks out of the trees onto a cliff edge, offering good views across and north up the lake. It then drops to a bridge over Devils Creek and continues next to the lake—high enough above it to feel airy. The views last only 0.3 mile, after which the lake is again hidden behind trees.

The next campground, Rainbow Point Camp, is 7.3 miles south of Lightning Creek. It's on the shore, below the trail. South of Rainbow the trail remains in forest, way back from the lake. At 8.2 miles it crosses May Creek on a footlog and passes a spur trail on the right leading down to a horse camp. Shortly after May Creek, you can glimpse the lake through the trees. Roland Creek Camp is at 9.5 miles. This one is above the trail, not on the lake. It's in trees, with one site near the creek. The creek crossing here is unbridged but should pose no serious difficulty.

It's a long, slow, steady ascent (700 feet in 2.7 miles) from

Roland Creek to 2500-foot Hidden Hand Pass, 12.2 miles south of Lightning Creek. Descending the pass you get a clear view south over Highway 20 to Ruby Mountain. At a four-way junction 1.0 mile below the pass a sign states RAINBOW POINT 6.0 - LITTLE JACK 6.0 - HIGHWAY 20 2.5 - ROSS LAKE 0.5. It's actually 4.5 miles from here up Little Jack Mountain and 2.9 miles to the highway. Turn right to reach Ross Lake at Hidden Hand Camp. To complete the hike, pass the trail to Little Jack and, following the sign directing you to the highway, angle left on a wide, smooth path. The trail contours southeast along Ruby Arm but offers no views. At 16.0 miles reach the bridge over Ruby Creek. Turn right (south), cross the bridge and ascend 100 feet in 0.1 mile to Highway 20 and the East Bank trailhead, at 1800 feet.

Information Sources

Maps and current trail reports are available at these offices. Budget cuts, however, could close any of them at any time, except the National Park offices. National Forest offices are usually open from 8:00 A.M. to 4:30 P.M. weekdays year-round, with extended hours during the summer. Hours for other offices are listed below, but are subject to change.

Cathedral Provincial Park
ph: (604) 494-6500
B.C. Parks Okanagan District Manager
P.O. Box 399
Summerland, BC V0H 1Z0 Canada
   Hours: 8:30 A.M.-4:30 P.M. weekdays year-round.

Chelan Ranger District
ph: (509) 682-2576
Route 2, Box 680
428 W. Woodin Ave.
Chelan, WA 98816

Darrington Ranger Station (for Glacier Peak Wilderness)
ph: (360) 436-1155
1405 Emmens St.
Darrington, WA 98241
   Hours: 8 A.M.-4:30 P.M. weekdays year-round; daily late May to Labor Day.

Entiat Ranger Station
ph: (509) 784-1511
P.O. Box 476
Entiat, WA 98822

Glacier Public Service Center
ph: (360) 599-2714
Glacier, WA 98244
   Hours: 8:30 A.M.-6 P.M. daily, late May to Labor Day.

Lake Chelan National Recreation Area
   Golden West Visitor Center
Stehekin District
ph: (360) 856-5703, ext 14

P.O. Box 7, Stehekin, WA 98852
  Hours: 12:30 P.M.-2 P.M. daily, March 15 - May 14; 8:30 A.M.-
  4:30 P.M. daily, May 15 - Sept 15; 10:30 A.M.-2 P.M. daily,
  Sept 16 - Sept 30.

Lake Wenatchee Ranger Station
ph: (509) 763-3103
22976 State Highway 207
Leavenworth, WA 98826

Manning Provincial Park Visitor Centre
ph: (604) 840-8836
B.C. Parks, Box 3
Manning Park, BC V0X 1R0
  Hours: 8:30 A.M.-4 P.M. weekdays year-round;
  8 A.M.-8 P.M. in summer.
  or, B.C. Parks Fraser Valley District Manager
ph: (604) 824-2309
P.O. Box 10
Cultus Lake, BC V0X 1H0 Canada
  Hours: 8:30 A.M.-4:30 P.M. weekdays year-round.

Mt. Baker Ranger District - North Cascades
ph: (360) 856-5700
2105 State Route 20
Sedro Woolley, WA 98284
  Hours: 8 A.M.-4:30 P.M. Monday through Friday year-round;
  8 A.M.-6 P.M. daily, late May to Labor Day.

North Cascades National Park Visitor Center
ph: (206) 386-4495
Newhalem, WA 98283
  Hours: 9 A.M.-4:30 P.M. daily is the minimum, mid-April
  through October; possibly open until 5:30 P.M. by the end
  of May; 8:30 A.M.-6 P.M. daily in July and August; 9 A.M.-4:30
  P.M. Saturdays and Sundays in November, and January
  through mid-April.

North Cascades National Park Service Complex -
Wilderness Information Center
ph: (360) 873-4500; (360) 856-5700 (winter)
728 Ranger Station Road
Marblemount, WA 98267
  Hours: 8 A.M. Sunday through Thursday. 8 A.M.-6 P.M.

Fridays and Saturdays, mid-May through June, and after
Labor Day until mid-October; 7 A.M.-6 P.M. Monday through
Thursday; 7 A.M.-8 P.M. Fridays, Saturdays, and Sundays,
July 1 through Labor Day; from mid-October through
mid-May, no regular hours.

Okanogan National Forest
ph: (509) 826-3275
1240 Second Ave. South, P.O. Box 950
Okanogan, WA 98840

Ross Lake Resort (for water-taxi reservations)
ph: (206) 386-4437
Rockport, WA 98283

Skykomish Ranger Station
ph: (360) 677-2414
P.O. Box 305
Skykomish, WA 98288

Tonasket Ranger Station
ph: (509) 486-2186
P.O. Box 466
Tonasket, WA 98855

Twisp Ranger Station
ph: (509) 997-2131
P.O. Box 188, 502 Glover
Twisp, WA 98856

Verlot Public Service Center
ph: (360) 691-7791
Granite Falls, WA 98252
  Hours: 8 A.M.-6 P.M. in summer.

Wenatchee National Forest
ph: (509) 662-4335
215 Melody Lane
Wenatchee, WA 98801-5933

Methow Valley Visitor Center
Winthrop District
ph: (509) 996-4000
49 Highway 20, Winthrop, WA 98862
  Hours: 9 A.M.-5 P.M. late May to Labor Day

INDEX

The Authors

Besides each other, hiking is Kathy and Craig's greatest passion. Their second date was a 20-mile dayhike in Arizona. Since then they've never stopped for long.

They've trekked through much of the world's vertical topography, including the Himalayas, Pyrenees, Alps, Dolomites, Sierra, and Rockies, as well as the mountains of New Zealand and the canyons of the American Southwest. They moved from the U.S. to Alberta so they could live next to the Canadian Rockies, the range that inspired their highly unconventional *Don't Waste Your Time* guidebook series. *Camp Free in B.C.* was their next book. They now live in British Columbia, within view of Mount Baker.

"We doubted any range could be as enrapturing as the Canadian Rockies," said Kathy. "But the North Cascades surpassed all our expectations. Skepticism gave way to fascination and eventually to awe and reverence."

Their enthusiasm for the joys of hiking and their colorful, unflinchingly honest writing make this an unusually compelling guidebook. To complete the research, they walked 1400 miles and ascended elevation equivalent to climbing from sea level to the summit of Mt. Everest nine times.

Joyful moment during the authors' odyssey

Your safety is your responsibility

Hiking and camping in the wilderness can be dangerous. Experience and preparation reduce risk, but will never eliminate it. The unique details of your specific situation and the decisions you make at that time will determine the outcome. This book is not a substitute for common sense or sound judgment. If you doubt your ability to negotiate mountain terrain, respond to wild animals, or handle sudden, extreme weather changes, hike only in a group led by a competent guide. The authors and the publisher of this book disclaim liability for any loss or injury incurred by anyone using information in this book.